The Economics of Environmental Degradation

The United Nations Environment Programme (UNEP) is built on a heritage of service to the environment. A productive consequence of the Stockholm Conference on the Human Environment in 1972, UNEP provides an integrative mechanism through which a large number of separate efforts of intergovernmental, non-governmental, national and regional bodies in the service of the environment are reinforced and interrelated.

From the very onset, UNEP recognized that environment could not be sectorized. Environment is a system of interacting relationships that extends through all sectors of activity and to manage these relationships requires an integrated approach for which present structures are not designed. Hence, while creating a basis for comprehensive consideration within the United Nations of the problems of the human environment, UNEP has also endeavoured to focus the attention of governments and the public opinion worldwide on the importance of environmental problems. Indeed, UNEP has been described as the environmental conscience of the UN system.

UNEP's uniqueness lies in its advocacy of environmental concerns within the international system. In this, it makes a particular effort to nurture partnerships with other UN bodies possessing complementary skills and delivery capabilities and enhancing the participation of the private sector, scientific community, NGOs, youth, women and sports organization in the achievement of sustainable development.

UNEP derives its extraordinary influence from the authority inherent in the importance of its mission. To the extent that governments face common environmental problems, are disturbed by environmental threats beyond their jurisdiction, or need to harmonize policies relating to the environment, UNEP has and will always continue to have a pivotal role.

Today, 24 years after the Stockholm Conference, the challenge before UNEP is to implement an environmental agenda that is integrated strategically with the goals of economic development and social well-being – an agenda for sustainable development.

UNEP's integrated work programme for the biennium 1996–97 emphasizes relationships between socio-economic driving forces, environmental changes and impacts on human well-being. Equipped with stronger regional presence and marked by a process of continuous monitoring and assessment of its implementation, UNEP's programme of work for 1996–97 focuses on the following areas: sustainable management and use of natural resources; sustainable production and consumption; a better environment for human health and well-being; and globalization of the economy and the environment.

The Economics of Environmental Degradation

Tragedy for the Commons?

Edited by

Timothy M. Swanson

Faculty of Economics and Politics, Cambridge University and CSERGE, University College London, UK

UNEP

Edward Elgar
Cheltenham, UK • Brookfield, US

Published by
Edward Elgar Publishing Limited
8 Lansdown Place
Cheltenham
Glos GL50 2HU
UK

Edward Elgar Publishing Company
Old Post Road
Brookfield
Vermont 05036
US

British Library Cataloguing in Publication Data
The economics of environmental degradation : tragedy for
    the Commons?
    1. Environmental degradation – Economic aspects
    2. Environmental economics
    I. Swanson, Timothy M.   II. United Nations. Environment Programme
    333.7

Library of Congress Cataloguing in Publication Data
The economics of environmental degradation : tragedy for the Commons?
    / edited by Timothy M. Swanson.
        Includes bibliographical references and index.
        1. Natural resources.   2. Environmental degradation.
    3. Sustainable development.   4. Externalities (Economics)
        I. Swanson, Timothy M.
        HC55.E355   1996
        333.7—dc20   96–6434
                                                                      CIP
ISBN 1 85898 486 6

Printed and bound in Great Britain by
Biddles Ltd, Guildford and King's Lynn

Contents

v

Illustrations

Boxes

Contributors

Raffaello Cervigni, Global Environmental Facility and CSERGE

Nick Johnstone, Associate Fellow, International Institute for Environment and Development

Robin Mason, Prize Research Fellow, Nuffield College, Oxford University

Mark Rogers, Research School of Social Sciences, Australian National University

Renata Serra, Faculty of Economics, Cambridge University

Timothy M. Swanson, Lecturer, Faculty of Economics and Politics, Cambridge University and Programme Director, CSERGE, University College London

Acknowledgements

The motivation for this volume was conceived originally by Hussein Abaza, Chief, Environmental Economics Unit at the United Nations Environment Programme (UNEP) and Professor David Pearce, UK Centre for Social and Economic Research on Global Environment, based at University College London and the University of East Anglia. This volume was commissioned by the Environmental Economics Unit with H. Abaza as the contracting officer who provided together with his colleagues in the unit numerous helpful comments, which have contributed extensively to the improvement of the initial manuscript. In addition I must express my thanks to those persons who worked with me on this project; their names are listed in the various chapters. Special thanks goes to Mark Rogers, a good friend, who contributed two chapters and assisted me with many of the more boring editorial tasks. I also thank Wendy Solomou who aided with the editing of the volume into its final form. I certainly appreciated, and needed, all of the assistance that I received in the production of this volume.

Finally, it would be a tragedy to overlook the contributions of two uncommon individuals: my parents. I would like to acknowledge that they have always been there with their love, support and encouragement. This is the most that any generation could ever want or expect from another.

Timothy Swanson
Cambridge University

Preface

How can tropical deforestation be halted? What can be done about the slaughter of African elephants? Why does the government continue to allow the trade in toxic wastes? Most of my students in the field of the environment have come to the subject with a set of questions such as these. Implicit in these questions is the belief that the changes that continue to wrack the natural world are the embodiment of environmental problems and that environmental policy should be addressed to stemming the tide of environmental change. This approach to environmental degradation traces its origins at least as far back as Pigou, who saw the developers of new polluting technologies as the source of the environmental problem. For the followers of this line of thought, the subject of environmental economics should be about how the existing state of reality is in conflict with the optimal. It is about analysing the imperfections that give rise to the resource and environmental decline that is witnessed, and internalizing these costs to the actors that generate them.

On the other hand, the field of natural resource economics has developed over the past twenty years in order to explain how natural resources will be exploited optimally across time. This discipline is focused on the issues concerning the predictable manner in which societies will alter their natural resource base. It assumes that resource exploitation will respond to signals of relative scarcity and that societal development will generate a support base that incorporates these scarcities. These assumptions imply an environment of continuous and possibly perpetual change, natural as well as social. Reaching back into the history of societal development, it probably even implies the general decline of the natural resource base as the support structure on which societies depend. In this perspective much of the general resource decline and environmental deterioration that is witnessed may be explained by reference to the societal development process. For example, deforestation is something that has occurred over virtually the whole of the so-called developed world in the past few millennia, for the development of agricultural lands and other societal assets; now that the remainder of the world is pursuing the same process, it would seem hypocritical (in this view) to prevent those countries from undertaking the same process as occurred earlier elsewhere.

How is it possible to reconcile these two views? When does resource decline equate with degradation and when does it equate with development? What are the fundamental problems with which environmental policy should be concerned? These are the problems and issues that are addressed in this volume. It represents an attempt at reconciling the 'externality' based approach of environmental economics with the 'development' based approach of natural resource economics. The object is to find the link between the two which will bring these two very different approaches together. The link identified here is institutions. It is institutional failure that results in the problem of persisting externalities. If co-ordinating institutions exist, then the impacts of non-co-operation in a commons will be recognised and internalized. It is the failure of an institution to accomplish this purpose that allows an externality to persist. Likewise, institutions will indeed lead societies to develop their natural resources down the right path, so long as those institutions are capable of recognizing and internalizing important resource scarcities. It is the failure of institutions to recognize resource scarcities and realize co-operative gains that allows societies to drift off the path of sustainable resource utilization.

This volume develops this thesis in the context of chapters one and two, and then demonstrates how it operates in various case studies on the causes of environmental degradation. It looks at other posited environmental problems (population, poverty, trade) and examines the extent to which these 'causes' are fundamental or examples of social problems channelled down the already existing conduit for environmental degradation, i.e. institutional failure. An underlying theme is: what is the source of the tragedy of the commons and is it ultimately avoidable? A dynamic approach to environmental degradation provides some interesting insights to the problems of the commons. Human opportunism will probably always be with us, and this approach indicates that the tragedy results whenever human institutions fail to keep pace with human opportunism. This is a contest that will never be won with finality, but may always be lost.

The volume is intended as a supplementary text for students and policy makers interested in the issues of environmental problems. It also provides a few new insights on the interface between environmental economics, natural resource economics and institutional economics for those working in any one of those fields. It is hoped that the volume will be of use and useful for the better understanding of environmental problems and that it will help to focus attention on the most important and fundamental problems yet to be resolved in this area.

Timothy Swanson
Cambridge University

1 The economics of environmental degradation: an institutional approach

Timothy M. Swanson

Introduction

In most parts of the world the quality of the environment continues to decline. In Asia newly industrialized regions spout massive amounts of pollution into previously pure air. In eastern Europe the infamous 'black triangle' stands as a monument to the excesses of the industrial policies of the regimes there, past and present. In sub-Saharan Africa the vast populations of the elephant were halved in the course of a single decade while its neighbour the black rhinoceros continues its slow slide into oblivion. The last great tropical forests located in south-eastern Asia, central Africa and the Amazon are submitting to the law of the chainsaw at a rate of millions of hectares per annum and with them goes perhaps the majority of the species that exist on earth. The problem is not restricted to the developing countries either. In the European Union there is pressure to revise the water quality standards simply because there are so many localities where chemical contamination is in violation of the existing standards. European lakes and forests continue to be destroyed by the phenomenon of acid rain. The quality of the water in the Ogalala aquifer in the central US, pristine for millennia, is now in many places unfit for consumption by infants by reason of nitrate contamination. There seem to be few, if any, regions or resources that are immune to this general trend of decline and despoliation; the 'commons' across the world appear to be uncommonly susceptible to tragic endings.

Current and future generations have even more to contend with than these locally based problems however. They must now come to grips with recognized environmental decline at the global level as well. Some of these problems have been long recognized but remain unresolved. For example, the world's open-sea resources, especially the fisheries, continue to be overexploited and undermanaged. Many other problems are only now being recognized, as societies begin to explore the impact of their technologies upon resources only recently identified. For example, it is now recognized that the introduction of various chlorine-based chemical compounds has had a degenerative impact upon various resources by virtue of their stability and persistence (originally, their most desirable characteristics) – the chlorofluorocarbons have thinned the ozone layer by reason of their reticence for reactivity and the organochlorines have accumulated within the biosphere, endangering many bird species, for the same reason. We are also beginning to explore the cumulative impact of fossil fuel-based industrialization and global deforestation in terms of the uncertainties and instabilities engendered by potential climate change. Similarly, the universal adoption of modern agricultural techniques and varieties is now seen to engender a threat to the maintenance of an adequate base of agricultural diversity, so as to be a threat unto itself. These examples illustrate that the decline of environmental quality and natural resources need not be immediately apparent at the local level in order to constitute a problem. Some of our most important commons now exist at the global level.

Why is this universally apparent decline of the commons occurring and why is it not being halted? Many observers will feel that the answers to these questions are obvious and that they are rooted in human short-sightedness and opportunism. That is, most people probably perceive the despoliation process as being rooted in the human proclivity to pursue personal pleasure and profit single-mindedly without adequate consideration of the social costs and consequences. In this view, the tragedy of the commons is the inevitable result of human shortcomings in reasoning and foresight in combination with the relatively opportunistic nature of the species. This is roughly what Garrett Hardin set forth as the basis of the problem in his seminal essay on the *Tragedy of the Commons* (Hardin, 1993).

There is of course more than a bit of truth in this paradigm of the source of commons problems; however, it also leaves a lot of unanswered questions to ponder. For instance, why are some resources managed as common resources if this form of management is systematically deficient? The answer to this question was given years ago – commons regimes are not routinely problematic and many of them operate very efficiently indeed. It is clearly *not* the case that every commons situation must result in tragedy (see Ciriancy-Wantrup and Bishop, 1975). Then why is it that human societies are able to manage the commons well in some circumstances and not in others? There is now a vast literature analysing common property systems that work very well in the context of presumably opportunistic human societies. This literature tends to focus upon the same broad set of factors in locating the basis of sound systems of commons management: recognition (of participants), exclusion (of non-participants), efficiency (of constraints on use), equity (in distribution) and so on (Ostrom, 1990; Hanna and Munasinghe, 1995). For our purposes the important question remains: why do some of these systems operate well when they are based on the same fundamental constituents as those that do not? That is, if the root of the commons problem does not lie with human short-sightedness and opportunism (since these do not always result in tragedy), then where is the fundamental root of the problem?

In explaining the tragedy of the commons, the economic framework focuses less upon the frailties of the individuals and more upon the imperfections in the social systems to which they respond. Economists are less convinced of the importance of human failings in determining social outcomes, simply because economists have believed in a special form of 'social synergism' since the time of Adam Smith. This synergism is the capacity of institutions (market-based and otherwise) for the co-ordination of the otherwise less-than-perfect intentions and activities of humanity; with institutions, the aggregate effect is much better co-ordinated than what was intended by any one of the individual parts. In other words, blemishes on the rationality and intentions of humanity are taken for granted by economists but these do not necessarily imply aggregate behaviour which will bring the species to the end that these imperfections imply.

How can institutions accomplish this important task? They do this whenever they are able to bring important resource scarcities within the decision-making framework of individuals and societies regarding their use. Institutions are able to achieve this effect by means of any mechanism (price, standard and so on) that is capable of signalling the increasing costliness of any resource which is becoming more scarce. For example, with regard to a standard discrete commodity, the market is able to reflect increasing scarcity simply by reference to the increasing prices that result from this scarcity, as well as the anticipated price increases (futures prices), which will induce individuals and societies to choose their activities in a manner that will economize on the resource relative to this increasing scarcity. For a more complicated resource, for example groundwater quality, it may be necessary for a governmental institution to generate the signals of relative scarcity by imposing water quality standards, emissions taxes or some other regulatory instrument which has the effect of signalling the increased costliness of accumulating further groundwater pollution. Any mechanism which brings the changing relative scarcity of the resource to the attention of the individuals making decisions regarding the resource will channel their individual intentions toward an outcome consonant with this increasing scarcity.

The problem of environmental degradation from the economic perspective is then 'to get the institutions right'. Human intentions and motivations regarding resources may range across the entire spectrum, from the selfish to the sublime, but they must be appropriately channelled by institutions so that (whatever the intended object) it is undertaken with the appropriate relative emphasis placed on the objective of economizing on the exploitation of various resources. From the economic perspective, it must be a combination of human and institutional imperfections that is capable of generating environmental degradation. The opportunistic nature of humanity is taken as a fixed parameter and the focus of the enquiry then becomes the development of institutions in a socially constructive direction.

What then are the fundamental sources of environmental degradation? The underlying causes of degradation will be found in those problems that systematically result in institutional failures. The failure of institutions will be seen to result from several limitations on the co-operative capacity of societies. First, there are the limits in terms of the costliness of institutional complexity. For very simple forms of resources that are readily commoditized, there is no significant costliness to recognizing and incorporating their changing relative scarcities within the economic system. For much more complicated resources, such as ecosystems, it is virtually impossible to generate the same sort of characteristics that assure their ready recognition. The complexity of the environment, together with the costliness of institutional complexity, generates the first general reason for co-operative failures at the societal level.

Secondly, there are the limits to individual co-operation mentioned by Hardin but channelled through institutions. That is, human opportunism is important not just in itself (as one of the fundamental reasons that institutions are required) but also on account of the institutional costliness it generates. Human opportunism is at the core of the costliness of the development of institutions and keeping them intact. The literature on commons problems makes this clear.

Finally, there is the myriad of other reasons that social conflict and non-co-operation persist: general civil strife, distributional problems and so on. These social problems generate the pressures that are often routed through the commons on account of the costliness of its regulation. Commons tragedies have their source in a diverse range of social phenomena, but are ultimately based in the problem of institutionalizing co-operation in regard to these resources.

This is the institutional approach to the problem of environmental degradation. It is an enquiry into the plausibility of the explanations for the widespread degradation that we are witnessing in the light of the fundamental explanation put forward here. It is important to examine all of the possible 'causes of degradation' (for example population, debt and poverty) but to do so within the context of a single unifying framework that allows the most fundamental source of the environmental problem to be identified. A careful assessment of societal capacity to resolve these various 'tragedies of the commons' can then be made.

Defining degradation: resource decline over time
Before it is possible to identify causes it will be necessary to define 'degradation', the phenomenon we are exploring. Are all of the examples of resource

decline cited in the previous section instances of environmental degradation? Many observers of the deforestation problem would view the current rate of decline of the great hardwood forests as a clear-cut instance of environmental degradation. The same reasoning would of course apply to the decline of many of the populations of large mammal species, such as the elephant. How could the loss of half a million African elephants in one decade not constitute one of the clearest examples of environmental degradation? The noticeable decline of many natural and environmental resources over time is one of the primary factors raising concerns for and consciousness of the degradation of the environment, and the decline of natural resources is usually equated with the problem of environmental degradation.

The problem with such an approach is that the passage of time includes other processes that may themselves have a systematic impact upon natural resources. The existence of other time-embedded processes impacting upon natural resources renders the equation between resource decline and degradation untenable. It is necessary to look carefully at the nature of the process resulting in resource decline. This is where the institutional approach is crucial to the investigation of causation. If the dynamic process being investigated is rooted in institutional failure, then the decline of the resource base may definitely be termed degradation. If the resource decline cannot be readily traced to an institutional imperfection, then it is necessary to take a closer look at the causation before it may be termed degradation.

It is necessary to analyse the relationship between resource decline and degradation because it is possible for the societal development process itself to be closely linked to change, natural as well as social. One important facet of societal development is the restructuring of the set of assets on which the society relies. Societal capital in its entirety is the base of assets (tools, technologies, humans and so on) from which human societies receive the flows of goods and services on which they depend. Clearly, given this definition, natural resources and systems constitute one important form of capital: they are the form that capital takes as it was endowed originally by nature. Humans for many millennia (as 'hunter-gatherers') took the entirety of their goods and services from a capital base that was almost exclusively natural in form. However, one of the most important facets of societal development has been the rearrangement of this capital base to incorporate more of other forms of capital. As a consequence natural resources necessarily declined as they were removed for investment and conversion into other important forms of capital (machinery, schools and so on) (Solow, 1974b). Social change and development, in the economic perspective, necessarily incorporate this sort of portfolio balancing and therefore imply substantial changes in the originally natural capital base. In this view it is entirely predictable that great forests will be cleared and large predators removed as a by-product of the process by which human societies re-make the world (that is when perceived solely as the societal capital base) into a form that generates a flow of goods and services more to their liking.

Even today societies that are continuing to reshape the asset base upon which they are building their societies will be 'investing' more heavily in some forms of assets and often 'disinvesting' in others. For example, a society may be in the process of restructuring itself away from a more traditional natural resource base and toward one based more upon industrial assets, or restructuring from an industrial base toward one more reliant upon human skills and services. In either case the relative emphasis of the development process in that society will mean that certain assets will be receiving more investment than others. The passage of time in the context of this form of societal development may imply substantial changes in the natural resource base of the society concerned. Development as well as degradation can be the source of natural resource decline over at least some period of time.

The degradation of the environment is a decidedly more complicated problem when viewed within a changing world. Change in itself is no longer an adequate indicator to warrant a determination of degradation. What is required is not simply a decline in resource quality but such a decline in combination with a demonstrable failure in the institutional apparatus controlling it. Environmental degradation clearly exists when the natural resource base is declining as the result of failures in management institutions. For this reason we will be examining other potential causes of degradation from the standpoint of their potential impact upon institutions and institutional failures.

Representing future generations: mining paradise?
One of the most fundamental problems of economic development and resource decline is the representation of future generations' interests within the current development process. What sorts of institutions can accomplish this task with respect to individuals not yet born? How should current generations' decision-making concerning the natural resource base be constrained in order to take into account the special concerns of future generations? These are once again very complicated issues that may be considered only within a dynamic context. The basic problem is: even if resource decline is linked to development rather than institutional failures, how can we be sure that this development process is correctly targeted? Does it point to an end that will meet the needs and desires of the generations that will exist when it gets there?

Consider the current case of one South Pacific island state that is quite literally mining itself out of existence. This tiny island had long supported an extremely limited and relatively impoverished population in a decidedly tropical lifestyle, due to its small size and thin natural resource base. However, over the past forty years all of this has changed as the island has been 'developed'. The development strategy chosen by the people on this south-sea island has taken a form that represents a parable for our times. On account of tens of thousands of years of guano accumulation, virtually the entirety of the island constitutes an extremely rich deposit of phosphate, a crucial ingredient for soil nutrients. The islanders have commenced mining the substance on a large-scale basis for export to other countries. As the mining process continues the island is to all intents and purposes becoming uninhabitable; the islanders are mining their homeland virtually out of existence, in return for the proceeds from the sales of the phosphate. They have accumulated immense stocks of wealth (for a relatively small population) while destroying the productivity and viability of their tropical island.

Does this mining process constitute development or degradation and, if it is part of the development process, should it be constrained in some manner to take into account its impact on future generations of islanders (who are potentially without an island)? The first important point to consider about this process is that the future of the current generation of islanders is becoming almost entirely detached from the natural resource base that was their past. The future of this generation (and all future generations) will instead be dependent upon the quality of their investments of the proceeds. This points to the first principle of sustainable development (the so-called 'Hartwick–Solow rule'): development requires that the proceeds from the mining of natural assets be invested in other forms of assets, rather than consumed by the current generation (Solow, 1974a). This much is obvious. Where would future generations live, and what would they depend upon if there were no compensating investments for the lost resource base?

Even assuming that the current generation of islanders invest the proceeds of their mining operations, consuming only the income from their investments, how can they ensure that the resulting portfolio of assets is of the nature that future generations would like to receive? One way in which to conceptualize this problem would be to consider the range of constraints that might be placed upon the current generation, in order to allow development to proceed within the context of the retention of some recognizable natural resource base. Consider an extreme example: should the current generation of islanders have been entirely prohibited from realizing any of the immense wealth obtainable from the mining of their island on the grounds that it would necessarily subtract from the wealth of future islanders? This seems restrictive, since it implies that nature's abundance must remain forever out of reach of all generations, not simply current ones. Some manner of constraint on the use of the proceeds from mining seems more sensible than a constraint prohibiting any mining at all. Should the current generation instead have been allowed to mine the island, but only in a manner or to an extent consistent with the maintenance of the productivity of the other natural resources on the island? This also seems restrictive, even from the standpoint of only future generations of islanders, as there may be other investments (schools and hospitals) which they might be happy to have in exchange for some reductions in other forms of investments. For instance, the islanders may be more than happy to give up all forms of agriculture on the island if their investments establish the island as the world's pre-eminent high-tech manufacturing centre (witness Singapore island-state). Should they then have been allowed to mine the island but only to the extent that opportunities existed for the investment of the proceeds on the island itself? Again, this intuitively appealing constraint seems artificial and unnecessarily restrictive on second thought, as a tiny island with massive wealth will not produce the same range of investment opportunities as are available on the whole of the world's financial markets. Small undeveloped states suddenly endowed with large quantities of financial capital may find it easiest to invest initially elsewhere while slowly developing the capital structure of the state itself (witness the small middle-eastern oil states such as Kuwait).

Any of these constraints placed upon the current generation of islanders would have limited the scope of their opportunities considerably and consequently limited the opportunities available to future generations as well. On the other hand, the adoption of any one of these constraints would have provided for the retention of some sort of homeland that was recognizable as a south-sea island for future generations of islanders. Allowing the islanders to consider the widest possible range of investment opportunities allows them to reshape their world beyond recognition, for better or for worse. Is there any reason to believe that future islanders would not want the current ones to make the selections that they do? The best analysis of this issue is probably the first: John Krutilla's works on the reasons for conserving natural environments (Krutilla, 1967). His arguments were based on the belief that the mining and conversion of natural resources might well increase the aggregate income and opportunities of future generations but that this enhanced income would generate increased demands for natural resource-based goods and services. Consequently future generations would be wealthier but, in the absence of natural capital, unable to have the range of experiences that they would prefer. For this reason it might be reasonable for current generations to adopt one of these constraints on their conversion of natural capital.

We all stand in the same position as these south-sea islanders. We have received an endowment of natural wealth which may be retained as it stands and thus remain on our own 'island earth', or alternatively this wealth may be invested in very different assets to support very different sorts of lifestyles.

To the extent that we select investment options very different from the naturally selected portfolio of assets, the world in which we live will be continuously and comprehensively altered. Unless we impose one of the above restrictions upon our investment options, the natural world around us will continue to change. Meanwhile, in the context of all of this change, we are also attempting to assess how well human systems and societies are cooperating within the context of our common environmental resources. Contemporaneous environmental change will sometimes camouflage the consequences of conflict; likewise, depletion and decline in the context of change will often be mistaken for degradation.

For these reasons the economic analysis of environmental degradation is a more complex matter than the mere identification of changing circumstances and declining resource bases. Environmental change is taken as the background against which environmental problems must be isolated. Then it is necessary to isolate the specific circumstances under which changes within the environment represent social problems. This does not mean that there will necessarily be many fewer cases of environmental degradation than would otherwise be expected but that there is a secondary level of analysis required (beyond simple environmental change) before the nature of the problem itself may be isolated. People are rightly concerned about the decline of environmental quality everywhere and the despoliation of the few remaining natural environments. However, the precise roots of these problems must be identified, and isolated from the change that is non-problematic, before social action can be appropriately directed.

Degradation and sustainability
This is where the issue of environmental degradation interfaces with the issue of sustainable development. Assessing whether resource decline constitutes degradation, against a background of change (societal and natural), requires an assessment of the underlying causes of that decline. That is, a necessary and sufficient condition for resource degradation is that the decline of a natural resource or environment can be traced to an identifiable institutional imperfection. In addition, this is also a sufficient condition for the existence of unsustainable development. Hence resource degradation may be seen as a subset of the possible paths to non-sustainability that a society may elect.

The sustainability of resource and environmental decline is something that has been commented upon for centuries now. Malthus and Ricardo were two of the first economists to note the importance of declining resource quality for economic sustainability, focusing on the pressures of rising populations on fixed agricultural bases. This was translated more recently into a concern about the 'limits to growth' placed upon economies by the naturally existing supplies of specific commodities, such as tin, zinc or oil, as was developed by the 'Club of Rome' group in the 1970s. In both cases, the subject of the enquiry was the impact of declining resource endowments on societal sustainability. However, during the 1970s a consensus was developed within much of economics that these were not the sorts of commodities for which scarcity was a real concern; markets apparently worked very well to register the scarcity of such tradables as mineral and agricultural commodities (Smith, 1979).

Today the focus of the debate on sustainability has shifted away from specific resources as commodities used in human production systems and toward natural resources as environmental systems upon which humans rely for sustenance as living beings. That is, concern has been extended from specific traded commodities towards less easily managed 'environmental systems', such as the services rendered by the ozone layer, the tropical forests and the global atmosphere. It is probably the case that an economic system might handle the former resource allocation problem quite well (for example the supply of forests for timber for housing construction) while managing the same natural resource very poorly for the latter purpose (for example the supply of forests for biodiversity). This is once again an illustration that it is not the decline of the resource so much as the institution managing the process that matters. Therefore, the issue of sustainability remains a matter of greatest debate in precisely the same region as the issue of resource degradation, i.e. where the weaknesses of institutions matter most. For this reason, the question of environmental degradation is a core concept in the solution of sustainability problems as well.

This volume addresses the question: what are the fundamental causes of environmental degradation? In the institutionalist's framework this translates into: what forms of resource and environmental utilization 'fall through the gaps' of existing economic and institutional systems? The pursuit of the causes of environmental degradation within this framework is seen to be a fundamental enquiry into the question of sustainability as well. It attempts to ascertain the *systemic reasons* for persisting threats to sustainability, in the sense that it attempts to identify the imperfections within existing systems that cause them to fail to register or to respond to important forms of scarcity.

This volume adopts a five-part approach to the investigation in order to illustrate the institutional framework and how it applies to various environmental contexts. The volume investigates each of the following potential pitfalls for sustainability: property, policies, population, poverty and prices. 'Property' is shorthand for the institutional deficiencies that contribute to continuing environmental problems, that is, why is it that the existing economic system does not generate solutions to environmental degradation? This is also referred to as the market's failure to provide a solution. 'Policies' refers to the failure of governments to intervene to supply resource management systems when natural resources are declining. Jointly, these two factors describe the externality-based view of degradation, that is, resource degradation as the result of systemic failures to account for important forms of scarcity.

The remaining approaches investigated are more straightforward: population growth, poverty and 'prices' (commercialization and trade). The investigation here will demonstrate that although these are more tangible and more easily linked intuitively to resource degradation, the relationship between these forces and resource degradation is far more indirect than in the case of the institutional factors. It is more often the case that these are indicators of other social problems that are allowed to work their harms through the environmental medium (by reason of a failed institutional set-up) than it is the case that they are environmental problems in and of themselves.

In short, resource degradation remains an important issue of concern in the analysis of economic sustainability, but this is because both problems have roots in the same source. The overarching problem society faces is the construction of institutions capable of registering and responding to all forms of important environmental scarcities. The limitations that prevent this from happening spontaneously are readily generalized: human limitations and institutional limitations within the context of environmental complexity. Nevertheless the precise specification of the nature of these limitations remains essential, if only to allow for the identification of situations where these problems persist.

Property: market failure and degradation
Market failure is a shorthand expression for the failure of management institutions to arise spontaneously in response to important resource scarcities. It is the failure of the economic system to solve its own problems. To a large extent, an economic system can in fact accomplish this task in many instances. One of the primary functions of a price system is the recognition and registration of relative scarcity. If a resource is becoming relatively scarce on account of a lack of management, then its relative price should be increasing and the incentive to increased management should likewise rise. By this logic, previously unmanaged resources will be overexploited, become relatively more scarce and more valuable and, for this reason, attract better management.

There are numerous examples of such spontaneously arising management institutions. Most forms of property systems are seen to be based on the relative scarcities prevailing in those societies. Changing prices, population densities and technologies have all resulted in the alteration of institutions (Anderson and Hill, 1975). A recent example is the extension of the 'territorial seas' from 12 to 200 miles. As the resources of these areas became more valuable with changing technologies and increasing scarcities, the institution of open access to the oceans and the resources that they contained was rendered obsolete. The incentive to develop a management regime for the oceans was too strong to ignore.

Environmental problems always generate incentives to better resource management but they do not always generate solutions. Wherever individuals interact with one another there is an incentive to manage that interaction. This is the meaning of the concept of 'externality': it is a signal that there is a benefit to be had from the management of that interaction. It is not always the case, however, that this signal is strong enough to overcome the hurdles in the way of co-operation. Externality is a term describing the situation where at least two parties are engaged in some manner of joint production in their individual pursuits and some choices that they are making impact upon one other. When making their decisions, this interaction is said to be external to their decision-making process in the sense that they do not take into account the impact of their actions upon others. Since the others are doing likewise, the could all benefit from a different form of decision-making – one that took these forms of interaction into account. It is in this sense that the parties are engaged in joint production: they would all gain from making their choices collectively where they are interactive.

The classic example is of course the fishery, where each fisherman acting in his individual interest would fail to take into account his interaction with the other fishermen through the medium of the fish stock. The act of catching a fish has an impact on all other fishermen through the reduction of the number of fish remaining in the sea, thereby increasing the unit cost of catching a fish and reducing the rate of regeneration for the next year's stock. An individual fisherman does not consider the impact of these stock effects on others using the resource; they are external to his decision-making process.

As the result of externalities, resources are necessarily overexploited in the sense that there would be less utilization of the resource if the decision were taken collectively. The stock of the resource is reduced below that which would be preferred ('degradation'), and complete exhaustion is a possibility. It is for this reason that externalities generate incentives for new management institutions. The parties interacting through a natural resource that is being degraded have an incentive to identify one another, agree with one another and then institute some form of regime that takes their interaction into account.

When do these incentives to better management fail? They fail whenever it is too difficult to perform any of the prerequisites to better management listed above: identification, negotiation and agreement. These difficulties are labelled 'transactions costs' and they are the fundamental reasons why some forms of market failure persist while others generate solutions. Therefore, they are the more fundamental reasons why resource degradation occurs under some circumstances and not under others.

Chapter Two outlines the various forms of transactions costs, and how they translate into resource degradation. One straightforward reason for persistent market failure is the difficulties that arise in the context of large numbers of interacting individuals. If the nature of the interaction is bilateral – two individuals making use of the same river, say – then the nature of the negotiations required is more straightforward than if the interactions involve numerous people. In part, this is simply because there are many more parties to identify and to consult. Chapter Two gives the example of the Swedish factory that agreed with an automobile factory to generate corrosive exhaust fumes only on those days when the wind was blowing away from the factory. Ironically, this management solution consisted of shifting the fumes away from a factory but toward a residential neighbourhood – the transactions cost of large numbers of negotiations at work.

Large numbers are costly however for more reasons than simply identification and consultation. There is also the added problem of bargaining costliness. Again, in bilateral bargaining this costliness is much reduced as the parties know that nothing will be accomplished unless they both agree. When large numbers are involved, there is always the incentive to 'free-ride' on the agreement of others, that is to allow others to engage in restraint while individually continuing with unconstrained exploitation. The problem here is how to differentiate between those whose recalcitrance for participation in a resource management regime is motivated by an interest in free-riding and those whose recalcitrance is driven by differential costliness. The problem of acid rain is a case in point. In Europe for much of the 1980s there was a 'club of 30 per cent' which jointly agreed to restrict sulphur dioxide emissions in order to reduce acidic rainfall. Several states and some of the largest emitters of sulphur dioxide (including the UK) initially declined to join this management regime. This recalcitrance limited the effectiveness of the regime and resulted in additional forest and lake degradation throughout continental Europe.

Were these countries free-riding on the agreement of others? The case of the UK is illustrative. Although the European continent would benefit immensely from the UK's involvement in the management regime, in this case there was little gain and substantial cost to the UK. This is because the benefits to resource management need not be symmetric. In this instance, the benefits of sulphur dioxide management depend largely on which way the wind is blowing and this is mainly in an easterly direction on the European continent. The UK's unwillingness to participate in sulphur dioxide management stemmed more from the lack of significant emissions to its west than any other factor. However, it is difficult to sort out each individual's or nation's initial position with regard to a common resource and this contributes to transactions costs and hence to resource degradation.

There is one more important form of externality that is difficult to internalize. This is the case where it is difficult to even identify the affected parties. Many environmental problems stem from diffusive forms of interaction, where it is difficult to ascertain who is affected by the degradation of the resource and who is not. This is why so many environmental resources are 'ambient': systems that flow evenly across large areas. Systems of this nature imply interaction between large numbers of poorly identified individuals. A good example would be the contamination of groundwater. This contamination can occur via numerous points of entry (rivers, lakes, ground) and can then affect large numbers of users. Even if it is clear that some polluter is having an impact on some user of the aquifer, it is still difficult to pinpoint precisely who is interacting with whom. In the absence of identification, it is difficult to commence negotiations.

A related problem exists where it is possible to identify the affected parties but not possible to have them involved in the negotiations; this is the nature of the problem in the case of future generations. These people are affected by resource utilization decisions every day but they have little capacity to voice their preferences in these matters. This much may seem obvious but it is important to speak with precision in this matter. It is not the case that future generations would necessarily contest all current natural resource utilization or even all resource exhaustion. This is because current societal utilization of natural resources is translated into both consumption and investment; although the consumptive portion of resource use is of no benefit to future generations, the portion that is invested can translate into important benefits in the future.

The forward-looking nature of societal investments is a crucial part of the argument concerning sustainability. That is, it is essential that resource utilization generates investments, and that these investments be forward-looking in the sense that they prepare the society for impending scarcities. Increasing scarcities and increasing prices should cause societies' investments to shift toward technologies and discoveries that economize on these scarcities. Therefore, it is not clear on first analysis that future generations would have any need for representation in the current generation's decision-making concerning resource utilization.

There are specific instances in which representation of future generations' interests remains important, that is, there are clear examples of 'inter-generational externalities'. These exist whenever the current generation is able to make a choice with little consequence for itself but implied costliness for the future. One such case is the problem of irreversibility. Some development decisions are one-way while other are not. In this case the mere fact of irreversibility implies a loss of resources for future generations; in essence, future societies will never have the breadth of choice that current generations have had. An example of such externalities is the conversion of wilderness lands. Such lands have been produced by means of a natural process extending over millions of years, and their naturalization is not reproducible by means of human construction. Therefore their loss represents a loss of breadth in choice for all future generations. The conversion of wilderness is an example of an activity with a cost for future generations imposed upon them by the present, and it is very difficult to have those individuals represented in the decision-making process.

In sum, market failure must be at the core of any problem of resource degradation, simply by definition. It is the failure of institutions to arise spontaneously to resolve resource management problems. The underlying causes of these market failures are more substantial explanations of resource degradation. Market failures exist wherever it is difficult for interacting individuals to collaborate for resource management. Chapter Two of this volume discusses in more detail the nature of these problems and identifies many examples in which such failures result in resource degradation.

Policy: domestic and global policy failures and degradation
When societies fail to generate management spontaneously in response to resource degradation, then it is the role of governments to intervene and to implement effective resource management. However, this does not always occur and such an event is termed a 'policy failure'. A policy failure is analogous to a market failure, that is it is the failure of a government to supply an effective institution in response to the emergence of a need for one. There are numerous examples, even vast literatures, citing examples of government policy failures that fail to manage resource exploitation and degradation (see for example Repetto and Gillis, 1988).

The classically cited example of policy failure is the set of incentives set in place by governments for the management of the tropical forest regions, such as the Amazon basin. In these areas the governmentally instituted incentives are clearly favouring the rapid removal of the forests. In Brazil, these incentives are created by means of direct subsidies to ranching operations that are developed within the region. In Ecuador and many other places these incentives are generated by means of a government grant of land titles to those who clear the forest. However, it is important to emphasize that the alternation of the naturally existing slate of resources does not automatically equate with the degradation of that environment. There is a crucial distinction to be made between degradation and conversion. Degradation exists whenever natural resources are lost due to a failure of societal co-operation; it equates with a net loss to that society. Conversion on the other hand may have the same observable effects, that is the clearing away of the natural resources, but with a very different source – conversion is motivated by the desire of a society to substitute one form of asset for another.

As mentioned previously, provision for future scarcities is effected by means of society's current investment patterns; society must invest in forms of capital that make provision for these scarcities. Natural resources are seen as one form of capital asset within this framework. They generate a flow of benefits to societies in the form of the goods and services that they render. However, natural resources must compete with all other forms in which societies might hold their capital (such as education, health and machinery). The retention of natural resources implies reduced investment in all of these other asset types because natural resources themselves are implicit investments.

The conversion of natural resources occurs whenever a society chooses to invest in another asset in preference to the natural one, that is the decision will reduce the stock of natural assets and increase the stock of another form of asset. These reductions in natural resource stocks do not necessarily represent net losses to the society and so they do not constitute degradation. Such conversion may take several forms. It can be direct, by means of mining the natural resource (such as a hardwood forest) for investment of the proceeds in other assets (such as a hospital or school). Alternatively it can be indirect, by means of the refusal to allot the required resources for the sustenance of a natural system because these resources are being invested elsewhere. An example of this would be the general biodiversity problem, which derives from the channelling of lands into agriculture and away from the support of many other species. These lands are being invested in other uses because the society views these other uses as affording a better prospect of future returns.

Even management failures may stem from decisions to convert assets. The management of a natural resource requires investment, in order to establish the institutions that are necessary for regulating resource exploitation. When it is decided to convert resources, one of the actions of a state might be to withhold the required management for the system. This is because the efficient management of every resource is not possible under severe financial constraints. Those resources which are deemed expendable might not be seen as valuable enough to warrant a managed disinvestment programme. This desire for conversion is the source of the 'policy failures' that have been occurring in the tropical forests. These governments perceive little benefit to the current state of these assets (little-used forests). Therefore, they adopt policies that subsidize the conversion of these lands to more intensively used agricultural lands in the hope that these investments will generate assets that yield better future returns.

A more subtle form of conversion occurs in the case of many unmanaged resources. The African elephant for example has been a substantial user of African savannas and management resources over the past century. If a government believes that there are better uses of these resources, then it is able to convert the use of these lands and governmental resources simply by withholding management of the elephant. This makes the resource *de facto* open access and results in the over-exploitation of the resource. Chapter Three demonstrates how a handful of African states practised this policy in the 1980s and managed to remove half of the continental population within a decade.

So, the question remains: when is governmentally induced resource decline degradation and when is it conversion? It is clear that several previously perceived policy failures cannot be so labelled (see for example Repetto, 1989). The mere fact that the full value of the resource is unappropriated when mined is not necessarily evidence of a policy failure, since it may not pay to invest in appropriation but it still might be worthwhile to convert the ancillary resources (lands, management) to other uses. Also, it seems unfair to engage in *ex post* evaluations of government investments, labelling any poor investment a failure; investment decisions should be evaluated under the range of information available at the time that they were made.

There is one very clear source of policy failure, however, and this derives from the failure of the global community to transfer its valuation of domestic resources. On many occasions the outside perception that a particular regime's policy is a failure derives from an asymmetry in the valuation of that country's resources. The domestic regime sees forests as sources of trees and savannas as sources of protein. The global community values them very differently, for their role in providing global services. The forests of the earth perform important functions in the climatic system and the evolutionary system. The savannas of Africa provide important lands for valued wildlife. These are important functions of these resources but they are of minor relevance to their host states in comparison to the other services that they render there. It is this externality between global and local communities that must be internalized in order to correct many policy failures. The asymmetry in perspectives with regard to the appropriate policy to pursue derives from the asymmetry in valuations. It is the responsibility of the global community to develop institutions that will internalize this externality within the decision-making framework of the local community and its state.

Therefore, policy failure is an important source of resource degradation but it is important to trace back government-induced resource decline to its fundamental source. A local government will often engage in policies to convert its natural resources to other forms of assets, and such decisions to alter the natural landscape are not always equivalent to degradation. However, if the government's policies are optimal only from a very narrow perspective then there is a policy failure, but it is not the failure of that government but rather the failure of other societies to bring the global values of the resource within that community's decision-making.

This points once again to the importance of the distinction between resource and environmental degradation. Environmental degradation refers to the loss of systemic benefits and these are the likely focus of concern for the global community. Policy failures often have their roots in the failure of the global community to internalize global values of environmental systems that consequently results in local decisions to engage in resource conversion. This disjunction between the local and the global optima results in resource conversion and environmental degradation; the former is the result of local policy and the latter the result of global policy failure.

Population: population, economic scale and degradation
Is the problem of resource degradation related to the 'scale' of an economy, that is its level of economic activity, its population, its rate of resource throughput? This is the question addressed in Chapter Five. The fundamental issue raised in this study is whether the only source of degradation is externality-based or whether there is another source: the limits to substitutability. If there are synthesizable substitutes that can perform all of the functions performed by natural resources, then it is possible to skirt continuously around scarcity. This is accomplished by always using the least scarce resources to synthesize substitutes for the most scarce ones.

This process is precisely what has occurred in the petrochemical industries. Although we have come to think of crude oil as a scarce commodity, it was only one hundred years ago that it was seen as a nuisance substance, generating useless tar pits. It was the sheer prevalence of the substance that generated its many uses. It was an organic compound of little-known value that could be used as a building block for many other, more scarce commodities. Thus, petroleum-based synthetics have come to replace a vast array of scarcer natural resource-based commodities: rubber, steel, aluminium, soil fertility and wood. The relative non-scarcity of the substance generated many low-cost substitutes for scarcer natural resources.

It is this building-block approach to substitutability that lies at the core of the sustainability paradigm. So long as it is possible to identify the function that a natural resource serves and to identify the essential physico-chemical nature of a substitute, then it is very likely possible to synthesize low-cost substitutes for that natural resource.

The limits to substitutability then become equivalent to the limits of the human capacity for analysis and imagination. For example, the age-old basis for the practice of medicine has been the use of the naturally generated biological interaction between plants and animals, but the question of substitutability goes to the capacity of the human mind to eliminate this step in the production of medicines. Over millions of years of evolution, plants have developed the capacity to affect animals' behaviour by evolving substances that affect them physiologically. It is the examination and utilization of these substances that has generated the practice of medicine over the ages. Part of the concern about biodiversity losses stems from the loss of plant forms which must by their nature contain novel forms of chemical interaction.

Human practices of medicine initially derived from clinical trials of plant-derived substances that were known to be biologically active. When an active chemical substance is identified, it has then usually been synthesized in a laboratory. However, over the past few decades scientists have begun to focus more on the analysis of the physiological basis for disease and the identification of useful chemicals commencing from an understanding of the mechanisms of the human body rather than the naturally generated chemical usefulness. If this process of 'rational pharmaceutical design' was 100 per cent effective, then it would constitute a building-block approach to the provision of medicine. The human understanding of the chemical processes within the body would substitute completely for the evolved usefulness of plant-based substances.

Therefore, for sustainability to be achievable human understanding and innovation must be able to construct bridges over the natural resource sector, and between non-scarce building blocks (basic chemicals, genes and energy sources) and the functions required to support human societies. That is, all of the functions of natural resources and natural systems must be replaceable with these more atomistic elements (in combination with human ingenuity). This is the meaning of the required 'substitutability' for sustainability. If such substitutability exists, then the only form of degradation that matters is that which derives from the existence of externalities. That is, the scale of an economy is irrelevant so long as it takes into account the full cost of all of the resources and systems that it exploits. Even global problems such as global warming and biodiversity depletion then devolve to the need to place values on systems that will encourage substitutability. The solution to global warming would then be independent of the scale of the global economy but would entail only the creation of an implicit price on the carbon constraint affecting the planet's climate. The economies of the world would then internalize the problem by substituting away from carbon-based production technologies.

The only means by which the pure scale of an economy might matter is through the existence of 'meta-resources' (Ehrlich, 1988). The term meta-resource represents the concept of non-substitutable resources and systems. A common example of a meta-resource is Net Primary Product (NPP) – the total amount of photosynthetic product available for the support of all life forms on earth. It is a fixed amount of product determined by the relationship between the solar energy received on earth and the earth's evolved capacity to make use of that energy. At present it is estimated that the human species appropriates fully 40 per cent of the terrestrial NPP (Vitousek et al., 1986). With another doubling of the human population expected over the near term, this figure is likely to increase somewhat proportionately as it is usually found that consumption relationships between different tiers of food chains remain relatively stable. Therefore, it would appear that NPP constitutes a meta-resource in the sense of a fundamental limit on further growth of the earth's human population.

However, two final points about this possible meta-resource will indicate the difficulty with assessing the limits to substitutability. First, although NPP is clearly limited and the human species remains dependent upon it for sustenance, these relationships need not continue once under pressure. Just as in the case of the pharmaceutical industry, it is possible for human production of nutrition to become subject to 'rational design' processes rather than natural production processes. Then the same basic building-block approach could be developed to utilize the least scarce elements to satisfy human nutrition requirements; human energy and nutrition requirements could be satisfied just as readily by design as are medicinal requirements.

The problem in both instances (medicinal and nutritional) is that humans are beginning to conceive of themselves as existing outside the systems of which they are a part. It is possible to imagine ourselves as existing outside the system, using it only as a source of inputs for our own system; however, this is not the case in fact. Humans are one form of life within a web of life forms. Even more fundamentally, the biosphere is only one system within a physical-chemical environment that consists of numerous interlinked systems, such as hydrological, chemical and solar. To place human society outside these systems, treating all other resources and systems as inputs to the human society, risks the possibility that this viewpoint is incompatible with reality. If we come to divorce ourselves entirely from the systems of which we are part, in fact as well as in theory, there must be a real risk of our continued viability. The risk is that, without a compatibility constraint, the path chosen for human society might be incompatible with the more fundamental systems to which it is tied. Unlike the case of the south-sea islanders, there may be no other system to which we may turn if we mine ours entirely out of existence.

Therefore, this analysis of scale points to a potential framework problem in the previous analysis. So long as resources and environmental systems are seen as mere inputs into a distinct and separate human system, then the only problem of degradation lies in pricing difficulties. If natural systems are merely means of producing secondary goods and services, then human societies are able to work around them by using primary goods (building blocks) to produce substitute secondaries. However, when natural systems are seen not merely as inputs into human systems but rather as fundamental constraints on the range of feasible options for that system, then substitutability becomes less important than compatibility. Then we must take the approach of imposing constraints on development very seriously indeed.

Poverty: poor people, poor societies and degradation

Poverty is clearly linked with degradation. Poverty in the individual context means a lack of assets and a corresponding lack of income. Although these deficiencies need not necessarily translate into more degradation than would exist in richer societies, the difference lies in the capacity of the poor person to respond to risk within the environment. Poverty implies fewer assets and hence fewer options in response to shocks, which implies an increased reliance on the 'mining' of existing assets including natural resources.

All people maintain a portfolio of assets to protect themselves against risk. The broader the range of assets, the more the variability in returns will be reduced. Poverty implies a lack of asset 'depth', that is, a relative lack of assets, and a consequent lack of breadth as well. Given that variability will result from this reduced range of assets, the necessity arises of mining assets in the event of failures. For example, if a family is subsisting on only the yields from a small herd of livestock grazed on communal lands, then the effect of a failure, for example, a drought, is twofold. First, given the single form of asset in which the family's wealth is held, the loss of return due to the drought corresponds with the fall in the family's income; that is, there are no other assets to rely upon in the event of the failure of the first. Second, given the precipitous drop in income, the family must then commence drawing down its asset holdings by overgrazing the pasture or consuming its herd. Therefore, poverty clearly implies increased degradation on account of the increased variability that derives from a lack of breadth in asset holdings and the consequent mining that this variability implies.

However, although poverty is closely linked with degradation, does this in fact imply that it is a cause of degradation? The issue here is whether a lack of assets, and the increased prospects for degradation that this implies, is an exogenous cause of that degradation or a linked outcome of other more fundamental causes. It is clear that the characteristic of poorness does not in itself generate degradation; many poor people and societies have been able to generate remarkably stable and resilient institutions for coping with the income variability that being poor implies. In many cases it is some other destabilizing factor (for example civil unrest) that generates both the paucity of income and the unstable institutions that result in degradation.

Therefore, poverty and degradation are more likely to be linked outcomes occasioned by other destabilizing forces, rather than cause and effect. This explains the vicious cycle of poverty and degradation, so often identified. When people are poor, it is more likely that they will need to mine the resources they possess, but further mining merely enhances their poverty and the prospects for future mining. To escape this cycle requires an analysis of the more fundamental forces within the society that initially place so few assets at a person's disposal.

At the societal level, resource degradation is more likely to occur in a poor society simply because there are increased constraints on the capacities of that society to manage its resources. This does not imply an increased level of all forms of degradation as degradation represents a net loss to poor societies as much as it does to rich ones. Rather, it implies that a poor society may not invest in the careful management programmes for resource conversions that a richer society could undertake. For example, this probably explains the reason for the lack of well-managed depletion programmes for the hardwood forests and large land mammals in many developing countries. Although there would be benefits resulting from the careful appropriation of the full values of these resources as they are mined, the investments in the management required to ensure such appropriation are not competitive with the returns available from other investments within the economy.

This is once again a case where local decision-making is only sub-optimal from a broader perspective. That is, the degradation that occurs in the circumstances of poor people and poor societies is not sub-optimal from their own perspectives; relative to their other choices, the resource mining that occurs is the best selection from a poor set of options. This is only degradation when looked at from the broader perspective of those people and societies with more assets to rely upon. Again, these mining and management problems are inefficient when considered from the perspective of the assets held by human society globally, but not so when viewed from the perspective of the few options available to the local society. It is again a form of global policy failure (or possibly a national one) in which the asymmetry in asset holdings generates distinct perspectives on the local approach to resources. Poverty-induced resource decline is degradation because it could be eliminated through global action.

Prices: trade and degradation

Trade is also closely related to degradation, but not in the manner that springs to mind. Flows of goods and services between countries is one of the interfaces that already exists between the different societies on earth. These flows therefore reflect some of the decisions being made locally about natural resources but, more importantly, they also provide an opportunity to influence those decisions. It was explained previously that individual societies make decisions concerning their natural resources based on the capacities of those resources to generate a return competitive with other assets in the economy. It is then the relative rate of return from a natural resource that determines whether it attracts investment or not.

This is only part of the story however because the investment decisions made by individual countries will be determined in part by investment decisions made by others. There is both a supply side and a demand side to this externality. On the supply side, the investment decisions made by other states will to some extent predetermine the range of resources in which it is profitable to invest. This is because those states will invest in some factors of production that confer positive externalities on other producers. Then a dynamic externality will exist that will bias state investments toward the same range of resources that attracted the first state's investments.

An example of this phenomenon is the range of domesticated livestock and cultivated crops used throughout the world. These resources were locally optimal attractors of investment in their countries of origin but later states had their decisions determined by those initial choices. This is because those initial states invested heavily in technologies that were closely tied to those species and which were freely available to successive users. Examples would be the basic knowledge of the traits, pests, diseases and dietary requirements of the cultivated and domesticated species. Since this information is freely available for these species but not yet developed for others, states making decisions about resource investments are biased towards these selected species. This is one reason for the spread of cattle across the face of the globe (now totalling 1.5 billion head), displacing innumerable other species from their lands.

Another means by which the choices of some countries affect those of others is related more to demand; this is the impact of comparative advantage on resource investment decisions. Although there is a tendency for global production forms to converge upon the same methods, there is also an incentive for different forms of production to be allocated to different countries. That is, there is an incentive for different countries to specialize in entirely different functions.

The precise specialization of any given country will be dependent in part upon the relative advantages of that country, such as its natural resource endowments, its human skills and its climate. However, another factor determining the relative advantage of a given country will be other countries' endowments. This means that the division of functions across the globe will depend not only upon natural endowments but also, crucially, upon societal preferences and the financial resources to support them. One nation may not have a natural superiority for a given function but still may have a market-based advantage if another country would prefer to export it (and has the financial capacity to do so). Such exportation of unwanted functions can be said to be equivalent to purchasing sustainability; it is once again a function as much of relative poverty as relative natural endowments.

A good example of this is the trade in toxic wastes. High-level toxic wastes have often been exported to small African states with little attention to their capacity for disposal of these chemicals. In fact, the relative factor endowments (natural, human and technological) probably favour the retention of the wastes in their country of origin, usually a large industrial Northern country. In these countries the necessary information, skills and technology exist in order to dispose effectively of the wastes. The problem is that there is such an asymmetry in the wealth levels between the two countries that the exporter can determine unilaterally the relative values of its own natural resource endowment and the other country's. If it creates a sufficient differential between the two, then the effect of the relative paucity in the other factors necessary for disposal (such as technology and skills) will be swamped. The wastes will be shipped simply because the exporter has the capacity to place such a high relative value on its own natural resources and virtually none on the other country's.

Does this form of 'imported sustainability' constitute resource or environmental degradation? It certainly does in the event of the various forms of externalities that might be generated, both inside and outside the country. For example, DDT specimens have now been found in the food chains in both arctic regions; poor disposal of persistent chemicals is certain to redound to the detriment of many societies other than the importing one.

Also important is the poverty-induced form of degradation that occurs in this situation. Shipping difficult-to-manage resources to poor countries makes little sense given the difference in management capabilities. It is only economically feasible if the local regime does not undertake the management necessary to deal with the wastes, because it is locally optimal to engage instead in unmanaged conversion of the state's natural resources. Then the wastes are shipped not on account of less expensive management but on account of non-management and a lower valuation of the nation's resources. From a global perspective, this is increasing the degradation of resources by exploiting the differential wealth levels in the world and is another example of poverty-induced degradation. A good example is the country of Guinea-Bissau which took imports of toxic substances from the US for five years for a fee that effectively doubled its national GDP.

Therefore trade is simply another form of resource utilization that can result in degradation if it falls within the criteria outlined above. The unique aspect of trade is that it provides one manner of interface between the global community and individual countries, an interface that might be used constructively to regulate degradation within individual countries. To a large extent, the debate on trade should be focused more on its constructive than its destructive capabilities.

The constructive use of trade has been proposed in many cases for numerous years. It has been used or studied in the case of fisheries, marine mammals, wildlife resources and forestry products. It has not been a successful movement to date for two reasons. First, in many cases trade regulation has been developed unilaterally rather than globally, as in the case of the US refusal of Mexican tuna catches. The point of this analysis is not that a developed country should substitute its judgement for a developing country's with regard to the latter's resources; the use of the trade interface for global regulation must be conducted on a multilateral basis. Secondly, trade regulation has been geared historically more toward trade refusal than trade rewards. The object of a global-local interface must be to correct differences in the values received from local investments. This implies increased returns to local investments in diverse resource stocks, not diminished ones. Therefore, Chapter Six concludes that trade might be used constructively as an instrument to halt resource degradation. It is one facet of the global-local interface which might be developed into a mechanism for correcting global policy failures and this is probably the most important facet of trade in the analysis of environmental degradation.

Conclusion: the causes of degradation

This volume now expands upon the themes developed within this framework. It shows in more detail and in more examples how these various factors (property, policies, population, poverty and prices) are associated with environmental degradation. The short answer provided here is that the framework of the economist demonstrates that there are numerous avenues to resource degradation but only one underlying source. This source is the institutional interface between human society and its environment. When this institutional structure is weak at recognising depletion or controlling utilization of some part of the environment, then there is an enhanced likelihood of degradation for the corresponding commons. Such weaknesses are usually based in the limitations of humans and institutions for responding to the complexities encompassed within many forms of resources.

The hypothesis of Hardin that the tragedy of the commons lay within the opportunistic nature of the human species is, in part, true (Hardin, 1993). One very important inherent weakness in commons management lies in the opportunities that exist for unilateral appropriation of the commons and the opportunism of individuals in pursuing these. On account of the complexity of these resources and the resultant difficulty in implementing effective management of them, there will always be opportunities available for their exploitation. The commons will continue to degrade so long as individuals exploit these opportunities. Societies will be faced with the prospect of either combating this opportunism perpetually or eliminating the commons, with the attendant costliness either implies. Commons remain commons largely because they tend to be complex resources; however, this complexity in itself implies continued and substantial costliness in combating the opportunistic strategies it enables. Commons institutions will have to be evolutionary in nature in response to these problems and it is probable that commons problems will be with us always.

It must be emphasized however that the commons is not always its own worst enemy. On many occasions the opportunism that is driving the degradation of the commons is not individual but society-based. That is, it is often the case that social problems are caused to work their costliness through the medium of a common resource. For example, fringe members of rapidly growing societies are sometimes pushed out onto 'frontiers' in order to mitigate social pressures. In these instances, social conflicts and their costliness are relegated to the commons rather than resolved. Then the costs of these problems become costs to the commons. It is a case of the society treating the commons as a wasteland, rather than a resource, and investing in neither the resolution of the problem nor in the resource. These are examples of broader social problems that need not, but often do, channel their costliness through the commons.

At base the problem of environmental degradation derives from the problem of sub-optimal social institutions. Institutions must continue to evolve in order to incorporate the increased knowledge that we have concerning environmental systems and in response to new human strategies of opportunism. However, it must also be recognized that it is never possible for institutions to reach 'first-best' in this context. There will always be further complexity recognized within natural systems and there will always be new and ingenious opportunistic strategies devised by human individuals. Each time that this is the case there will be the need for another step along the long road toward institutional refinement. This journey can never come to an end within the context of changing natural and social environments. There will always be one more tragedy awaiting the commons.

Bibliography

Anderson, D. and Hill, L. (1975), 'The Evolution of Property Rights', *Journal of Law and Economics*, **18**, 163.
Barzel, Y. (1990), *Economic Analysis of Property Rights*, Cambridge University Press: Cambridge.
Baumol, W. and Oates, W. (1988), *The Theory of Environmental Policy*, Cambridge University Press: Cambridge.

Cheung, S. (1970), 'The Structure of a Contract and the Theory of a Non-Exclusive Resource', *Journal of Law and Economics*, **13** (1), 49–70.

Ciracy-Wantrup, S. and Bishop, R. (1975), 'Common Property as a Concept in Natural Resources Policy', *Natural Resources Journal*, **15** (4), 713–29.

Conrad, J. and Clark, C. (1987), *Natural Resource Economics*, Cambridge University Press: Cambridge.

Daly, H. (ed.) (1992), *Toward a Steady-State Economy*, (2nd edn), Island Press: Washington, D.C.

Dasgupta, P. (1982), *The Control of Resources*, Blackwell: Oxford.

Dasgupta, P. and Heal, G. (1979), *Economic Theory and Exhaustible Resources*, Cambridge University Press: Cambridge.

Dorfman, R. and Dorfman, E. (eds) (1993), *Economics of the Environment: Selected Readings*, Norton & Co.: New York and London.

Ehrlich, P. (1988), 'Meta-Resources', *Ecological Economics*, **1**, 1–10.

Hanna, S. and Munasinghe, M. (1995), *Property Rights and the Environment*, The World Bank: Washington.

Hardin, G.J. (1993), 'The Tragedy of the Commons', reprinted in Dorfman, R. and Dorfman, E. (eds) (1993).

Hartwick, J. and Olewiler, N. (1986), *The Economics of Natural Resource Use*, Harper Collins: New York.

Heal, G. (1975), 'Economic Aspects of Natural Resource Depletion', in Pearce, D. and Rose, J. (eds), *The Economics of Depletion*, Macmillan: London.

Hotelling, H. (1931), 'The Economics of Exhaustible Resources', *Journal of Political Economy*, **39**, 137–75.

Krutilla, J.V. (1967), 'Conservation Reconsidered', *American Economic Review*, **57**, 777–86.

Krutilla, J.V. and Fisher, A. (1975), *The Economics of Natural Environments*, Johns Hopkins University Press: Baltimore.

Libecap, G. (1990), *Contracting for Property Rights*, Cambridge University Press: Cambridge.

Ostrom, E. (1990), *Governing the Commons*, Cambridge University Press: Cambridge.

Panayotou, T. (1989), *The Economics of Environmental Degradation: Problems, Causes and Responses*, Harvard Institute for International Development, Cambridge, Massachusetts, (reprinted in Markandya, A. and Richardson, J. (eds) (1992), *Environmental Economics*, Earthscan: London).

Pearce, D.W. (1988), 'The Sustainable Use of Natural Resources in Developing Countries', in Turner, R.K. (ed.), *Sustainable Environmental Management: Principles and Practice*, Belhaven Press: London.

Pearce, D.W. (1991), 'An Economic Approach to Saving the Tropical Forests', in Helm, D. (ed.), *Economic Policy Towards the Environment*, Blackwell: Oxford.

Pearce, D.W., Barbier, E. and Markandya, A. (1990), *Sustainable Development: Economics and Environment in the Third World*, Edward Elgar: Aldershot.

Pearce, D. and Warford, J. (1993), *World Without End*, Oxford University Press: Oxford.

Perrings, C. (1991), 'Ecological Sustainability and Environmental Control', *Structural Change and Economic Dynamics*, **2**, 275–95.

Repetto, R. and Gillis, M. (1988), *Public Policies and the Misuse of Forest Resources*, Cambridge University Press: Cambridge.

Repetto, R. et al. (1989), *Wasting Assets: Natural Resources in National Accounts*, World Resources Institute: Washington.

Smith, V.K. (ed.) (1979), *Scarcity and Growth Reconsidered*, Johns Hopkins University Press: Baltimore.

Smith, V.K. (1972), 'The Effects of Technological Change on Different Uses of Environmental Resources', in Krutilla, J.V. (ed.), *Natural Environments: Studies in Theoretical and Applied Analysis*, Johns Hopkins University Press: Baltimore.

Smith, V.K. and Krutilla, J.V. (eds) (1982), *Explorations in Natural Resource Economics*, Johns Hopkins University Press: Baltimore.

Solow, R. (1974a), 'Intergenerational Equity and Exhaustible Resources', *Review of Economic Studies*, Symposium Issue on Depletable Resources, 37–48.

Solow, R. (1974b), 'The Economics of Resources or the Resources of Economics', *American Economic Review*, **64**, 1–2.
Vitousek, P. et al. (1986), 'Human Appropriation of the Products of Photosynthesis', *Bioscience*, **36** (6), 368–73.

2   Market failure and environmental degradation

Robin Mason

Introduction

This chapter develops the framework for understanding why environmental degradation exists and, especially, why it persists. That is, it addresses the fundamental question of why individual activities that generate obvious environmental costliness continue unabated. Why does some sort of societal response not arise spontaneously to solve such problems?

This is the problem of 'market failure': the failure of a decentralized society to generate solutions to particular problems. Market failures are said to exist whenever some significant economic factor is 'unpriced', that is, when economic activity is undertaken without consideration of the full impact of that activity (due to the absence of a price on some input to or output from that activity). Market failures are important because they harm all society. Underpricing or non-pricing of a resource leads to its systematic over-exploitation. Over-exploitation results in the degradation of the resource. The degradation of a resource, as opposed to its managed use, cannot be of benefit to society. Therefore the absence of regulatory institutions (pricing mechanisms) leads inevitably to the degradation of environmental resources such as air, water and wildlife and thus to social costliness.

The purpose of this chapter is to demonstrate why it is that the solutions to social problems of this nature are difficult to achieve. The implementation of environmental regulation, even when the benefits to be derived are obvious, is not a given. The parties whose interests are at stake must be identified and they must agree and enforce a new regime of regulation. The difficulties involved in accomplishing these simple tasks often forestall effective regulation and ensure continued degradation of the environment.

Externalities

The most important form of market failure for the issue of environmental degradation is the existence of externalities. An externality arises when the decisions of some economic agents (individuals, firms, governments), whether in production, consumption or exchange, affect other economic agents and are not included in the priced system of commodities, that is they are not compensated.[1] An alternative way of expressing this problem is to say that economic agents consider only their private (marginal) costs when making decisions and not the total or social (marginal) costs of their actions. For example, a polluter will only consider its own cost of burning coal, not the pollution costs inflicted upon its neighbours. It is the gap between private and social marginal costs that gives rise to the problem of externality (see Figure 2.1).

Externalities result in market 'failure': a distortion in the market's allocation of resources. This market failure translates into resource degradation by reason of the excessive exploitation of the unpriced factor; that is, Q-private is greater than Q-social in Figure 2.1. Thus it is in the interests of the whole of society to correct for externalities.

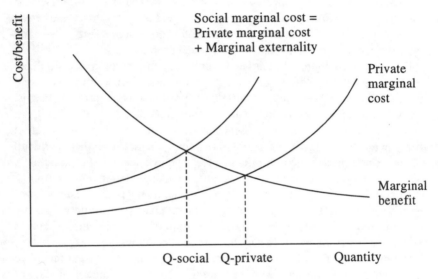

Figure 2.1   The gap between private and social marginal costs

The institutional nature of externality
A valid question to ask is: why do externalities exist? That is, if externalities are truly 'costs to society', then why don't societies always act to eliminate them? The answer to this question is known as 'transactions costs' and is the subject of this chapter. In essence, if it is as costly to eliminate an externality as it is to retain the externality (due to the various forms of transactions costs), then the externality will persist. In the absence of these costs, co-operation between members of a society can successfully eliminate all significant externalities (the so-called Coase Theorem).[2]

For example, if two firms are situated on the same river, one using the water for the operation of its brewery and the other as a receptacle for its waste products, then an externality may exist. However, it would be antici-pated that (in many such cases) the two parties would be able to identify the nature of their interaction and to act jointly to co-ordinate their usage of the common resource, that is, the river. When the parties achieve such co-opera-tion (in the manner of the Coase Theorem) the externality will be removed by reason of their joint action.

The discovery of persistent externalities therefore boils down to the search for situations in which the Coase Theorem does not hold. Baumol and Oates (1988) quote an example which illustrates both the benefits and limitations of bargaining:

> On the outskirts of Gothenburg in Sweden, an automobile plant is located next to an oil refinery. The automobile producer found that when the refining of lower quality petroleum was under way and the wind was blowing in the direction of the automobile plant, there was a marked increase in corrosion of its metal inventory and the paint of recently produced vehicles. Negotiation between the two parties *did* take place. It was agreed to conduct the corrosive activities only when the wind was blowing in the other direction *toward the large number of nearby inhabitants who, naturally, took no part in negotiation.*
> Emphasis in the original, p. 11.

Transaction costs arise from three sources. First, when many individuals are affected by the same externality, separate bargaining with each 'victim' would be prohibitively expensive and this costliness is reflected in the above quota-tion. Second, there is the possibility of free-riding. Suppose that a bargain exists between a single polluter (a factory producing smoke, say) and many victims (for example householders), which involves the householders making a payment to the factory to reduce smoke emissions. However each indi-vidual householder has little incentive to join the collective bargain but in-stead will hope that all other victims are sufficiently damaged by the smoke and will therefore pay a little bit more to ensure that the bargain is made. The non-paying householder then gains the benefit of a smoke-free environment without having to pay his share of the bargain. At the limit, no bargain at all will take place as everybody attempts to be a free-rider; in intermediate cases, more than the efficient level of smoke production occurs. Third, there is the problem of identification and representation. That is, even if the parties wish to make an effort at co-operation, it may be costly or impossible to identify those parties to the interaction. This is often the case, for example, with respect to pollution of ambient media such as groundwater where it can be virtually impossible to trace the pollution back to its source. Finally, even if it is possible to identify the parties affected, it may still be impossible to bring them into the bargain. This is the problem of representing future generations' interests in an environmental resource.

The conditions under which bargaining will fail to internalize externalities are sufficiently common to merit attention. This chapter examines externalities and the failure of bargaining in four sections: externalities between individuals, locations, countries and generations. Each section contains detailed case studies to highlight the principles that are presented.

Externalities between individuals: the tragedy of the local commons
What happens to resources when no property rights have been awarded? Such resources are free to be used by anyone who wishes and, being free and of finite capacity, they are used excessively. This problem was labelled 'the tragedy of the commons' by Hardin (1968) and occurs frequently in resource economics. It will be encountered once more when externalities between countries (the 'global commons' problem) are considered. On an individual, local scale, overgrazing, overfishing and the depletion of trees and shrubs from common land for use as fuel are familiar problems.

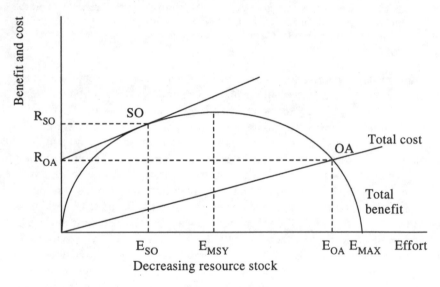

Figure 2.2   The tragedy of the commons

The 'tragedy of the commons' is illustrated in Figure 2.2. In this diagram, total benefits and total costs are shown against effort expended in harvesting the resource (for example cutting down trees for fuel). The amount of effort expended in harvesting is monotonically and inversely related to the remaining stock of trees. The total benefit curve is drawn as an inverted U, signifying that there exists a critical effort level, or stock of trees, beyond which the population starts to decline. The harvest at this critical level (marked E_{MSY} in

Figure 2.2) is known as maximum sustainable yield. Harvests in excess of this level deplete the resource stock.

Three points on this diagram are of interest. First, E_{MAX} is the maximum level of effort and corresponds to a zero stock of trees. Second, suppose that the entire forest were given to a single owner who then aims to maximize 'profits' (the differences between total benefits and costs). This situation would bring about point SO – the point at which the difference between benefits and costs is the largest. The effort level employed is E_{SO}, corresponding to a resource stock of R_{SO}. Third, suppose that no one individual possesses the property right to the forest and access is open, free and unrestricted. In this case, anyone who can make a 'profit' (obtain some net benefit) by harvesting will do so. That is, whenever total benefits are greater than total costs, someone will find it worth their while to expend effort to chop down trees. They will stop only when total costs exceed total benefits – to the right of point OA. The effort level employed is $E_{OA} > E_{SO}$, and the corresponding resource stock is $R_{OA} < R_{SO}$.

What is the source of the externality in this problem? It is that the individuals in the open-access regime consider only their own private (marginal) costs and benefits, assuming that their individual actions will not have any significant effect on the resource stock. The impact of their actions on others is ignored. In the terminology of economics, individuals attach a zero shadow price to the resource, and therefore use it excessively.[3] The single owner (or social planner), on the other hand, takes into account the effects of his or her actions on the resource stock, that is s/he attaches a non-zero (positive) shadow price to the resource.

Real life will undoubtedly be more complex than this simple diagram. Commons are rarely completely open-access but are owned by a community and operate under agreed rules of behaviour (although it is not guaranteed, however, that everyone will adhere to these rules). In this case, the actual amount of effort expended will be less than E_{OA} and the resource stock greater than R_{OA}. It is possible for a common property regime to result in excellent resource management. However an open-access common, for which no management regime exists, will lead to excessive harvesting of the resource.

Why does the Coase Theorem not apply in this situation, that is why don't individuals bargain privately to achieve a better outcome than under open-access ('market the externality')? The problem lies in the costs of bargaining. Is it conceivable that a large number of people will agree on rules to use the commons? In certain circumstances, this may be so – if, for example, the majority recognizes that extinction is the imminent consequence of continued unfettered usage. Of course, as discussed previously, even if the parties wish to make an agreement, it may be costly to do so and this is the problem of transactions costs. In addition unless the 'contract' is legally binding, peer pressure is the only mechanism by which over-exploitation can be prevented – an unenforceable contract is no contract at all. These factors mean that, while there may be some decrease in E below E_{OA}, bargaining and the Coase theorem will not always provide us with a solution to the problem of the commons.

Case study: Southeast Asian fish stocks

The 'tragedy of the commons' is seen clearly in the depletion of fish stocks in Southeast Asia (see Pearce and Warford, 1993). Catch rates per unit of fishing effort have declined by at least a factor of ten for most species since 1961. Pauly and Thia-Eng (1988) show that 60 to 70 per cent of the decline in catches is due to overfishing, mostly by large numbers of small trawlers using nets with meshes that catch many of the species' young. Figure 2.3 shows clearly how the amount of effort (measured by the mean annual fleet horse-

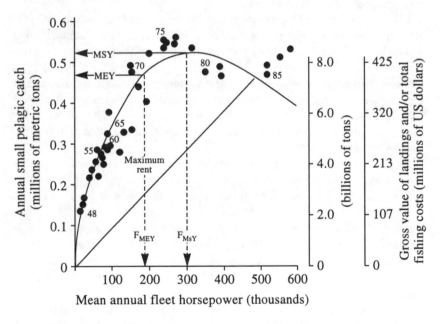

Note: Beginning in the 1970s, fishing effort went beyond the maximum economic profitability yield (MEY), and even beyond the maximum sustainable yield (MSY) and approached open-access catch rates. In both the demersal and the pelagic fisheries, the profit rate is zero. Significant increases in profits could be achieved by reducing catch rates.

Source: Pauly and Thia-Eng (1988). (Reprinted in Pearce and Warford, 1993).

Figure 2.3   Overfishing in pelagic fisheries of the Philippines

power) expended in harvesting pelagic fish in the Philippines is well beyond the point of maximum profitability for the industry and is approximately at the level predicted by the simple open-access model of Figure 2.2. Bans have now been put into effect in parts of Southeast Asia in an attempt to reduce catches, allow fish stocks to regenerate and increase the income of fishermen.

To conclude this section, it should be noted that the externality encountered in the commons problem occurs frequently in other contexts. The situation where co-operation is socially optimal but where individuals have incentives not to co-operate, is not unique to the use of environmental resources. In economics, the situation is known as the Prisoners' Dilemma (see, inter alia, Kreps, 1990, for a discussion) which can be applied to many interactions between economic agents.

Recognizing environmental degradation as a case of Prisoners' Dilemma shows that co-operation can never be achieved by private unmonitored agreement between individuals since each will have an incentive to deviate and over-harvest. Instead, an external agency (for example government) is required to monitor and enforce any agreement to restrict harvesting. We shall return to this setting in a later section of this chapter concerning the regulation of global resources.

Externalities between locations
When individuals are in physical proximity (using the same resource) and can identify the source of the externality, it might still be difficult, if not impossible, to create a socially efficient outcome through private contracts. The limitations of bargaining become even more severe when we consider the case where activities in one location affect individuals in another location.

Two problems arise: first, as in the case of externalities between individuals, bargaining costs due to the large number of victims may be high. A small amount of externality-generating activity in one location may give rise to a large number of victims in many different locations. An obvious example is a factory releasing chemical waste into a river – everyone downstream will suffer from the pollution created by a single release of chemicals. As before, these costs may preclude an efficient outcome being reached through contracting. Second, it may be difficult for the victims of the externality to identify the offender(s). In the example of the chemical-dumping factory, an individual some fifty miles downstream may take some time to realize that the pollution originates from the offending factory. In addition, by the time the pollution has reached the victim and the origin has been identified, the offender may no longer exist (in this case, the factory may have gone bankrupt). Moreover, even when the location of externality generation can be identified, geographical separation confers anonymity on the offender. For example, consider the case where several factories operate on a river. Pollution downstream evidently originates upstream but which of the factories is the culprit?[4]

In this case the costs to bargaining (monitoring to find out who is creating the externality and then forming a contract) may be so high that no contract is formed at all. Once again the Coase Theorem can offer no help in these situations.

We will consider two examples of externalities between locations: the use of agricultural chemicals (such as pesticides and insecticides) and the deforestation of areas of Amazonia.

Case study: use of agricultural chemicals

The value of the global, end-user market for pesticides was approximately US$20.5 billion in 1988 (see Conway and Pretty, 1991). In developing countries in particular, the use of pesticides is growing very rapidly – for example, pesticide consumption in Indonesia grew by 30 per cent between 1980 and 1985 (ADB, 1987). Pesticides undeniably play a crucial role in world agriculture. In the industrialized nations they have helped (along with mechanization) to drive down the variable costs of farming. In developing countries crop yields have increased as pesticide use has grown.

The use of pesticides, however, has not been an unqualified success. The effectiveness of certain pesticides has been eroded by the buildup of resistance. At the same time, the effect of pesticides on the environment has become a matter of increasing concern. The very nature of pesticides makes their use extremely hazardous. Pesticides are usually designed to be non-selective, to maximize the range of uses of the chemical and to minimize the costs of development of the pesticide. They work by interfering with basic biological processes that are common to a wide range of organisms, including wildlife and often humans. As Conway and Pretty conclude, 'the safest assumption is that every pesticide is harmful to all organisms unless the contrary is proved' (p. 17). Pesticides are also often designed to be persistent, thus avoiding the need for repeated applications by farmers. It is this characteristic, combined with the high water solubility of many chemicals, that presents the greatest danger to the environment at the moment.[5]

Pesticides can enter the environment by several routes (see Figure 2.4). The method of application determines how much chemical reaches the crop and how much escapes. Aerial spraying, for example, often achieves less than a 50 per cent application rate inside the target field due to spray drift. Once on the crop chemicals can be absorbed by the crop or by weed seeds (the aim of application), but they can also evaporate to the atmosphere, run off with surface water, biodegrade or hydrolyse, and leach through the soil layers to groundwater. It is this last action which is currently causing so much concern

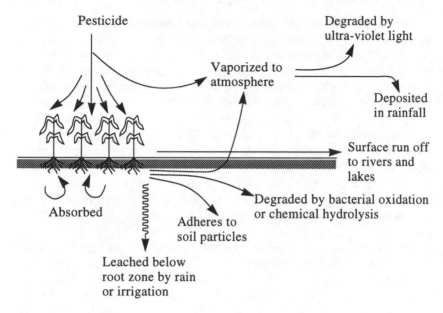

Source: Conway and Pretty (1991).

Figure 2.4   Fate of pesticides after application

in Europe and the US (although the other effects are, of course, important). Once chemicals reach groundwater they may become extremely persistent – there is little biodegradation, due to the lack of oxygen, and obviously no photolysis. For example, the half-life of DDT in soil is between one and two years; once it reaches groundwater, however, the half-life extends to 25 to 40 years (Wheatley, 1965). Atrazine, a herbicide used in maize cultivation, has a half-life above ground of 90 days; in groundwater, this becomes three years or more. Fortunately, the solubility of DDT in water is not that high, so little of the chemical makes its way to groundwater. Many chemicals are highly soluble however (atrazine is but one example), and have been accumulating over many years so that now they have reached alarming concentration levels. Once in groundwater, chemicals travel through underground water reservoirs and reach rivers, lakes and drinking water supplies. Even low doses of these pesticides remain in the base environment for long periods, allowing higher animals (birds, mammals) to accumulate these substances at higher and higher rates, even far from the treated area. The accumulation of these substances leads to population reduction in some animals (for example birds of prey), changed behavioural patterns in others (for example salmon and trout) and even to high concentrations in many humans.[6]

What is the origin of the externality (market failure) in this case? There is an in-built market mechanism which attempts to calibrate society's costs and benefits in the use of chemicals in agricultural production, that is, the farmer. In determining the proportion of chemicals to use in generating any given level of output, the farmer will weigh the costs of additional chemical usage against the prospective benefits from its use.

The costs which the farmer will consider are derived from the price to him of an additional application of chemicals. To a degree, this price represents society's costs as well because the farmer will have to pay enough for the chemicals to divert their use to agricultural purposes as any petrochemical product can be used in a variety of different fashions (such as plastics and fuels). The price that each of these industries pays must be sufficient to bid the petrochemical away from the others. This is the 'opportunity cost' of the chemical.

The farmer does not, however, consider the costs of the potential health risks to persons other than himself – he considers only the costs of depriving the plastics and fuels industries of the petrochemical resource. The health cost is not reflected in the price which he has to pay for the chemical input, resulting in excessive use of pesticides. Therefore, as depicted in Figure 2.1 earlier, there are 'externalized costs' within the farmer's decision-making process resulting in social costliness.

This externality cannot be corrected by bargaining à la Coase. A single application of chemicals by a farmer has the potential of affecting many others (if, for example, the chemical reaches groundwater and travels then to drinking-water wells). Our previous arguments indicate that bargaining in this situation will be prohibitively costly, even when property rights have been established.[7] In addition, identification problems are severe. The time lag for pesticides to travel from the point of application to drinking water sources may be long – concentrations of atrazine in drinking aquifers in the north of Italy are still increasing, despite a complete ban imposed in 1990 (Zanin et al., 1991). Many farmers may work in the same area. Both factors make identification of the perpetrators (the other side of the bargain) difficult and any potential contract unenforceable. Therefore it is very difficult for the market to generate spontaneously a solution to the pesticide pollution problem.

Case study: Amazonian deforestation

Unofficial estimates of alteration and deforestation of Brazilian Amazonia suggest that about 10 per cent of the original forest (some 290,000 km^2) has been altered. This trend is not confined to Amazonia, however, and rates of tropical deforestation are high and increasing in all parts of the world (see Table 2.1).

Table 2.1 Rates of tropical deforestation (closed forest only)

	Figures in million hectares per annum		
	Late 1970s	Mid-1980s	Late 1980s
South America	2.67	9.65	6.65
Central America	1.01	1.07	1.03
Africa	1.02	1.06	1.58
Asia	1.82	3.10	4.25
Oceania	0.02	0.02	0.35
Total	6.54	14.90	13.86
Remaining forest	0.6%	n.a.	1.8–2.1%

Note: Figures cover 34 countries accounting for 97.3% of the extent of tropical forest in 1989.

Source: Pearce and Warford (1993).

Cattle-raising and timber exploitation explain the majority of the forest's disappearance. The contribution of pasture formation to the total area of altered forest may be as high as three-quarters (Barbier, 1989). Although timber exports in Brazil demand only a few species of tree (mahogany in particular), the low population density of any particular species means that extensive forest damage results from the search for a limited number of trees.

For all this effort, the economic impact is small – Brazilian Amazonia contributes only 5 per cent to the country's GNP and forest timber makes up only 10 per cent of the country's exports of industrial timber. For these minor benefits, the costs are inordinately high. There are, of course, environmental quality losses – the reduction in the biodiversity of the area and alteration of locations with unique cultural and aesthetic features. In addition there are more tangible effects, for example, the loss of productivity and other economic damage due to water run-off and soil degradation following deforestation. Watersheds, previously protected by the water retention, flow regulation of water pollution, and organic nutrient cleansing provided by dense forest, are depleted. Moreover, the effects are not confined to one particular area. A net loss of water in central Brazil may subsequently affect agriculture in south-central Brazil (and other South American regions), due to the complex interdependence of the Amazonian ecosystem.

Market failure in this case, as in the others previously considered, lies in the non-valuation of socially important factors when (private) individuals are buying and exploiting land and natural resources. Choice of land use is biased in favour of those that have marketed outputs, such as ranching and timber exploitation. The market value of this land fails to reflect the lost environmental benefits such as watershed protection. If owners had to pay the full social cost of developing forested land, the outcome would certainly be different. Instead forest land is clearly underpriced and the result is too much conversion of forest to farm areas, over-exploitation, and under-investment in the natural management of forest land.[8]

Externalities across frontiers

Environmental systems have no respect for man-made borders. In many cases, an environmental problem will not confine itself conveniently to one area but will overlap areas of jurisdiction and control. In the absence of one single authority to control and prescribe the solution to the problem, international externalities will be plagued by lack of co-ordination and concomitant inefficiency.

International externalities can take many forms (see Mäler, in Helm, 1991).[9] For example, a pollutant may move across a border, carried by rivers, sea currents or winds. A pollutant (for example waste materials) is often transported by humans across national frontiers, with the danger of accidental spillage. Pollution or environmental degradation in one country may simply be of concern to other countries. For example, Brazilian deforestation causes concern in the West for the preservation of tropical forests (more often for cultural and aesthetic reasons than the effects on the global climate). Finally, there may be economic side-effects to environmental policy (for example the impact on international trade – see Chapter Seven).

Solutions to trans-frontier problems must, in general, come from voluntary agreements between states (multilateral contracts). The problem is, as we shall see, that the structure for bargaining is often biased towards failure (the Prisoners' Dilemma situation). That is, the nations sharing an environmental system (joint airspace or water supply) may have a collective interest in effectively managing the resource but none has the individual incentive to take the action to invest in the resource. The absence of incentives to collective action makes it unlikely that the international externality will be internalised.

We shall concentrate on two case studies: acid rain (an example of a regional reciprocal externality) and global warming (an example of the 'tragedy of the global commons'). The key question that we shall ask in each case is: what are the incentives for (voluntary) co-operation?

Case study: acid rain

Sulphur and nitrogen oxides are emitted when fossil fuels are burned and in some industrial processes. The oxides are oxidized in the atmosphere and from there are carried long distances. They may be absorbed in the dry state by surface water, land or crops (dry deposition), or washed out of the atmosphere by rainfall (wet deposition). Both forms of deposition are acidic, and both are referred to as 'acid rain'.

The nature and extent of damage caused by acid rain is still a subject of some debate. There seem to be three effects (see Pearce and Warford, 1993). First, acidic deposition reduces the pH of lakes and rivers, with effects on aquatic life. Second, these depositions cause direct damage to leaf surfaces of crops and trees. Third, the increased acidity of rainfall causes greater solubility of soil ions; consequently forest soil is both stripped of nutrients and left with toxic ions (aluminium in particular) which, through run-off, can affect rivers, lakes and eventually human drinking water.

Both North America and Europe are afflicted with the problem of acid rain. In the former, acid compounds located in the atmosphere of the northeastern US and eastern Canada have (it is claimed) increased because of emissions in the central and southern US. In Europe, emissions in the central belt and east of Europe have caused soils to acidify in Scandinavia in particular. In both cases, forest damage may be a result although the evidence is, as yet, inconclusive.[10]

Acidification of soil and rivers in both continents is, less controversially, a result of acid rain depositions, although the damage that this causes is not clear. We mention the effects above but the extent to which this acidification causes economic and/or environmental damage is still unclear. Three conclusions can be reached however: acid rain is undesirable, acid rain is no respecter of international boundaries and, therefore, international agreement is necessary to combat the problem of acid rain.

A digression on the Prisoners' Dilemma

Let us concentrate on the problem of acid rain in Europe. First consider the case where two countries emit sulphur and nitrogen oxides in equal amounts and impose an acid rain externality on each other to the same extent.[11] This problem is familiar – it is, once again, the Prisoners' Dilemma. The 'payoffs' to the game are shown in Table 2.2 in the form of a 'game matrix' (the numbers in the table representing the payoffs to countries A and B, respectively, given each country's selection of a strategy).

The reasoning behind the payoffs is as follows. If both countries maintain emissions at the current level (the *status quo*), then both suffer from the acid rain externality and their payoffs are correspondingly low ((–5, –5) in the game matrix). If both reduce emissions, then both are made better off (by the

Table 2.2　The Prisoners' Dilemma game matrix

		Country B	
		Reduce Emissions	Maintain Emissions
Country A	Reduce Emissions	0, 0	–10, 5
	Maintain Emissions	5, –10	–5, –5

same extent) since the externalities are removed and their payoffs become (0, 0). If however, one country reneges on the bargain and maintains emissions while the other reduces, then the reneging country does even better – it keeps the private benefits of the *status quo* (for example higher levels of industrial production or lower expenditure on emission-abating technology), while not incurring the cost of the externality imposed by the other country. The exact converse is true for the 'honest' country – it both loses its private benefit and bears the externality cost. The payoffs are therefore (5, –10) respectively.

This is the standard Prisoners' Dilemma story. In the language of game theory, {reduce emissions, reduce emissions} with a payoff of (0, 0) is the Pareto (socially) efficient outcome. However {maintain emissions} is a 'strictly dominating strategy' for both players, and so {maintain emissions, maintain emissions} with its payoff of (–5, –5) is the (Nash) equilibrium of the game.

If there are no solutions to this problem, how are agreements ever reached (for we do indeed see agreements made)? No sophisticated argument is needed to see that Coase fails here, for there is no way (in the absence of some international body which is recognised and obeyed by all[12]) that property rights can be established. Both countries will claim the right both to carry out polluting activities and to have clean air (no acid rain from the other). Any agreement must be voluntary, but we have just shown that voluntary agreements will not always be followed as there are individual incentives to deviate.

The solution to this problem arises from interaction that will continue indefinitely. When this is the case, the benefits of a co-operative strategy will be seen to be the receipt of others' co-operation. The fact that future co-operation is important renders current co-operation feasible.

The Prisoners' Dilemma and European acid rain
Now consider the possibility of asymmetry in a Prisoners' Dilemma situation, that is where different individuals or countries perceive the nature of

their interaction very differently. This is the case for European acid rain – sulphur and nitrogen oxides are produced in varying amounts by all countries. Some countries, however, are more 'downwind' than others. For example, the UK is very much 'upwind' in Europe and therefore receives little acid rain; Sweden, on the other hand, is 'downwind' and suffers from a large amount of acid rain. Abstracting from informational problems, so that all countries know the costs and benefits to each of reductions in acid rain, will a co-operative outcome (voluntary agreement to reduce sulphur emissions) ever be reached? Mäler (1991) calculates the net benefits to individual European countries from the full co-operative solution as follows:

> The full co-operative solution would require a Europe-wide reduction in sulphur emissions of around 40 per cent; but notice that the load is spread very unevenly amongst the countries, as are the benefits. The UK in particular, since it receives little acid rain from other countries, but donates much to others, would be required to cut emissions by over 80 per cent at a net (dis)benefit of DM336 million. It seems unlikely, therefore, that (all other things being equal) the UK would participate in this agreement voluntarily.

Table 2.3   Net benefits from full co-operation in the European acid rain game

Country	% reduction in sulphur dioxide	Net benefits (DM million)
Bulgaria	43	–7
Czechoslovakia	75	152
Finland	14	–2
France	10	879
German Democratic Rep.	80	11
Germany, Fed. Rep. of	86	328
Italy	33	–83
Netherlands	62	565
Poland	27	599
Soviet Union	2	1 505
Spain	14	–29
Sweden	4	606
United Kingdom	81	–336
All Europe	39	6 290

Source: Pearce and Warford (1993).

In fact, five countries – Bulgaria, Finland, Italy, Spain and the UK – have incentives to 'free-ride', that is to enjoy the benefits of the co-operative reduction in emissions by other countries while continuing to produce sulphur dioxide themselves (see Table 2.3). The individual incentives to deviate results in a loss of social welfare of DM1,110 million.

This conclusion is a little stronger than the earlier Prisoners' Dilemma result. There, co-operation was desirable for both players but not voluntarily sustainable (in the short-term); here, for some countries at least, not even co-operation is beneficial. The solution, although simple in words, is difficult in practice. There must be transfers from those who benefit to those who lose under the co-operative outcome. For the UK, this transfer must be somewhere in excess of DM300 million. In the jargon, the full co-operative outcome must be a potential Pareto-efficient equilibrium – another way of saying that the gain to the 'winners' must exceed the loss to the 'losers', so that the former can compensate the latter and still be better off than under the non-cooperative outcome. Exactly how this transfer is arranged is another matter. Indeed, whether this transfer is acceptable may be a problem as, in this case, it is to advocate that the victim pays. Payments to polluters may in themselves create incentives to generate more pollution.

Table 2.4   Net benefits from free-riding (non co-operative outcome)

Country	Emission reduction (%)	Net benefit (DM million)
Co-operating countries		
Czechoslovakia	75	125
German Democratic Rep.	80	−47
Germany, Federal Rep.	86	78
Poland	27	544
Sweden	3	478
Total for co-operators	37	4 933
Defecting countries (non-participants in solution)		
Italy		150
United Kingdom		87
Total for detectors		247
Total for Europe	28	5 180

Source: Mäler in Helm (1991).

To summarize, the 'acid rain game' has shown the complexities of bargaining when (i) countries do not consider the costs that their actions impose on other, neighbouring countries, that is a transfrontier externality exists; and (ii) when no recognized (or obeyed) international body exists to establish property rights and enforce contracts.

Case study: the tragedy of the global commons
The analysis of the previous section can be extended readily to the case of global commons (such as global warming or biodiversity). As in the tragedy of the 'local commons', unrestricted access to a resource will typically lead to excessive use. The situation is, in almost all respects from an economic analysis point of view, identical to the regional reciprocal externality that we considered in the acid rain game.

There are three crucial differences however (see Pearce, 1991). First, the scale of the problem is much larger – global rather than continental or regional. The potential is for universal harm rather than 'merely' trans-national damage. Second, many of these global effects are irreversible because they affect global systems, for example induced warming, once it occurs, is here to stay whether future generations like it or not. Finally, consequences are uncertain – the only thing that is known is that there is a risk of risk. There is no previous experience with the degradation of these resources.

Two things are certain however: that the breadth of global commons problems magnifies the bargaining costs discussed in the previous section, making voluntary agreements all the more improbable; and that the international nature of the problems requires the creation of incentives to enter into voluntary but enforceable international environmental agreements. It is the crucial importance of international environmental agreements that distinguishes the problems of the global commons.

Externalities between generations
Hetch Hetchy Valley in Yosemite National Park was considered by many to be as remarkable a natural phenomenon as the lower Yosemite Valley. In 1914 however it was flooded to provide a reservoir for the city of San Francisco. Many people now wish that Hetch Hetchy could be restored to its former natural glory.

Most of the major consequences of externalities, particularly those which are global, will fall on the next generation and beyond. Yet the decision to exploit natural resources rests solely with the present. Even if Americans of today were willing to transfer part of their (greater) wealth to the decision-makers of 1914 in order to preserve Hetch Hetchy, there is no feasible way such an inter-temporal transfer could be arranged. Another way of stating the problem is that the Coase Theorem fails to provide a solution to an externality-based market failure when the other side to the bargain (future generations) does not yet exist.

This issue of inter-generational equity has attracted great attention from philosophers and social scientists alike. We shall consider three aspects of the problem (using the 'tragedy of the global commons' as the canonical example): discounting, irreversibility and uncertainty.

Discounting

Discounting is a familiar concept – the notion that one dollar in the pocket today is better than one dollar in the pocket tomorrow. In the context of environmental degradation, however, the notion has been challenged on two grounds. First, what are the inter-generational equity effects of discounting and second, how is the discount rate determined?

A standard argument by environmental conservationists is that discounting biases present decision-making against future generations. It is easy to see why this might be. Discounting assigns diminishing weights to a given benefit or cost as that benefit or cost stretches into the future. This means two things – it is desirable for benefits to come quickly so that investments with long gestation periods before benefits appear will not be particularly attractive, and it is desirable for costs to be incurred in the future, that is by future generations. Both effects mean that today benefits at the expense of tomorrow, both in terms of a lack of long-term investments and a shifting of environmental costs.

These arguments are not new as Pigou (1932) suggested that conservation of (exhaustible) natural resources might be achieved through lowering the discount rate. This is not the whole story, however. As Markandya and Pearce (1991) note, lowering the discount rate (which would reduce the inter-temporal bias claimed by conservationists) could accelerate environmental degradation if investment is material/energy intensive. Arguing for a zero discount rate, the logical conclusion of (pure) inter-generational equity considerations, ignores the effects of altering the balance between consumption and investment.

If not zero, then what? What determines the discount rate? There are, in general, two reasons why the value of one dollar today is greater than the same sum tomorrow; they are referred to as time preference and the opportunity cost of capital.[13] Time preference, as the nomenclature suggests, signifies some sort of impatience: for an individual, a desire to have his/her cake today rather than waiting until tomorrow. On an individual level such time preference is difficult to justify, as Markandya and Pearce (1991) point out. Discounting time because of impatience is irrational. Moreover, the fact that individuals (perhaps behaving irrationally) prefer benefits today rather than tomorrow is no reason why society as a whole should do the same. It can be argued, however, that the prospect of death for an individual or ruin for a society may justify a positive value of time preference. The immediacy of needs in some developing countries, even with already severe environmental problems, favours the use of time preference as a factor in determining the discount rate.

In addition to pure time preference, the social rate of time preference differs from the individual rate by a term which indicates how much society values growth in consumption. Algebraically, the social rate of time preference is:

$$r = e.g. + tp$$

where tp is the rate of pure time preference, g is the rate of growth in real consumption per capita, and e is the elasticity of social marginal utility of consumption (the percentage decrease in additional utility derived from a percentage increase in consumption). This first term arises because if g is large (that is society tomorrow will be much richer than society today), then society today will be less willing to forgo present consumption for the benefit of future generations, that is the discount rate will be high. In practice, estimating the three components of r (e, g and tp) is a matter of some debate. For example, if g is large but negative (that is consumption per capita will fall), does this mean that the social discount rate should be negative? This highlights the limitation of the above expression – it is only meaningful when sustainable changes in real consumption per capita can be expected. In other circumstances no clear rules can be used to determine the social rate of time preference.

An alternative justification for discounting comes from considering the opportunity cost of capital. Since capital is productive, a dollar's worth of resources now will generate more than a dollar's worth of goods in the future. This is also referred to as the marginal productivity of capital argument. The discount rate for any project is then determined by the rate of return that could be achieved if funds were invested in an alternative project of similar risk. In developing countries the opportunity cost tends to be high, due to a shortage of capital.

Criticisms have been levelled at this rationale for discounting. First, it is argued that the underlying assumption is that project returns are reinvested rather than consumed. This is fair criticism which has led many economists to advocate weighted discount rates which incorporate this effect. Second, environmentalists argue that damages or costs relating to a project's activities can be discounted only if compensation for these damages is actually paid. Economists disagree with this argument – the issues of actual and potential compensation are quite distinct. What is of importance is that the project generates sufficient benefits to potentially compensate any victims. Whether any compensation is actually paid is irrelevant to the choice of the discount rate.

The discount rate debate remains unresolved despite substantial argument and debate. Two general points emerge however. First, it is overly simplistic to argue that high discount rates increase environmental degradation. As Markandya and Pearce (1991) show, how the choice of discount rate affects the overall use of natural resources is ambiguous. Second, determination of the discount rate typically assumes sustainability, for example in evaluating the social rate of time preference. This indicates the next step of the discount rate argument – the rate should be determined either by time preference or capital productivity factors, subject to some sustainability constraint (Page, 1977). The form of this constraint will, of course, be the subject of much debate.

Irreversibility

We have already noted that global externalities often incur (potentially) irreversible losses of natural resources. Global warming is a one-way process and reductions in biodiversity may lead to losses that can never be recouped. Present decisions will rarely consider the effects of irreversibility and, in particular, the value denied to future generations by the destruction of the resource.

What is this value and in what ways can the preservation of a natural resource contribute to (future) societal welfare? There is the obvious benefit of continued appreciation of natural beauty. Fisher and Hanemann (1987) identify two other factors. First, preservation of, for example, plant and animal populations preserves genetic information which may become useful at some stage in the future. Second, removal of a natural resource (a species of animal, for example) may cause a systemic break-down because that species had evolved a set of characteristics which were essential to the functioning of the system. In these two cases there is gain to be had in the future, either through realising the benefits of (genetic) information or from system sustainability, that would be forgone if development brought about irreversible change.

The value of the information that arises after the development decision has been made was labelled the quasi-option value by Arrow and Fisher (1974).[14] To see the value of information, consider a two-period situation where the first period represents today and the second period the future. A planner has to decide how much of a tract of wild land should be developed. Let development be a binary choice, that is to either develop fully during a period or not develop at all. In addition, assume development is irreversible.

Two possibilities exist for the first period – either develop or do not develop. If development is chosen and irreversible change consequently occurs, only development can be chosen in the next period; conversely, if conservation ('do not develop') is chosen, either conservation or development may be chosen in the second period. In between the two periods, information may arise that enhances the value of preservation (for example a scientific discovery about the linkage of the tract of land with wildlife stocks). The first period expected value of this additional information, conditional on 'no development' being chosen, is the quasi-option value of the natural resource in question.[15]

Decisions that incur irreversibilities must therefore take into account this quasi-option value, otherwise, an externality is imposed on future generations. Two questions are of interest: will this inclusion necessarily lead to conservation of natural resources and how is the quasi-option value to be estimated? The answer to the first question is: not necessarily. Additional information gained through non-development may either discourage future development or indicate that there is no significant cost to the exploitation of the natural resource. Moreover, as Viscusi and Zeckhauser (1976) show, some development can provide information about whether development is in fact irreversible. These considerations mean that development decisions that incorporate quasi-option values will not necessarily be more conservationist than those that ignore them altogether. Natural resources will not necessarily be conserved by eliminating externalities.

The answer to the second question – how to estimate quasi-option values – has not yet been provided. Although Fisher and Hanemann (1987) claim that the value can be estimated empirically and that it is likely to be significant, no study has yet determined the quasi-option value for a natural resource. Johansson (in Helm, 1991) concludes: 'such analyses are probably among the most important and challenging for environmental economists' (p. 123).

Uncertainty
In a deterministic world, evaluation of environmental degradation would be relatively easy. In reality, even if the direct costs and benefits (for example revenue to be gained from industrial production, cost of pollution abatement) of natural resource exploitation are known, indirect values (the likely effect of continued pollution, the benefits of reduced CO_2 emissions) are unknown. How do we know an externality is being imposed on future generations if we do not know the effects of present activities? How can we possibly correct for externalities when we are unable to assess alternative actions?

The presence of uncertainty can be compensated for in two ways: either by altering the discount rate or by adjusting cost/benefit values. We have already dealt with one type of uncertainty in considering discounting, that is the effect of the chance of death or ruin on the time preference rates of individuals and society. Other types of uncertainty exist. There may be uncertainty about the size of future benefits and costs. It is a familiar notion that a benefit (or cost) is worth less the more uncertain is its occurrence. This suggests that the discount rate should be raised to incorporate higher levels of uncertainty. This approach has two important disadvantages however. First, it imposes on risk a particular time profile – since discounting is an exponential exercise it forces the risk premium to be exponential over time as well. This is a restrictive, although seldom noticed, assumption. Second, it ignores the distorting and undesirable effect that a change in the discount rate might have on the balance between consumption and investment in the economy (see the previous discussion on discounting). The theoretically correct method of treating uncertainty in this case is to adjust the stream of benefits and costs, replacing each entry with its certainty equivalent value.[16]

There might also exist uncertainty about future preferences. Of course, preferences for certain goods will remain roughly constant – food, water, and other subsistence items will always be required. Future generations may, however, value environmental conservation (the sights of Hetch Hetchy Valley) more than the present generation values development (improved water supply from reservoirs). Krutilla (1993) was the first to make an argument that preferences systematically alter over time with increasing development. How is it possible to provide for the consideration of such predictable change? The approach favoured by economists, first suggested by Weisbrod (1964), is to include an option value, reflecting a risk premium arising from uncertainty as to the value attached to the resource in the future. The use of the phrase 'risk premium' makes clear that the value of the option derives from risk aversion on the part of society (contrast this with the irreversibility origin of the quasi-option value).

An externality arises, therefore, when present generations do not incorporate this option value in their decisions. The concept of option value has its limitations however. As Johansson (1987) shows, under certain circumstances the option value may be positive, negative or equal to zero, regardless of whether a project is worthwhile or not or whether individuals are risk averse.[17] This is because option value is an attempt to place a value on two potential 'time-paths' for development and there are risks and opportunity costs associated with the selection of either.

Externalities across time – conclusion
In this section we have discussed the issues underlying the problem of externalities between generations. The arguments put forward by conservationists for a zero discount rate have not been found to be convincing – there is no simple relationship between high discount rates and environmental degradation. The discount rate should be determined by society's rate of time preference or the opportunity cost of capital, subject to some sustainability con-

straint. The irreversible consequences of development should be incorporated into the decision-making process by the inclusion of quasi-option values. Uncertainty about future values should be dealt with by replacing uncertain cost/benefit streams with their certainty equivalents. Uncertainty about future preferences calls for the use of option values. All of these concepts are still the subject of some debate and suffer from severe difficulties in their estimation. They will undoubtedly form the basis of the ongoing debate between economists and environmentalists.

Conclusion
Market failures exist on account of the failure to price correctly some economic factor. When that factor is an environmental resource, the absence of an effective pricing mechanism leads inevitably to the degradation of the resource and social costliness.

This chapter has demonstrated why it is that problems of this sort exist and persist. Whenever the market fails to supply a ready price for a commodity (such as air quality), it is virtually guaranteed that some degradation of the resource will exist due to over-exploitation.

The same problem will persist, that is continue after notice, only if there is costliness implicit in its removal (transactions costs). In this chapter we have identified three basic forms of costliness that allow environmental problems to persist. First, there is the costliness of 'large numbers bargaining', as in the case of the Swedish oil refinery. Therefore, environmental degradation will almost always occur on a diffuse basis, affecting large numbers of people similarly situated with respect to the resource. Second, there is the problem of 'free-riders' in bargaining, as in the case of acid rain. It will almost always be the case that the first-best option will be to allow others to solve environmental problems while pursuing 'business-as-usual' individually. The solution to environmental problems requires the involvement of *all* individuals and societies dependent upon the resource. Third, there is the problem of identification and representation, as in the case of wilderness preservation. It is very difficult to work out agreements in the present with parties who will not exist until some time in the future.

Therefore, environmental problems and the consequent degradation persist on account of these difficulties within the process for generating solutions. At base, all environmental degradation must exist (in part) on account of these market failures.

Notes
1. For a concept which is used so extensively by economists, there is remarkably little agreement as to the precise definition of an externality. We ignore this debate here but refer the interested reader to Baumol and Oates (1988), chapter 3. Note that we refer only to 'technological externalities' in what follows.

2. The complete statement of the Coase Theorem is: if costless negotiation is possible, property rights are well defined and redistribution does not affect marginal values, then the final allocation of resources will be Pareto-efficient and independent of the initial allocation of legal rights.

3. This assumes a large (infinite) number of resource users, such that individual actions have an insignificant effect on the resource stock.

4. Such moral hazard and monitoring problems do, of course, exist in the local commons problem of the previous section – we mentioned that individuals may ignore community and act out of self-interest. However these problems are exacerbated by the additional uncertainty introduced by geographical separation.

5. Toxicity has not been mentioned explicitly in this discussion. Many of these chemicals exhibit low toxicity (a herbicide such as atrazine is no more toxic than aspirin), although some, of course, are highly toxic (for example the insecticide endrin). The greatest danger comes not from the toxicity of a single (small) dose but rather from steady accumulation to risky concentrations. See Conway and Pretty, 1991.

6. The consequences of groundwater pollution for humans vary with the substances involved and the anticipated use of the contaminated water source. The effects of detectable pesticide concentrations in drinking water are only partially understood – liver, kidney and central nervous system damage, birth defects and cancers are potential hazards associated with chemicals found in pesticides. No adverse effects have yet been found at current pesticide concentrations however. Little is known about the effects of pesticide concentrations in groundwater used for irrigation, industrial and other non-potable water uses. See Saliba, 1985.

7. The rights to pollute groundwater (or, alternatively, to have chemical-free groundwater), are often not defined. An exception is the US, where entitlements to groundwater are defined by law in certain states.

8. To say that forest land is underpriced is undoubtedly true – land is awarded free to claimants and title is given for three times the area that has been cleared. This 'first come, first served' basis of allocation encourages claims for large tracts of land (any free good is overused – refer back to the example of the 'tragedy of the commons'). Further, clearance of land serves to deter squatters. This, along with the favourable treatment granted to forest developers by the Brazilian government, means that the deforestation of Brazil is caused not just by market failure but also by government policy failure (see Chapter 3).

9. Acid rain can be either a reciprocal (e.g. in Europe) or unidirectional (e.g. in North America) externality. In the former countries impose externalities on each other, in the latter one country imposes an externality on others. An example of a unidirectional externality is the appearance of the pesticide lindane in Lake Mashu, an isolated lake in Japan. As this pesticide has not been used in Japan since its ban in 1971, the only source must be agricultural activities in China and Korea, some 1500 km away (see Conway and Pretty, 1991).

10. Forest damage may be caused by a variety of factors other than acid rain. For example, ozone pollution may well be a significant contributor to forest damage in both North America and Germany. It is fair to say, however, that acid rain, while perhaps not the primary cause of forest damage, is certainly a contributing factor.

11. This is not a very realistic setting and we shall relax the symmetry assumption below. It is, however, the way in which environmental problems are often presented – as a (symmetric) Prisoners' Dilemma game. We examine symmetry initially to show, later in this section, the effects of asymmetry.

12. If the cost of setting up an international body were sufficiently small, it might be in the interests of both countries to establish such a co-ordinating institution. It is not clear, however, in this 'one-shot' situation, that the reneging country will necessarily obey the institution, or pay any penalties imposed. We are back to the observation that an unenforceable contract is no contract at all.

13. Although in a perfect world (efficient markets and no taxes) the two factors would give rise to the same discount rate, in practice time preference rates tend to be lower. Uncertainty and risk are omitted here, to be discussed in a later section.

14. The option value is 'quasi' to distinguish it from the option value that arises from uncertainty. See the next section.
15. Although the concept of quasi-option value relies implicitly on the existence of uncertainty (the value derives from improved information about some uncertain, stochastic variable of the system), the assumption of risk aversion is not used. The value derives not from individuals' or society's attitude towards uncertainty and risk but from the information loss caused by irreversible change. See the next section for a consideration of uncertainty.
16. Such calculatins are, however, very complex and of limited operational use (see Anderson, 1989 and Dixit and Williamson, 1989).
17. Despite this theoretical indeterminacy, the sign of the option value for a resource stock may be expected to be positive if the future demand for the resource is certain and future supply is uncertain.

Bibliography

ADB (1987), *Handbook in the Use of Pesticides in the Asia-Pacific Region*, Asian Development Bank: Manila.

Anderson, D. (1989), 'Economic Aspects of Afforestation and Soil Conservation Projects', in Schramm G. and Warford J. (eds), *Environmental Management and Economic Development*, Johns Hopkins University Press: Baltimore.

Arrow, K.J. and Fisher, A. (1974), 'Environmental Preservation, Uncertainty and Irreversibility', *Quarterly Journal of Economics*, **88**, 312–19.

Barbier, E.B. (1989), *Economics, Natural-Resource Scarcity and Development: Conventional and Alternative Views*, Earthscan: London.

Baumol, W.J. and Oates, W.E. (1988) (2nd edn), *The Theory of Environmental Policy*, Cambridge University Press: Cambridge.

Cheung, S.N.S. (1973), 'The Fable of the Bees: An Economic Investigation', *Journal of Law and Economics*, **16** (April), 23ff.

Coase, R.H. (1960), 'The Problem of Social Cost', *Journal of Law and Economics*, **3**, (October), 1–44.

Conway, G.R. and Pretty, J.N. (1991), *Unwelcome Harvest: Agriculture and Pollution*, Earthscan: London.

Dixit, A. and Williamson, A. (1989), 'Risk-Adjusted Rates of Return for Project Appraisal', PR Working Paper 290, World Bank.

Fisher, A.C. and Hanemann, W.M. (1987), 'Quasi-Option Value: Some Misconceptions Dispelled', *Journal of Environmental Economics and Management*, **14**, 183–90.

Hardin, G.J. (1968), 'The Tragedy of the Commons', *Science*, **162**, 1243–8.

Harsanyi, J.C. and Selten, R. (1972), 'A Generalised Nash Solution for Two Person Bargaining Games with Incomplete Information', *Management Science*, **18**.

Helm, D. (ed.) (1991), *Economic Policy Towards the Environment*, Blackwell: Oxford.

Johansson, D.O. (1987), *The Economic Theory and Measurement of Environmental Benefits*, Cambridge University Press: Cambridge.

Kreps, D.M. (1990), *Course in Microeconomic Theory*, Harvester Wheatsheaf: London.

Krutilla, J. (1993), 'Conservation Reconsidered', reprinted in Dorfman, R. and Dorfman, E. (eds), *Economics of the Environment: Selected Readings*, Norton & Co.: New York and London.

Mäler, K-G. (1991), 'International Environmental Problems', in Helm, D. (ed.), *Economic Policy Towards the Environment* , Blackwell: Oxford.

Markandya, A. and Pearce, D. (1991), 'Development, the Environment and the Social Rate of Discount', *World Bank Research Observer*, **6** (2), 137–52.

Page, T. (1977), *Conservation and Economic Efficiency*, Johns Hopkins University Press: Baltimore.

Pauly, D. and Thia-Eng, C. (1988), 'The Overfishing of Marine Resources: Socio-economic Background in Southeast Asia', *Ambio*, **17** (3), 200–206.

Pearce, D. (1991), 'An Economic Approach to Saving the Tropical Forests', in Helm, D. (ed.), *Economic Policy Towards the Environment*, Blackwell: Oxford.

Pearce, D.W. and Markandya, A. (1989), *The Benefits of Environmental Policy: Monetary Valuation*, OECD: Paris.

Pearce, D.W. and Turner, R.K. (1989), *Economics of Natural Resources and the Environment*, Harvester-Wheatsheaf: London.

Pearce, D.W. and Warford J.J. (1993), *World Without End: Economics, Environment and Sustainable Development*, Oxford University Press: Oxford.

Pigou, A. (1932) (4th edn), *The Economics of Welfare*, Macmillan: London.

Saliba, B.C. (1985), 'Irrigated Agriculture and Groundwater Quality – A Framework for Policy Development', *American Journal of Agricultural Economics*, **67**, (5), December, 1231–7.

Viscusi, W.K. and Zeckhauser, R. (1976), 'Environmental Policy Choice Under Uncertainty', *Journal of Environmental Economics and Management*, **3**.

Weisbrod, B. (1964), 'Collective Consumption Service of Individual Consumption Goods', *Quarterly Journal of Economics*, **78**, 471–7.

Wheatley, G.A. (1965), 'The Assessment and Persistence of Residues of Organochlorine Insecticides in Soils and their Uptake by Crops', *Annual of Applied Biology*, **55**, 325–9.

Zanin, G., Borin, M., Altissimo, L. and Calamari, D. (1991), 'Simulazione della contaminazione da erbicidi nell'acquifero a Nord di Vicenza (Italia nord-orientale)', Paper presented at the 25th Annual Meeting of *SIA*, Bologna.

3 Policy failure and resource degradation

Timothy M. Swanson and Raffaello Cervigni

Introduction

This chapter analyses the role of the state in determining resource degradation, that is, why some resources within a state are subject to degradation while others are not. It should be clear from the discussion in the preceding chapter that degradation is the consequence of an absence of management. Since it is the function of the state to provide or authorize such management, it is essential to analyse carefully the circumstances under which this management is withheld. 'Policy failure' is here defined as the failure of the state to provide the institutions required for the management of a particular resource, consequentially resulting in its degradation.

This chapter builds upon the analysis provided in the preceding one to explain why it is that a society will allocate its efforts toward the resolution of some environmental problems and not toward others. In short, in the developing world this is in part the result of severe financial constraints which limit the range and number of resources which may be subjected to effective (and costly) management. Financial constraints necessarily limit the number of resources that may be managed, and many of those that go unmanaged will suffer over-exploitation and consequent degradation. However it is equally true that identities of the particular resources that are routinely degraded derive from particular views of the appropriate pathways to development held throughout the world. Certain resources are perceived to be less worthy of attention and investments than others and these are the ones that are destined for over-exploitation and degradation. Therefore many examples of 'policy failure' are in fact predictable degradation resulting from societal investment and management decisions. It is the purpose of this chapter to demonstrate this point.

Of course these investment decisions are not the only sources of policy failures that result in environmental degradation but they are the most systematic ones. Other sources would include vested interests, ignorance and pure stupidity. However it is not possible to systematically explain the existing direction of policy-based resource degradation by reference to these factors. It will have to suffice to state that existing policy failures exist in part because societal preferences (given financial constraints) result in the management of certain resources and not others and also because existing policies do not reflect societal preferences. The latter problem was considered more generally in Chapter Two and this chapter considers the former problem.

The theory of resource over-exploitation and degradation

Initially, Gordon (1954) and Scott (1955) presented models of the impact of heavy exploitation pressures on wildlife resources. Both Gordon and Scott developed their models in order to explain the over-exploitation of ocean fisheries and Clark went on to demonstrate how the same models might be used in order to explain human-sourced degradation and extinctions (Clark, 1973).

How does the Clark model explain the degradation and possible extinction of a resource? It does so in relation to three factors:

1. open access to the resource;
2. relative price to cost of harvested resource; and
3. relative growth rate of resource.

These three factors alone are sufficient to produce a bioeconomic model of the stock of the resource that will exist in an equilibrium between societal and natural forces. In short, so long as there is open access to the resource, a price of the resource that remains high relative to its cost of harvest, and a relatively slow rate of resource growth, then there is the prospect that the steady-state stock will be much lower than existed in the 'natural' state (that is, prior to human intervention). The resource will be degraded. In essence, these conditions create incentives for continued harvesting of the resource, even to an extent incompatible with the capacity of the resource to regenerate itself.

Figure 3.1 demonstrates the Clark model of resource degradation. In this figure, two variables are demonstrated to be functions of the stock level of the resource: the harvesting rate and the growth rate. With regard to the harvest function, as the stock level increases, the harvesting rate increases because the costliness of locating and capturing a unit of the resource diminishes. With regard to the growth function, the resource multiplies more rapidly with initial increases in stock (due to increasing reproduction opportunities) but then this rate of growth declines with successively increasing stock levels (as the carrying capacity of the resource is approached).

The upper line in Figure 3.1 indicates the nature of the possibility of 'economic extinction'. In the case of this harvesting function, there is no intersection between the growth function and the harvest function at any stock level. This means that the incentives to harvest the resource exist at all stock levels and the growth of the resource is insufficient to maintain a population in the face of these pressures. The basic principle is: low growth

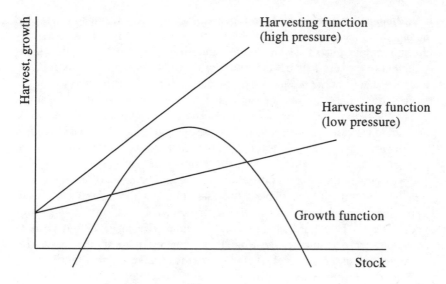

Figure 3.1   Clark model of over-exploitation

rates combined with high price–cost ratios within the Clark model result in forces pointing to reductions in the stock levels of the resource. That is, the resource will be degraded through this combination of forces.

Addressing the fundamental causes of resource degradation
Existing policies concerning resource degradation (which are built upon the Clark model) fail to reach beyond the surface of the problem. They are dealing with proximate, rather than fundamental, causes of resource degradation. It is necessary to broaden the analysis to consider the fundamental reasons for resource degradation. When this is done it is readily apparent that all resources share the same common threat, that is, human inattention and underinvestment. Humans are now investing most of their attention, resources and management on an increasingly narrow range of natural resources, leaving many others without the basic resources required for their sustenance. It is the examination of this fundamental problem that is required in order to understand the nature of the human-sourced problem of resource degradation.

Degradation as conversion
Degradation is implicitly the result of human investment strategies. Humans now select the resources that will be subject to human investment and those which are not. When the naturally occurring resources are not included within the human investment portfolio, they (or the resources on which they depend) are converted to other, selected resources.

Although the fundamental force generating resource degradation may be human investment decision-making, the proximate cause of a given resource's decline may be one of several consequential types. Exclusion implies disinvestment in the resource, but the nature of the disinvestment process depends upon the nature of the resource and its relationship to human society.

First the resource may be seen as valuable but not as an asset (that is, not as a resource with potential for growth). Consequently it will be perceived to be optimal to harvest the entire stock of the resource in order to invest the return in another, more productive asset. This is known as resource mining, for the purpose of the conversion of its value to another, preferred asset.

An example of this form of disinvestment would be much of the deforestation of slow-growing hardwoods that has occurred throughout the world. These hardwood forests have immense market value but very slow growth rates (one to three per cent per annum). In this instance it makes more economic sense to market the timber and convert it to another asset (for example cash in the money markets) in order to receive a higher return.

Second, a resource may not be perceived as valuable, as an asset or otherwise, and thus it will not be worthy of substantial investment in its maintenance. That is, even if the resource itself has no intrinsic market value, it may still be the case that some of the other resources on which it depends have such a value. The resource may then be degraded when its 'base resources' are converted. The most obvious requirement for the survival of many living resources is an allocation of the natural habitat that it requires for its sustenance. All lands have a conversion value (that is, a value in an alternative use) and the resources naturally dependent upon a given area of land must be able to generate a flow of comparable goods and services in order to avoid the conversion of the land to these other uses.

An example of this form of disinvestment would probably be the projected losses of general biological diversity (such as unclassified insects and plants) set to occur in the tropical zones over the next century. All of these projections are based upon estimates of land-use conversion trends within these zones. The problem lies in the capacity of cattle to generate appropriable returns whereas the plants and insects do not. Under these circumstances, it is predictable that the use of the lands will be converted from the naturally occurring plants and insects to the cattle.

The third source of conversions may occur where the resource may be seen as valuable, but not valuable enough to warrant the allocation of resources required for a management programme. The resource will again incur disinvestment but on this occasion the disinvestment will occur by reason of the lack of investment in the management of access to the resource or its habitat. This results in what is commonly called 'open access over-exploitation'. This is another statement of the 'institutional failure' problem identified in the previous chapter. In essence, it is costly to provide effective management regimes for resources and, depending upon the perceived value of the subject resources, this level of management will not always be supplied. An absence of management results in over-exploitation and resource degradation.

An example of this form of disinvestment would probably be the decline of many of the large land mammal resources throughout Africa, such as the rhinoceros and the elephant. These resources have historically had substantial market values (up to $1000 per kg for rhinoceros horn) but they are also expensive to manage. On account of this, they have remained largely outside effective management regimes.

Policies promoting conversion
Although these three routes to degradation are the visible layer of causation in resource degradation, the more fundamental forces lie below these with the decision-making process regarding society's investments. Policies that emanate from these fundamental forces are truly 'failures' when they result in inferior management regimes, but it is important to recognize nevertheless that all such policies may be seen as deriving from the opportunity costs involved in acting otherwise. The maintenance of an environmental system, even one part of an original endowment from nature, often requires that the host state forsakes the conversion of those resources to their first-best uses. In this sense, even inferior management regimes may be 'optimal' from the perspective of the domestic regime.

The extent to which this 'process of conversion' is being put into place is indicated by the rates and locations of recent land-use conversions. During the twenty years from 1960 to 1980, the whole of the developing world saw the proportion of its land area dedicated to the specialized agricultural land uses increase by 37.5 per cent, while that same proportion remained constant in the developed world where the conversion process is complete (Repetto and Gillis, 1988). At the 'forested frontier' these rates of conversion are even greater than the average, and continuing to the present time. For example during the 1980s, Paraguay (72 per cent), Niger (32 per cent), Mongolia (32 per cent) and Brazil (23 per cent) have all experienced significant rates of conversion of lands to specialized crops and Eucador (62 per cent), Costa Rica (34 per cent), Thailand (32 per cent) and the Philippines (26 per cent) have all experienced significant conversions of lands to specialized livestock (World Resources Institute, 1990). The extent to which land use conversion contributes to environmental problems is indicated by Table 3.1. The projections of mass extinctions all derive from extrapolations from current land use trends. The aggregate impact of resource conversion is a force for global change.

Therefore one of the most fundamental forces for natural resource degradation is the force for conversion. It often operates through the policies

Table 3.1   Estimated rates and projections of biodiversity losses

Basis	Rate (%)	Projection (%)	Source
forest area loss	8	33–50	Lovejoy (1980)
forest area loss	5	50	Ehrlich & Ehrlich (1981)
forest area loss	–	33	Simberloff (1986)
forest area loss	9	25	Raven (1988)
forest area loss	5	15	Reid & Miller (1989)

Note: The rates are given as percentage losses of total number of global species per decade. The projections are based upon the extrapolation of this trend through to the total conversion of the examined forested area.

selected by the domestic regime, policies which encourage conversion to other uses through the degradation of the naturally existing resources and systems. Before describing a few examples of such domestic policy failures, this chapter will analyse in more detail the forces for conversion and the way in which they translate into natural resource degradation.

The forces for resource conversion – resources as assets
A more generalized model of resource degradation focuses on the investment potential of different forms of resources and, importantly, their ultimate substitutability. This model analyses degradation as the result of human choice regarding the assets to retain in the society's production portfolio. Then the society's policies, and perceived policy failures, may be explained in part by the better understanding of the forces driving its decision-making.

Asset selection – substitutability between assets
In essence, any resource on earth is potentially replaceable by a more productive asset, even another natural resource. In terms of strict functional value, what matters is the capacity of the resource to generate a competitive return relative to other assets (Hotelling, 1931). The vast majority of biological resources, for example, are threatened or endangered by reason of their potential replacement by another biological resource better suited to the production of appropriable value for human use.

This insight generates models that relate a resource's stock levels to its ability to generate a return competitive with the returns available from other investments within the economy. Given that the stocks of all natural assets commence at a point other than zero, investment, within this framework, can take the form of either active stock increases, or simply benign non-conversion.

In any event, investment occurs whenever there is a refusal to convert the entire standing stock of one natural asset to another. The decision not to convert must then equate the returns between assets.

In the steady state, the resource would be maintained at a stock that equates the return from that stock with the return from other assets. In the first instance, the return to a stock of a given resource is generated by at least two stock-dependent factors;

1.   the relative growth rate (which slows as it reaches carrying capacity), and
2.   the costs of harvest (which decline with increasing stocks).

The combination of these two stock-dependent factors means that for any given stock level a different rate of return is implied by its retention. An asset-based model indicates that each biological resource would be kept at the steady-state stock level that equilibrates its returns with that of all other productive assets in the economy. That is, stocks will be maintained (invested) to the extent that the marginal unit will yield a return equivalent to its immediate harvest and alternative investment (i.e. the market interest rate).

Within this framework it is equally obvious what the nature of degraded resources would be. The lower line in Figure 3.2 represents a very slow growing resource which fails to reach the general market rate of return on assets within the economy. In the steady state there is no stock of this resource that generates an economic return; it is optimal to convert the

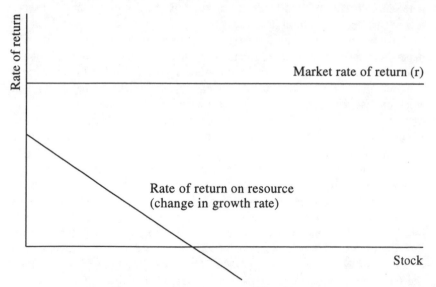

Figure 3.2   A natural resource with a non-competitive return

entirety of the asset to other, more productive forms in order to acquire a better return.

Therefore, slow growth relative to other assets in the economy is in and of itself a route to resource decline. This is true even from the perspective of a perfectly well-managed resource. Resources, even biological resources, must be competitive as productive assets if they are to be retained in a world of scarce resources (see Clark, 1976; Spence, 1975).

The opportunity cost of base resources (land)
The previous model must be revised in order to focus on the fundamental importance of investment in resources other than stock levels for resource conservation. The constraining investment factor is unlikely to be stock levels in every instance because there are other resources on which there are likely to be more pressing demands. It is often the case that a resource will be 'undercut' before it is 'over-exploited'.

Specifically, it is important to revise the model in order to provide for the possibility of competing uses for the resources that a resource relies upon, and therefore to provide for the necessity of realizing a competitive return for the resource's implicit 'use' of these resources.

The implicit assumption in bioeconomic models was that environmental resources were 'free goods' that did not require investment. It was believed that environmental and ecological services resulted from natural processes deriving from the existence of the system. This is definitely true in an aggregate sense. The earth does produce a continuous flow of environmental services as the result of natural processes.

However, the particular form that those services will take is critically dependent upon relative investment rates, that is on the rate at which base resources are provided to individual resources. At the level of the individual resource, investment is the crucial flow variable determining whether a given stock of that resource will continue to exist. Investment must also take the form of the provision of a natural resource base for sustenance of environmental systems. Without that natural resource base the resource will be undercut, resulting in its inevitable decline.

This implies that the optimal investment criterion for any given resource will equate its growth rate with the real cost of investment *in any necessary factor*. For biological production, one of the necessary factors is a stock of the resource for reproduction but other factors are equally necessary, such as land, light and water. The resource must be able to pay a competitive return on each of these factors, otherwise it will be denied its use. When such a denial occurs with regard to *any one* of these biologically necessary factors, the resource is doomed to extinction by reason of being cut off from its resource base.

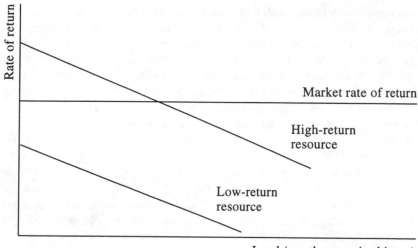

Figure 3.3   The returns to investment in land or management for a natural resource

Consider initially that the resource base resource requirements may be met so long as it is provided with a quantity of land. Then the condition for survival is that the resource's growth must be sufficient to cover the real opportunity cost of the land (the opportunity cost of capital multiplied by the price of land divided by the net return per unit of output). This is simply the familiar investment condition that the marginal value product from investment must be equated with the nominal cost of capital. In short, the condition says that the resource must compete for the base resources upon which it relies.

Figure 3.3 shows the rate of optimal investment in the base resources (land) made available as habitat for two different resources, one with high growth (for example, cattle) and the other with low growth (for example, indigenous wildlife). Assuming initially that each resource has the same unit rental value, there will be different rates of investment in the two different land uses according to their relative growth rates. The low growth resource, as shown in this diagram, is not competitive enough as a productive asset to warrant provision of the base resource. It is undercut in the process because it is implicitly excluded from society's investment portfolio. The resource becomes degraded because its habitat is converted to use for other resources.

The opportunity costs of other national resources

There are other resources which must be supplied for the maintenance of environmental resources. One of the more important is the provision of management institutions. The economic analysis of commons exploitation indicates that efficient societal use of any resource requires institutions which efficiently restrict the aggregate exploitation of the resource. After allocating the flow from a resource, it is necessary to supervise the allocations in order to prevent cheating. The efficient exploitation of individual renewable resources requires management institutions which perform these functions on an ongoing basis.

These institutional commitments require scarce national resources for their implementation. The management of the production of any one resource is itself an individual problem requiring investment for its solution. The optimal level of spending on management institutions could be demonstrated in a diagram identical to Figure 3.3 but with the horizontal axis representative of investments in resources other than land, for example management. In that case, the relevant opportunity cost would not be the price of land but rather the wages of the monitors. Again, the costliness of developing production methods and management institutions tailored to any individual resource may be too great to warrant the investment in that resource, given its relative rate of return.

Without the necessary allocation of management resources, the resource may be subjected to pressures that it cannot withstand and it will be threatened through over-exploitation. Although the resource may be degraded as a result of these unmanaged pressures, this is only the proximate and not the fundamental cause of its decline. The adoption of an open access regime for management means that the asset is being treated as if it is unable to generate a competitive return on institutional investments. The result for the resource is unmanaged access, which ensures over-exploitation. The fundamental cause of the decline of the resource is its uncompetitiveness as an asset but the immediate cause is unmanaged over-exploitation.

This is often the first factor to become operational in the case of a usable resource and it creates the general perception that the early theories of exploitation-based degradation were accurate. However, at base, even degradation which is clearly linked to over-exploitation must be the result of refusals to invest in the resource.

Earlier theories have taken the choice of institution to apply to a particular resource as an exogenous decision. However, it is important to ask why productive assets potentially worthy of investment would be subjected to such a regime. Within this framework the answer is straightforward. From the perspective of an investment-based model, open access regimes are often caused *by* decisions not to invest in certain resources, rather than a cause *of* such decisions. Policy failures can therefore be the result of more fundamental factors.

The decline of the African elephant – a case study
During the decade of the 1980s, the populations of African elephants declined precipitously according to most estimates. In aggregate, the number of elephants on that continent declined from about 1.3 million to roughly half that number (approximately 600 000) over a period of 10 years. What have been the causes of this decline and what are the policies needed to arrest it? This section outlines the facts of the African elephant's decline from the perspective of each of the competing theories above.

An application of the Clark model of resource degradation?
At first glance, the recent decline of the African elephant appears to be a good example of the workings of the Clark model of over-exploitation resulting in resource degradation. There is no doubt that the immediate cause of most elephant deaths during this decade was a high-powered weapon and that the motivation for the slaughter was the procurement of ivory. During the 1980s the trade in ivory reached a peak of over 1,000 tonnes per annum, after averaging nearer 600 tonnes per annum in the previous decade (ITRG, 1989).

It is also clear that the incentives for over-exploitation were in place over this period. During the 1980s the price of elephant ivory soared, reaching more than $140 per kg in Japan, while the cost of harvesting (indicated by the prices paid to poachers) was more in the order of $5–10 per kg (Swanson, 1989).

Finally, the growth rate of the African elephant is relatively slow (RRAG, 1989). It has a life span of 60 years and reaches fecundity at the age of 13 with five year birth intervals. Studies indicate that a maximum population growth rate of 6 per cent is all that is feasible.

The congruence of these characteristics spells resource degradation in the context of the simple Clark model. The high price/cost ratio of harvesting combined with the low growth rate of the resource makes extermination the likely economic outcome. This model would explain the commencement of the downward spiral in elephant populations as the result of a technology shift, that is the widespread availability of high-powered weaponry, causing the cost of harvesting to fall precipitously. With this one-time shift in the harvest cost function, it is possible that the new bioeconomic equilibrium would not be established prior to the extinction of the resource. In essence the harvesting function (on account of the technology shift) has shifted up (as shown in Figure 3.1), resulting in a lower population in the steady state and, possibly, extinction.

The application of this paradigm leads to some fairly straightforward policy conclusions. A quick remedy for the endangered resource within this frame-work is the enforced criminalization of the production process, as well as a ban on the international trade in its outputs. This policy reform is believed effective because it is intended to have two important positive impacts within the context of the model. First, by withdrawing the consumers' support for the resource's products it reduces the demand and hence the price paid for these products. Second, by encouraging domestic enforcement of this criminalization it increases the costliness of accessing the resource. There-

Table 3.2   Estimates of African elephant populations (selected countries)

	1979	1989
Central Africa	497 400	277 000
of which:		
Cameroon	16 200	22 000
CAR	63 000	23 000
Zaire	377 000	112 000
East Africa	546 850	110 000
of which:		
Kenya	65 000	16 000
Sudan	134 000	22 000
Tanzania	316 300	61 000
Southern Africa	282 200	204 000
of which:		
Botswana	20 000	68 000
Mozambique	54 800	17 000
South Africa	7 800	7 800
Zambia	150 000	32 000
Zimbabwe	30 000	52 000
Western Africa	17 090	19 000
of which:		
Burkina Faso	1 700	4 500
Ghana	3 500	2 800
Total	1 343 345	609 000

Source: ITRG (1989).

fore, the policy of enforced criminalization is intended to have positive impacts working on both sides of the price-cost ratio. The hoped for result is that the ensuing downward shift in the harvest function will be sufficient to restore bioeconomic equilibrium at a stock greater than zero.

This is precisely the policy shift that has occurred as a result of the decline of the African elephant in the 1980s (see Table 3.2). The international community acted to impose an international 'ban' on the trade in ivory effective from 1990. Acting within the context of the Convention on International Trade in Endangered Species, the parties passed a resolution to list the African elephant in Appendix I of that treaty, effectively disallowing all further trade in that resource's products (Barbier et al., 1990).

A more fundamental explanation of the elephant's decline
An alternative theory would place the elephant's decline within the context of the broader forces operating across its range. Although the immediate cause of death of each elephant was some hunter's pursuit of its ivory, the more fundamental causes concern the reasons why these hunters were allowed unmanaged access to the elephant herds and why the ivory harvest was not better managed for the benefit of the elephants' 'owners'.

This framework provides an alternative explanation for the decline of the African elephant. In short, the African elephant makes little economic sense as a biological asset for investment purposes. Each elephant requires about one-half of a square kilometre of good grazing land for its sustenance (Caughley and Goddard, 1975). Average life expectancy is about 55 years (Hanks, 1972). Therefore, it represents a substantial commitment of ancillary resources to provide for a single elephant's livelihood. The resources required for the sustenance of the millions of these creatures that recently roamed Africa would represent a substantial portion of that continent's land area. In addition, few elephants are stationary within an area of a few hectares; they travel widely in search of food and crops are at particular risk. For these reasons there are substantial negative externalities experienced by those living in the rural areas of a country that has a significant elephant population. Also, the management of access to the population would be more expensive than in the case of a more sedentary animal.

Combined with its slow growth rate and the absence of significant international markets for its products, the pressures for the removal of a substantial portion of the African elephant population from the lands of Africa must be intense. The resource will very likely be replaced by a more specialized biological asset, such as cattle, goats or even grain.

In short, elephants do not demonstrate the characteristics that make an asset worthy of the substantial investments (of natural and governmental resources) that this resource requires for its sustenance. This is the fundamental force underlying its decline. The absence of incentives for investment made the resource a candidate for non-management.

It is the case that the prevailing management regime in most African range states has been 'open access'. Open access, in the context of terrestrial resources, is largely a function of the efforts and expenditures of the putative owners. That is, open access occurs when the *de jure* owners fail to allocate sufficient resources to create barriers to accessing the resource or its habitat. In the case of the African elephant the *de jure* owners are the governments of the African range states, who without exception claim exclusive title to the elephant as 'wildlife'. However, governmental spending on park and habitat protection has been insufficient to regulate access in all but a couple of states, resulting in *de facto* open access regimes.

This fact has been demonstrated empirically. Poaching pressure and resource decline has been shown to be closely related to the governmental spending levels on park protection. In the case of the heavily poached rhinoceros populations of sub-Saharan Africa, spending on management was shown

Table 3.3   Park management spending by selected African states

	Year	Level of Spending ($/km²)
Botswana	1984	10
Burkina Faso	1986	132
Cameroon	1986	5
CAR	1984	8
Ethiopia	1984	57
Ghana	1984	237
Kenya	1984	188
Malawi	1986	49
Mozambique	1984	19
Niger	1984	5
Somalia	1984	50
South Africa	1984	4 350
Sudan	1986	12
Tanzania	1984	20
Uganda	1984	357
Zaire	1986	2
Zambia	1984	11
Zimbabwe	1984	277

Source: Bell and McShane-Caluzi (1984); Cumming et al. (1986).

to be inversely related to the decline of the rhino population in those localities (Leader-Williams and Albon, 1988). This relationship indicated a zero
population change level at spending of about $215 per square kilometre. The
information that is available indicates that the spending on park monitoring is
in fact much lower than this in most African states (see Table 3.3).

Open access regimes are better thought of as implicit determinations to not
invest in the particular resources, with the object of converting to others that
are perceived to be more productive. That is, it is likely to be the decision to
deplete a natural resource that generates the open access regime, not the other
way around. In the 1980s few of the range states perceived the elephant as an
asset worthy of the investments necessary to maintain existing stock levels.

Unofficial open access policies have been a good method for mining the
vast numbers of surplus elephants from the perspective of an aid-sensitized
African government. The criminalization of the off-take of ivory preserves
international appearances, while the absence of resources applied to elephant
protection allows the mining to continue apace. There is, in addition, the side
benefit of the revenues derived from sales of seized ivory. Virtually the
entirety of the trade in ivory during the past decade (ranging between 500 and
1000 tonnes per annum) has derived from poached ivory sales that were
'licensed' after seizure. This arms-length approach to the industry preserves
appearances while fostering the removal of the resource from the land.

In short, the elephant's decline has been largely the result of an implicit
decision to undertake mining on the part of some of the range states. For
example, in the 1980s four countries alone – Tanzania, Zambia, Zaire and
Sudan – are estimated to have lost 750,000 elephants between them, equal to
the overall continental losses (ITRG, 1989). The above table indicates that
these states spent $20, $11, $2, and $12 per square kilometre, respectively, on
park monitoring in the year surveyed. The decline of the African elephant
during the 1980s, and the ivory trade it spawned, was a direct result of these
official non-investment decisions.

Other African states, on the other hand, chose to invest in their elephant
populations and with quite different results. In fact populations increased by
almost one hundred per cent in one southern African state that invested
heavily in its elephants, namely Zimbabwe. The relationship is not exact but
it is apparent that most instances of elephant population declines were prede-
termined by government refusals to invest meaningfully in the resource.

This is also consistent with the nature of the observed threats of large-scale
losses to less well-documented biodiversity. Throughout Latin America, for
example, much of the force for conversions derives from governmental policies that encourage deforestation and the substitution of specialised agriculture. In Brazil and many other Latin American states, property right regimes
are only substituted for open access regimes on the condition that the land is

cleared and used for specialised agriculture (Repetto and Gillis, 1988). Throughout many parts of Latin America it is 'illegal' to trade in all wildlife products and yet large-scale trade flows from the continent (Swanson, 1991). The impact of such unenforced laws is simply to enshrine open access with respect to these resources so that it is impossible for the local populations to foster them as economic resources.

In summary, even in the case of a resource such as the elephant that is apparently well-suited to the over-exploitation framework for extinction, the underlying rationale is actually one of underinvestment. This has resulted in the mining of the resource from arms' length over the past decade. The absence of investment incentives has generated this open access institutional framework.

Discrimination against indigenous resources

In many developing countries it is illegal to hunt, capture, trade or export any part of the wildlife resource. This is true for most of the states of South and Central America. For example Brazil and Bolivia have total bans on all wildlife exports, as does Mexico. Many of their neighbours have partial or full bans in place (IUCN Environmental Law Centre, 1985b). Also, in sub-Saharan Africa there are half a dozen states with complete wildlife exportation bans in place, and many others with severe use restrictions (IUCN Environmental Law Centre, 1985a).

Many of these wildlife exploitation bans actually pre-date the Convention on International Trade in Endangered Species (CITES). This is because many of the wildlife laws in the developing world remain as a part of the colonial legacy in these areas. In that era, the local communities were increasingly disenfranchised from the wildlife resource and this resource was given protected status in parks, in practice for the exclusive use of foreign colonials and tourists (Marks, 1983). In Latin America and in Africa in particular, this legacy often continues in the form of wildlife legislation which disallows indigenous peoples' use of the resource.

In general there is a widespread prohibition on the development of diverse resources as economic resources, particularly in those parts of the world where they might still play a significant role in the economy. These domestic prohibitions are often supported by international restrictions on the same trade, such as those found within CITES.

At base, all of these domestic policies (non-management and non-exploitation) are based on decisions to convert the indigenous resources. The decision not to invest management resources results in the over-exploitation of valuable resources and their consequent decline, as in the case of the African elephant. Just as certainly, the decision not to allow legal exploitation of valuable resources also enhances the prospects for conversion. Even if public management of the resources is withheld (by *de jure* ownership and *de facto* open access), it remains possible if not likely that local communities will establish effective management regimes for valuable resources. Making the exploitation of specified resources officially illegal renders such investments too uncertain and hence makes them unlikely. The combination of non-management and non-exploitation policies is the surest means of encouraging conversion in the absence of direct subsidies. Of course, direct subsidies to conversion are the clearest example of this societal preference for conversions and some examples of this are provided in the next section.

Classic policy failures: subsidies to conversions
From the point of view of the private decision maker, the choice between conservation and conversion is in general determined by a comparison of the net present value of the two alternatives. The purpose of this section is to show, with very simple examples, how policy can affect the valuation of the alternatives and how in some cases it can lead to the rejection of the decision that would 'normally' be taken. It is by influencing such decision making that government policies increase the rate of conversions.

We can consider two separate dimensions of the problem: the origins and the effects of policies. On one hand the incentive for conserving natural

Table 3.4   Examples of impact of policies on resource degradation

	Incentive to conserve	Incentive to deplete
Policies in sectors involving natural resources	I Establishment of property rights or of systems for sharing revenues from sustainable uses of natural resources (examples: Thailand, Zimbabwe)	II Concessions that encourage selective and non sustainable harvesting, low government capture of the rent from timber extraction (example: Indonesia)
Policies in other sectors	III	IV Real exchange rate devaluation; (example: Malaysia) Subsidies for alternative land uses such as agriculture, cattle ranching (example: Brazil)

resources can be modified by policies either implemented in sectors directly involving biological resources such as forests, or initially enforced in other sectors such as the infrastructure or the agricultural sector. On the other hand, both types of policies can either encourage conservation or discourage it.

Table 3.4 summarizes the above discussion and its entries give examples of policies that provide incentives to conserve and deplete. Some of them will be analysed in the rest of the chapter. This section is mostly concerned with cells II and IV of Table 3.4 which list a few case studies to illustrate how government policies, directly or indirectly, result in increased rates of natural resource conversion.

Policies that encourage conversion of natural resources

Property rights and land tenure   There are two ways in which the property rights system can affect deforestation, namely, property rights may not be established at all or they can be assigned in the 'wrong' way. In the first case forests can be made into 'open access resources' and, in the absence of binding common property resource management systems, there are no incentives for sustainable use of the forest resources. On the other hand, the manner in which property rights are awarded can encourage deforestation.

In Costa Rica for instance, title to occupied public land has been assigned on the basis of a legal procedure called *informaciones posessorias*. A provision of the law (abolished in 1986) suspended the requirement to prove proper acquisition if less than 50 per cent of the claimed land was covered by forest. This clearly gave the incentive to people to cut 50 per cent or more of the forest cover (see Peuket, 1991, p. 7).

In Brazil, similarly, the so-called *direito de posse* establishes a link between deforestation and claims to land. The law states that a squatter (*poseiro*) who lives on unclaimed public land and uses it 'effectively' for at least one year and one day, has a usufruct right over 100 hectares (Binswanger, 1989, pp. 5–6). So long as clearing land from forest is proof of effective use, there is a clear incentive to deforest to acquire land title.[1] These incentives are even stronger in some regions. In the Grande Caryas area, for example, a claimant who lives on the land may obtain a title *for up to three times* the area which he has cleared of forest (Binswanger, 1989, p. 6).

Concessions   Forests can also be publicly owned, and assigned to private concessionaires for economic use. Clearly, the way concessions are determined influences the incentives to exploit forests in a sustainable way.

In Indonesia the concession agreements represent the most significant part of the whole forest management system.[2] Two elements of the concession system are of particular importance: the size and duration of the concession, and the way in which royalties on concessions are collected. Concessions are normally agreed on plots of large size (the average figure reported by the World Bank study is 100,000 hectares) and for a duration of twenty years.

The problem is that large concessions are quite difficult to monitor. Furthermore, the growing cycle of commercial tropical hardwood is such that a second harvest should be delayed 25 to 35 years after the initial harvest but this is a period that exceeds the length of the concession. As a consequence, concessionaires have no incentive to maintain long-term forest productivity.

The second problem is related to the royalties system. Concessions are allowed by the Forestry Department, which also manages the collection of royalties. These are *ad valorem* taxes based on timber removals and the rate is uniform regardless of the species actually logged. This system entails three problems. First, it relies largely on concessionaires' reports to assess the amount of timber logged, which gives concessionaires a considerable incentive to under-report log extraction. Second, royalties are based on timber removals, rather than on the stock of merchantable stems in the stand which would constitute a much more reliable measure of the actual economic value of the concession. Finally the uniform *ad valorem* taxes apply to all species in the same way and hence give a strong incentive to log only the most valuable species.

Policies enforced in other sectors inducing conversion of natural resources
As previously mentioned, depletion of natural resources can occur not only because of mis-management of sectors, like forests, with a high 'natural resources content', but also as a consequence of modifications of the incentive framework implemented in other sectors. In particular, making alternative land uses such as annual cropping or cattle ranching particularly attractive will clearly have a detrimental effect on conservation so long as their return is perceived by individuals as higher than the return from sustainable uses of forested land.

The case of Brazil is probably one of the most useful for illustrating this point. Brazilian authorities have implemented large-scale programs for encouraging resettlements in the Amazonia Region and exploitation of its natural resources. Several types of incentives have been used, including subsidized loans, tax credits and tax deductions.

Forested land is cleared mainly for conversion to agricultural uses. Among these, the two more significant are conversion to pasture for cattle ranching and conversion to crop cultivation. Agricultural incomes, in general, benefit from a very favourable tax treatment. It has been calculated that by using several provisions of the income tax code, 'corporations and individuals can exclude up to 80 and 90 per cent respectively of agricultural profits from their

Table 3.5 Fiscal and credit incentives to livestock in Brazil

Year	Fiscal incentive (FINAM) (1990 US$ million)	Subsidised livestock credit (1990 US$ million)	Total (1990 US$ million)	Real interest rate (%)
		Direct incentives to livestock		
	Fiscal incentives (FINAM) and subsidized credit, 1972–87 (millions of 1990 US$)			
1972	214	71	285	-2.7
1973	131	89	220	-2.6
1974	209	76	285	-16.4
1975	238	151	389	-13.0
1976	265	229	494	-23.0
1977	108	152	261	-17.8
1978	134	164	298	-19.0
1979	88	183	271	-35.6
1980	102	99	201	-38.8
1981	174	97	270	-25.6
1982	250	137	387	-27.3
1983	134	91	225	-36.1
1984	168	53	221	-1.6
1985	153	52	204	-3.8
1986	303	204	507	-35.5
1987	156	100	256	n.a.

Note: Deflated by IGP-DI to 1977, then converted to 1990 US$.

Source: Schneider (1991).

Table 3.6   Economic and financial analysis of government assisted cattle ranches in the Brazilian Amazon

	Total investment (US$)	NPV (US$)	NPV Investment
Economic analysis			
Base case	5 143 700	−2 824 000	−0.55
Sensitivity analysis			
Cattle prices assumed doubled	5 143 700	511 380	+0.10
Land prices assumed to rise 5% per year more than general inflation rate	5 143 700	−2 300 370	−0.45
Financial analysis			
Reflecting all investor incentives: tax credits, deductions and subsidised loans	753 650	1 875 400	+2.49
Sensitivity analysis			
Interest rate subsidies eliminated	753 650	849 000	+1.13
Deductibility of losses against other taxable income eliminated	753 650	−658 500	−0.87

Source: Repetto (1988)

taxable income' (Binswanger, 1989, p. 2). Moreover, other provisions regarding depreciation of fixed investment, animals and machines lead to the conclusion that 'almost all agricultural incomes escape taxation' (Binswanger, 1989, p. 2). If this is compared to the tax rates applicable to other sectors, where corporate profits are subject to a rate between 35 and 45 per cent, then the incentive to convert lands to agricultural activities is quite clear.

Conversion to cattle ranching   Table 3.5 provides some figures on the direct government incentives for livestock operations in the North Region of Brazil.[3] The incentives take the form of subsidized credit and regional fiscal incentives. Subsidized credit consists of loans with interest rates below the market rates and often negative in real terms. Fiscal incentives are tax credits matching firms' investments in approved projects in the north.

It has been frequently observed that cattle ranching activities undertaken within this incentive framework are intrinsically non-economic. Table 3.6 gives an economic and financial analysis, based on a fifteen-year project life and a 5 per cent real discount rate, of a typical cattle ranch project benefiting from government incentives in the Brazilian Amazon (Browder, 1988). The top panel shows that the typical project has negative returns from the point of view of society, unless cattle prices are doubled. From the point of view of the individual, however, government incentives lead to a net present value nearly two and a half times higher than the total investment outlay, which explains why projects have actually occurred. Government investment subsidies render conversions feasible that could not otherwise occur.

Whose policy failure – domestic or global?

Policy-based resource degradation is caused, fundamentally, because societies convert resources to alternative uses. They do this because those resources (the land, the management or even the funds represented by the stocks of the species) are perceived as being more highly valued in other uses within the economy. All natural resources are part of a society's stock of assets, that is, they are natural forms of capital (Solow, 1993). Many times a society will reformulate its portfolio of assets in the process of development, disinvesting in those which are 'inferior' and investing further in those which are perceived to be 'superior'. To a large extent, the problem of 'policy failure' derives from the prevailing perception that certain resources constitute inferior forms of capital for a developing society to retain.

The framework that this analysis implies focuses on the *perceived investment-worthiness* of the resource. In essence, in the context of owner-states all questions of policy-based resource degradation are based in the incentives for underinvestment. That is, the fundamental problem is that owner-states do not invest in the management of these resources and this gives rise in turn to the perception that such investments are not important for national development.

This indicates that at the very core of the problem of policy failure are the *external values* of the degraded resources: global and domestic. Disinvestment by one party appears as degradation to another when there exists a difference in the perceived values. If the owner of the resource is only able to appropriate a small portion of the value that is perceived by outsiders, then this asymmetry in perspectives provides the basis for disagreement about the appropriate choice of management regime. That is, if the value of the resource is viewed identically both within the relevant state and without (for example the smallpox virus), then the choice of policy is also viewed similarly (in this case, eradication). However, if there is a profound difference in viewpoints on the value of a particular resource, then opinions on the appropriate management regime will also differ. Again, the case of the African elephant is instructive. In that case, the values of the species outside of its home states vastly exceeded that which it attained there, due to the negative externalities it imposed on neighbouring villages and the positive existence value it generated in Europe and the US (the 'Save the Elephant' campaign generated more donations for conservation organizations than has any other single fundraising campaign). Hence, those within Africa demonstrated a very different preference regarding elephant management than those outside Africa.

The real policy failure lies in not capturing these 'global values' of natural resources and not transferring them to their host states. If investments in natural resources are to be optimal from the global rather than the local perspective, this is what is required.

The optimal policy for regulating the conversion decisions of individual owner-states is the creation of systems that result in the internalization of the global stock effects of natural resources in the owner-state's decision-making framework. The rationale is that if an owner-state considers the global benefits rendered by diverse resources when making its conversion decision, then it will only decide in favour of conversion when that is globally optimal. The internalization of externalities has the effect of making the perceived local optimum coincide with the global optimum.

Therefore many resource degradation problems that appear to be sourced in domestic policy failures are better described as the result of institutional failures at the global level, as were described in the preceding chapter. For example, the problem of deforestation in Brazil may be seen as caused by inefficient subsidies to conversion or, more fundamentally, by the failure of the global community to create institutions that will transfer global values to Brazilians. The value of a hectare of Brazilian forest land has been estimated to be in the region of $120 to $250 for the purpose of cattle ranching while the value of the same land for purposes of carbon sequestration has been estimated at some $1000 per hectare (at current estimates of carbon taxes) Schneider et al., 1992). The value of forest for the purpose of its contribution to medicinal plant production alone has been estimated at between $20 and $50 per hectare (Pearce, 1994; Balick, 1994). If institutions were put into place that transferred these global values to local decision makers, there would be little prospect of the domestic policy failures currently witnessed in the Amazon. To a large extent, domestic policy failures are a mere symptom of global ones.

Conclusion

Environmental degradation is often caused by choices made by governments. Sometimes these policies are direct and apparent, as with the subsidies paid for the clearance and conversion of natural resources. Sometimes these policies operate more indirectly and discreetly, as with the failure to fund adequate management regimes for specific resources. In either case the effect is to degrade the resource subject to the governmental policy.

These policies are failures in the sense that they are inefficient from some perspective, that is, there is a management regime that would be more efficient in regard to the subject resources under some conceivable circumstances. However many policy failures are not failures in the sense that they are irrational or arbitrary applications of poor policy-making practices. They derive instead from rational determinations of investment patterns for individual countries operating under severe financial constraints. From this perspective they represent decisions promoting conversion (something widely practised across the developing world) rather than policies failing to halt degradation.

Conversion itself is a form of degradation from some perspectives. In particular, from the global perspective many forms of conversion which are optimal from the local perspective will be suboptimal. That is, if the decision in regard to the natural resources was to be taken in light of global resources, natural and financial, then it is likely that the domestic policy would be reversed.

Therefore, many policy failures are more properly seen as global failures than domestic ones. This is because it is the responsibility of the global community to bring the global values of natural resources within the decision-making framework of the domestic regime, that is, it is the responsibility of global society to internalize a global externality. Many domestic policy failures will require the creation of international institutions before they will be 'corrected' from the global perspective.

This is not meant to imply that the sole cause of inefficient domestic policies is international institutional failure. It is just as likely, for example, that a state will be ignorant of the external values that emanate from an environmental system internally as well as internationally. It is of course important to ensure that national policies are built upon a sound base of local and national information. This was the point of the principles developed within Chapter Two, that is, that environmental degradation can result from various sources that make the internalization of externalities costly. In that chapter, it was pointed out that a watershed might have diffuse environmental benefits (geographically) but entirely within one state, and that these benefits should be internalized within any policy made from the management of that system.

The point is that there is a clear void of institutions for the management of the global benefits of environmental resources and systems and this absence of institutions will necessarily result in inefficiencies in resource management. One form of inefficiency that will necessarily result from non-existent international institutions will be inadequate domestic ones. This chain of policy failures generates inefficient environmental degradation within every country on the planet.

Notes
1. According to Schneider (1991), p. 29, since 1989 deforestation is no longer proof of land occupation.
2. According to the World Bank (1992) there are presently over 500 concessionaires with an average size of 100,000 hectares.
3. States of Brazil's North Region are Acre, Amapa, Amazonas, Para, Rondonia and Roraima.

Bibliography
Balick, M. (1994), 'Ethnobotany and the Use of Medicinal Plants', in Swanson, T. (ed.), *Intellectual Property Rights and Biodiversity Conservation*, Cambridge University Press: Cambridge.

Barbier, E., Burgess, J., Swanson, T. and Pearce, D. (1990), *Elephants, Economics and Ivory*, Earthscan: London.

Barton, J.H. and Christensen, E. (1988), 'Diversity Compensation Systems: Ways to Compensate Developing Nations for Providing Genetic Material', in Kloppenburg, J. (ed.), *Seeds and Sovereignty*, Duke University Press: Durham.

Bell, R. and McShane-Caluzi, E. (eds) (1984), 'Funding and Financial Control', in *Conservation and Wildlife Management in Africa*, Peace Corps: Washington D.C.

Binswanger, H. (1989), 'Brazilian Policies that Encourage Deforestation in the Amazon', The World Bank, Environmental Department Working Paper No. 16, Washington D.C.

Browder, J.O. (1988), 'Public Policy and Deforestation in the Brazilian Amazon', in Repetto, R. and Gillis, M., *Public Policies and the Misuse of Forest Resources*, Cambridge University Press: Cambridge.

Caughley, G. and Goddard, J. (1975), 'Abundance and Distribution of Elephants in Luangwa Valley, Zambia', *African Journal of Ecology*, **26**, 323–7.

Clark, C. (1973), 'The Economics of Overexploitation', *Science*, **181**, 630–34.

Clark, C. (1976), *Mathematical Bioeconomics: The Optimal Management of Renewable Sources*, John Wiley: New York.

Cornes, R. and Sandler, T. (1984), 'Easy Riders, Joint Production and Public Goods', *Economic Journal*, **94**, 580–98.

Cornes, R. and Sandler, T. (1986), *The Theory of Externalities, Public Goods and Club Goods*, Cambridge University Press: Cambridge.

Cummings, D., Dutoit, R. and Stuart, S. (1986), *African Elephants and Rhinos*, IUCN: Gland.

Dasgupta, P. (1985), *The Control of Resources*, Blackwell: Oxford.

Dasgupta, P.S. and Heal, G.M. (1979), *Economic Theory and Exhaustible Resources*, Cambridge University Press: Cambridge.

deBeer, J.H. and McDermott, M. (1989), 'The Economic Value of Non-Timber Forest Products in Southeast Asia', Netherlands Committee for the International Union for the Conservation of Nature (IUCN), Amsterdam.

Dixon, J. and Sherman, P. (1990), *Economics of Protected Areas*, Island Press: Washington D.C.

Ehrlich, P. and Ehrlich, A. (1981), *Extinction*, Random House: New York.

El-Ashry, M. (1992), 'Global Environmental Facility Makes its Debut', *Development Forum*, **20**, (2), 3.

Gillis, M. (1988), 'Indonesia: Public Policies, Resource Management and the Tropical Forest', in Repetto, R. and Gillis, M., *Public Policies and the Misuse of Forest Resources*, Cambridge University Press: Cambridge.

Gordon, H. (1954), 'The Economic Theory of a Common-Property Resource', *Journal of Political Economy*, **62**, 124–42.

Hanks, J. (1972), 'Reproduction of Elephants in the Luangwa Valley, Zambia', *Journal of Reproduction and Fertility*, **30**, 13–26.

Hotelling, H. (1931), 'The Economics of Exhaustible Resources', *Journal of Political Economy*, **39**, 137–75.

ITRG (1989), 'The Ivory Trade and the Future of the African Elephant', Report to the Conference of the Parties to CITES, Lausanne.

IUCN Environmental Law Centre (1985a), *African Wildlife Laws*, IUCN: Gland.

IUCN Environmental Law Centre (1985b), *Latin American Wildlife Laws*, IUCN: Gland.

Katzman, M.T. and Cale, W.G. Jr (1990), 'Tropical Forest Preservation Using Economic Incentives', *Bioscience*, **40**, (11), 827–32.

Leader-Williams, N. and Albon, S. (1988), 'Allocation of Resources for Conservation', *Nature*, **336**, 533–5.

Lovejoy, T. (1980), 'A Projection of Species Extinctions', in Barney, G.O. (ed.), *The Global 2000 Report to the President. Entering the Twenty-First Century*, Washington, D.C.: Council on Environmental Quality.

Mahar, D. (1989), 'Government Policies and Deforestation in Brazil's Amazon Region', The World Bank, Washington D.C.

Marks, S. (1983), *The Imperial Lion: Human Dimensions of Wildlife Management in Central Africa*, Westview Press: Boulder, Colorado.

Pearce, D. (1994), 'Economic Value of Medicinal Plants in Pharmaceuticals', in Swanson, T. (ed.), *Intellectual Property Rights and Biodiversity Conservation*, Cambridge University Press: Cambridge.

Peuket, A. (1991), 'Public Policies and Deforestation in Costa Rica', draft, The World Bank, Washington D.C.

Raven, P. (1988), 'The Scope of the Plant Conservation Problem Worldwide', in Bramwell, D., Hamann, O., Heywood, V. and Synge, H. (eds), *Botanic Gardens and the World Convervation Strategy*, Academic Press:

Reid, W. and Miller, K. (1989), *Keeping Options Alive*, World Resources Institute: Washington, D.C.

Repetto, R. (1988), 'Economic Policy Reform for Natural Resource Conservation', The World Bank, Environmental Department Working Paper No. 4, Washington D.C.

Repetto, R. and Gillis, M. (1988), *Public Policies and the Misuse of Forest Resources*, Cambridge University Press: Cambridge.

Repetto, R., Magrath, W., Wells, M., Beer, C. and Rossini, F. (1989), 'Wasting Assets: Natural Resources in the National Income Accounts', World Resource Institute, Washington D.C.

RRAG (1989), 'The Impact of the Ivory Trade on the African Elephant Population', in Cobb, S.

(ed.), *The Ivory Trade and the Future of the African Elephant*, Report of the Ivory Trade Review Group to the CITES Secretariat.

Schneider, R. (1991), 'An Economic Analysis of Environmental Problems in the Amazon', draft, The World Bank, Washington D.C.

Schneider, R. et al. (1992), 'Brazil: An Analysis of Environmental Problems in the Amazon', The World Bank: Washington D.C.

Scott, A. (1955), 'The Fishery: The Objectives of Sole Ownership', *Journal of Political Economy*, **63**, 116–24.

Sedjo, R.A. (1988), 'Property Rights and the Protection of Plant Genetic Resources', in Kloppenburg, J. (ed.), *Seeds and Sovereignty*, Duke University Press: Durham.

Sedjo, R. (1992), 'Preserving Natural Resources as a Resource', *Resources*, Winter, 26–9.

Simberloff, D. (1986), 'Are we on the verge of a mass extinction in tropical rain forests?', in Elliott, D. (ed.), *Dynamics of Extinction*, John Wiley: New York.

Solow, R. (1993), 'The Economics of Resources or the Resources of Economics', reprinted in Dorfman, R. and Dorfman, E. (eds), *Economics of the Environment: Selected Readings*, Norton & Co.: New York and London.

Spence, M. (1975), 'Blue Whales and Applied Control Theory', in Göttinger, H. (ed.), *System Approaches and Environmental Problems*, Vandenhoeck: Göttingen.

Swanson, T. (1989), 'Policy Options for the Regulation of the Ivory Trade', in *The Ivory Trade and the Future of the African Elephant*, ITRG: Lausanne.

Swanson, T. (1991), 'Animal Welfare and Economics: The Case of the Live Bird Trade', in Edwards, S. and Thomsen, J. (eds), *Conservation and Management of Wild Birds in Trade*, Report to the Conference of the Parties to CITES, Kyoto, Japan.

Swanson, T. (1993), 'Regulating Endangered Species', *Economic Policy*, April.

Swanson, T. (1994), *The International Regulation of Extinction*, Macmillan: London.

World Bank (1992), *World Development Report*, World Bank: Washington D.C.

World Resources Institute (1990), *World Resources 1990–1991*, Oxford University Press: Oxford.

4 The causes of environmental degradation: population, scarcity and growth

Renata Serra

Introduction

Population growth inevitably has a distinctive impact on the environment, multiplying pressure on space and resources, emitting more wastes and absorbing an increasing share of the sun's energy. The current demographic explosion therefore raises the issue of its consequences on resource depletion and environmental pollution. Despite this fact it is clear that many environmental problems have less to do with population growth than with technological, economic and institutional elements governing human societies. However, with the prospect of world population doubling in size by the end of the next century, reaching the astronomic figure of ten billion, the connection between population growth and environmental stress has often been singled out for analysis. According to an early exponent of the anti-population growth view, 'the causal chain of the deterioration [of the environment] is easily followed to its source. Too many cars, too many factories, too much detergent, too much pesticide, multiplying contrails, inadequate sewage treatment plants, too little water, too much carbon dioxide – all can be traced easily to too many people' (Ehrlich, 1968).

Although the theoretical existence of an ultimate limit for the growth of human society is universally acknowledged, the object of contention lies in the definition of this limit and of its time horizon. This is due to divergent and often opposing views on the earth's capacity for sustaining the needs of a growing population, and on the ability of the institutional and economic systems to compensate for natural scarcity. The terms of the debate refer to recent concerns that environmental and technological problems, along with other problems affecting social and institutional organizations, may have grown to the point of being disruptive for the future of civilization on earth. Unfortunately theoretical divergence, here more than in any other field, cannot be easily reconciled by means of empirical studies.

Rapid population growth and demographic transition

Today the world population is 5.4 billion. Most of the increase in world population has occurred during this century (see Figure 4.1), due to both uninterrupted exponential growth and an increase in the growth rate itself.

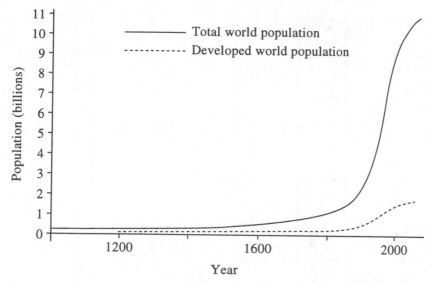

Figure 4.1   Past and projected world population, AD 1000–2150

Any quantity following an exponential growth pattern increases in each given period by a constant percentage of its current size. Therefore, although the initial level may be very low it will reach high figures rapidly. In addition, while world population in 1700 was growing at around 0.3 per cent per annum, by 1900 this had risen to 0.6 per cent and in the last thirty years it has increased to 2 per cent per annum (Table 4.1).

Human population, as with any other biological species, never increases by a constant growth rate; trends and fluctuations are caused by changes in fertility and mortality. In addition, the age structure of the population also plays an important role. For example even if the rate of reproduction were to decline to replacement levels in the near future (which is unlikely given the continuing high birth rates), total population would continue to grow for another century. This is due to the phenomenon known as 'population momentum'. This momentum exists since 40 per cent of the current population is now less than fifteen years old and the real explosion will occur when these young enter their reproductive years. Demographers expect ten billion people by the year 2100 and a static population of 12 billion people soon afterwards.

Regional differences make the effects of these prospective trends appear even more problematic. Most of the increase (95 per cent) in world population over the last quarter of this century occurred in less advanced economies, with detrimental consequences for their resource use and environmental conservation. In countries striving to improve their per capita consumption standards, rapid population growth amplifies the resource scarcity problems and

Table 4.1 World population growth since 1600 and forecasts to 2025

Year	Population (millions)	Annual growth rate (%)	Year	Population (millions)	Annual growth rate (%)
1600	545	—	1975	3 698	1.96
1650	545	0.00	1980	4 450	1.74
1700	610	0.23	1985	4 854	1.74
1750	720	0.33	1990	5 292	1.73
1800	900	0.45	1995	5 766	1.71
1850	1 200	0.57	2000	6 251	1.62
1900	1 625	0.60	2005	6 729	1.47
1950	2 565	0.91	2010	7 191	1.33
1955	2 752	1.80	2015	7 640	1.21
1960	3 019	1.86	2020	8 062	1.08
1965	3 336	1.99	2025	8 467	0.98
1970	3 698	2.06			

Source: Data from 1600 until 1950 are from McEvedy and Jones (1978); data from 1955–2025 are from United Nations, estimates and projections as revised in 1988.

Table 4.2 Average annual growth of population and GNP per capita for selected world regions

Region	Average annual population growth (%)				Average annual growth of GDP (%)			
	1973–80	1980–90	1990–2000	2000–2030	1973–80	1980–90	1990	1991
Low/middle income	2.1	2.0	1.8	1.3	2.7	1.2	–0.1	–2.1
Low income	2.1	2.0	1.9	1.3	2.6	4.0	2.9	2.1
Middle income	2.2	1.8	1.5	1.2	–	0.5	–1.0	–3.4
Sub-Saharan Africa	2.9	3.1	3.0	2.4	0.9	–1.3	–1.4	–0.6
East Asia	1.7	1.6	1.4	0.9	4.8	6.2	5.3	5.0
South Asia	2.4	2.2	1.9	1.3	1.7	3.2	3.3	–0.7
Latin America	2.4	2.0	1.7	1.1	2.2	–0.4	–1.4	1.7
Middle East/N Africa	3.0	3.2	2.9	2.2	1.7	–2.0	–0.2	–1.3
High income countries	0.8	0.6	0.6	0.2	2.1	2.3	1.6	0.3
World	1.8	1.7	1.6	1.2	1.3	1.2	0.5	–0.1

Source: World Bank (1993).

exacerbates the trade-off between efforts to increase crop yields and attempts to combat desertification, soil erosion, deforestation, waterlogging and salinization. The world demographic divide coincides approximately with the economic divide (Table 4.2), requiring particular attention to the connection between population growth on one side and development and environmental concerns on the other.

This divide is explained by the theory of 'demographic transition'. This theory envisages a relationship between reductions in death and birth rates and the stage of socio-economic development, measured in terms of output per head, the relative importance of the industrial to the service sector, the degree of urbanization, improvements in infrastructure (transport, schools, hospitals), the expansion of education and the development of credit and insurance markets. The transition is characterized by two phases. First there is a decline in mortality rates due to improvements in material living conditions (for example nutrition and medical care) and this increases the population growth rate. Second, after a period of time which varies according to the specific conditions of the society, birth rates also decline, considerably lowering the growth rate.

While the industrialized countries have experienced the complete demographic transition (their population growth rate is now less than 1 per cent), the developing countries have still to go through the second phase of the transition. Given the rapid mortality decline after the Second World War and the continued high fertility rates in most developing countries, population growth rates have increased to levels (2 to 4 per cent) never before experienced by any society. Although in some regions, for instance in eastern and south-east Asia and parts of Latin America, fertility rates have decreased, they are still above replacement levels. The average number of children in developing countries is now about four, with the highest figures found in sub-Saharan Africa (the region with the highest rates of growth of about 3 per cent) with an average of six to seven children (United Nations, 1990).

Population and degradation: ecologists' warnings and Malthusian models

According to many ecologists and natural scientists, human population is the key variable in determining the exploitative use of resources, which implies not only the rapid exhaustion of non-renewable resources but also the utilization of renewable resources beyond their regenerative capacity. In addition, high rates of world consumption undermine the stock of natural capital. Societies become accustomed to living on income generated by mining that capital. Moreover, the impact of human societies on the earth's natural ecosystem reduces its ability to support vital services, such as climate regulation, soil creation and disposal of wastes. This section surveys the range of im-

pacts potentially resulting from the increasing scale of human populations and activities.

The addition of more than 95 million people to the world population each year depends upon the expansion of food production. Although total food production in developing countries has increased rapidly in recent decades, in per capita terms growth has been low (0.4 per cent per annum in the period 1960–80). Furthermore, in many low-income countries, such as Bangladesh, Nepal and twenty seven out of thirty nine countries in sub-Saharan Africa, have experienced declining food production per capita (Table 4.3).

The green revolution has succeeded in tripling world food production since the Second World War by diffusing the use of intensive methods of agriculture, applied to high-yield crops. However, this effort has placed the land itself under severe strain. The intensive use of pesticides and fertilizers masks rather than solves the problems of lost nutrients and soil erosion. Irrigation can also have potentially negative effects such as salinization. Moreover there are serious constraints to bringing new lands into cultivation, due to its marginal nature and low productivity. Within the past thirty five years, during which the world population doubled, an initial abundance of arable land has been reversed. According to some estimates the amount of arable land has declined slightly in

Table 4.3   *Growth rates of food production by region, 1960–80*

Region	Total annual change		Per capita annual change	
	1960–70 (%)	1970–80 (%)	1960–70 (%)	1970–80 (%)
Developing countries	2.9	2.8	0.4	0.4
Low income	2.6	2.2	0.2	−0.3
Middle income	3.2	3.3	0.7	0.9
Africa	2.6	1.6	0.1	−1.1
Middle East	2.6	2.9	0.1	0.2
Latin America	3.6	3.3	0.1	0.2
South East Asia	2.8	3.8	0.3	1.4
South Asia	2.6	2.2	0.1	0.0
Industrial market economies	2.3	2.0	1.3	1.1
Non-market industrial economies	3.2	1.7	2.2	0.9
World	2.7	2.3	0.8	0.5

Source: World Bank (1992).

the past twenty years, due to losses from erosion, salinisation, urbanisation and desertification (Brown et al., 1989) – see Box 4.1.

Box 4.1   Desertification and degradation in developing countries

Desertification and degradation of land are essentially a developing country phenomenon. Over 80 per cent of the six million hectares undergoing desertification each year takes place in less advanced economies (The Global Outlook 2000, 1990). Tucker et al. (1990) estimated that the Sahara desert and the Saharan-Sahelian transitional zone expanded from 8,633,000 km^2 in 1980 to 9,269,000 km^2 in 1989. This expansion results only in part from natural factors such as rainfall shortage. Adverse human impacts have proved very significant when short-term subsistence needs, combined with a highly uncertain environment, lead people to give little weight to the long-term environmental costs of their actions. When marginal land is cleared and put under cultivation the result can be rapid loss of its soil nutrients in addition to the reduced forest cover. The loss of services provided by forests causes more problems, since destruction of vegetation and burning contributes to siltation, flooding of river basins, and desertification. Shifting cultivation, with the damaging practices of slashing and burning, may be the only available method for populations lacking technology and capital. The projected increase in the number of people engaged in it (over 450 million in the year 2000) will lead to further extension into marginal lands. Another serious cause of degradation is the over-population of grazing animals, which eat the grass faster than it can grow and destroy vegetation with their movements. However cattle may represent the only form of asset for many families and its expansion is welcomed as an immediate wealth improvement.

There have been several empirical investigations of the link between deforestation and population growth and density (Allen and Barnes, 1985; Capistrano and Kiker, 1990; Constantino and Ingram, 1990; Palo et al., 1987). Both cross-sectional and time series studies have revealed a significant relation between deforestation and population pressure (and in some cases with food production). The forest cover on earth declined from six billion hectares at the time of the agricultural revolution to four billion hectares today, with half of this loss occurring in the last forty years (Brown, 1991). During the 1980s tropical deforestation took place at an average of 0.9 per cent per year (World Bank, 1992).

The impact of population pressure on deforestation is motivated not only by agricultural expansion but also by rising demand for fuelwood, which still represents the main source of energy for more than half of the world's population. Cheap and abundant energy from fossil fuels is now becoming increasingly scarce, the effects of which are more pronounced for poor people in low technology economies who are forced to cover greater distances in order to collect fuelwood (see Chapter Five for a case study on fuelwood).

Population growth also has significant global effects such as greenhouse warming (Schneider, 1989; Abrahamson, 1989), acid rain (Harte, 1988), depletion of the ozone layer, vulnerability to epidemics and reduction of biodiversity (Ehrlich and Ehrlich, 1981; Wilson, 1988). With its expansion, humankind competes with plant communities and animal populations for 'basic resources', converting to human use many resources which are the natural habitat for other species (Pearce et al., 1993).

The evidence of the negative effects associated with human expansion has recently awakened old concerns and pessimistic views proposed by classical economists about the limits of human population growth and the implications of possible diminishing returns to scale. According to the research undertaken by one of the followers of this tradition, the so-called Club of Rome (an informal organization of personalities from different disciplines who met for the first time in Rome in 1968), if growth rates of population, industrialization, pollution, food production and resource depletion continue unchanged, the planet will reach its limits to growth by the next century, with a collapse in both population growth, induced by famines and epidemics, and industrial production (Meadows et al., 1972 and 1992). Their work consisted of the construction of a world model which simulated different paths for population growth, economic and environmental variables into the future. The model results are dependent on the assumptions about upper limits on resource supply, energy and absorption of wastes. Although these limits may be considered fluid to some extent, the Club of Rome's view is that they cannot be shifted much further since many resources and pollution flows have already grown beyond their sustainable thresholds.

A related approach is the concept of carrying capacity. This consists of an attempt to identify a limit to the number of people who can live within a designated environment. According to the definition of UNESCO and FAO (1985), carrying capacity indicates 'the number of people sharing a given area or territory who can, for the foreseeable future, sustain the existing standard of living through the utilisation of energy, land, water, skill and organisation'. Referring to the whole earth, carrying capacity is determined by the characteristics of soil and other resources capable of ensuring a minimum living standard. The concept does not define any desirable size of population, which would in turn depend on the level of living standards desired. In fact, it is this aspect of the notion which has been criticised, on the grounds that these 'calculations are clearly mere exercises having little or no relation to reality. They appear to assume that the goal of mankind is to

Box 4.2   FAO/UNFPA/IIASA analysis of carrying capacity

The best known analysis of this concept has been carried out by FAO, UNFPA and IIASA (see Higgins, 1983). However, their analysis does not look at the earth as a whole but considers the distinct carrying capacity for 117 countries for the year 2000. The estimates were made by firstly deriving potential food production for each country corresponding to three different levels of technology applied to agriculture, namely: low, medium and high level. The carrying capacity for each country is then derived by dividing the potential calorie output by the per capita calorie intake recommended by the World Health Organization.

If the low and traditional agricultural practices are assumed, the countries in south Asia, Africa and Latin America would be able to support 1.6 times the expected population for the year 2000 (on the basis of the present rate of population growth). If high technology is applied, like that used in mechanized North America, 9.3 times the expected population could be sustained (see table below).

Number and population of critical countries – year 2000

	Africa	Southwest Asia	South America	Central America	Southeast Asia	Total
Total countries	51	16	13	21	16	117
Countries with:						
Low inputs	29	15	–	14	6	64
Intermediate inputs	12	15	–	7	2	36
High inputs	4	12	–	2	1	19
Percentage of population exceeding the potential supporting capacity:						
Low inputs	32.9	40.7	–	8.4	3.7	14.0
Intermediate inputs	6.2	29.7	–	3.2	0.4	3.9
High inputs	0.3	15.8	–	0.2	0.2	1.3

Source: Higgins et al. (1983).

maximise the number of people, and that in order to do so, every available resource must be turned into food. Yet there is no country in the world in which people are satisfied with having barely enough to eat' (Davis, 1991). Underlying this approach is the tendency to view mortality as the mechanism through which numbers adjust to resources, thus underplaying the role of preferences regarding living standards.

Nevertheless, the various estimates of the earth's carrying capacity differ significantly from each other, in correspondence not only to levels of per capita consumption, but also to different assumptions relating to arable land availability, its productivity per hectare and (especially) future technological improvements. The estimates of the earth's population carrying capacity range from an unrealistically high figure of 40 billion (Revell, 1976) to as low as three billion (Gilland, 1983). Perhaps more realistic estimates suggest a carrying capacity of 7.5 billion, well below the population projections for the next century.

Carrying capacity remains a controversial concept on account of the ambiguous measure of welfare on which it is based and due to the real difficulties in envisaging the constraints that will apply in the future (especially in regard to such an unpredictable phenomenon as technological change). The FAO/UNFPA/IIASA research on carrying capacity (Box 4.2) has received criticisms on similar grounds.

The neoclassical view
Most economists manifest a different view from that implied by pessimistic models such as the one created by the Club of Rome, strongly disagreeing with their assumptions, methods and conclusions. The main criticisms are expressed by Nordhaus (1992) as follows:

1. The equations and definitions of variables are based neither on sound scientific knowledge nor on plausible assumptions about behavioural and institutional responses.
2. The assumptions on production are too pessimistic, since they do not allow for significant substitutions or expansion in arable land and technological change is essentially ruled out.
3. There is no attempt to consider the enormous and complex implications of the behaviour of non-linear systems, with the result that the model is extremely sensitive to small changes in specification and parameters.

Nordhaus has shown that technology-induced growth of 0.25 per cent per year is sufficient to overcome the negative impacts of resource constraints, land scarcity and population growth and reverse the model's conclusions (Nordhaus, 1992, pp. 15–16).

Ideologically, economics has been developing since the last century as a pro-growth discipline, dismissing the aspects of the 'dismal science' developed by Malthus and other classical economists. The record of almost two centuries of continuous economic developments seemed to offer living proof of the feasibility of unlimited expansion. Scientific progress, fundamental discoveries and more efficient ways of exploiting nature's services have not been impeded by population growth. It is these 'dynamic' effects of human society that have the greatest capacity for influencing resource scarcity.

The fundamental question addressed by economists is whether natural resources, collectively or individually, are becoming more scarce in an economic sense. From a theoretical perspective, technology and the market mechanism are believed to prevent the scarcity of natural resources becoming a constraint on long-term growth. Technological progress, by identifying more efficient methods, new applications and new resources, allows the productivity of resources to increase more or less exponentially over time, enabling the world almost to 'do away' with natural resources (Solow, 1974). Their supply is not a fixed constraint but a function positively related to prices and the supply can be artificially 'augmented' through technological innovations.

The market is supposed to provide the necessary mechanism through which the co-ordination of all economic activities is reached, maximizing collective welfare. When reserves of a non-renewable resource are approaching exhaustion (that is, when supply of the good is low relative to demand) its price goes up. The rising price increases the incentives to save on the use of the resource and also to search for substitutes, both of which delay the time of its exhaustion. This argument rests on the twin assumptions that prices reflect scarcity and that there are always substitutes for a scarce resource. Since there are no supposed limits on the feasibility of expanding the supply of human-produced factors of production, reproducible capital enters as a near perfect substitute for land and other exhaustible resources.

Growth-limiting pressures may also be relieved by trading abundant resources for scarce ones. Populations living on infertile land may be able to grow and develop by selling their abundant product, such as minerals and labour. This possibility has expanded with the widening of communication networks, which enable factors to be employed where their efficiency is maximized. South Korea and Taiwan represent two countries which, although poor in agriculture resources, were able to develop their economy and their population by importing technology and trading in labour-intensive products. However, while trade can alleviate local scarcities, it cannot do anything for global scarcity.

The debate between optimists and pessimists concerning resource scarcity, however, can be furthered only by means of empirical analysis. According to

Hotelling's theory of natural resource pricing, if markets are competitive the prices of exhaustible resources rise so that net royalties (prices minus costs of extraction) rise at the rate of interest. Comparing actual price movements to this postulated rate and to the movement of other prices in the economy is a measure of underlying scarcity.

One of the most important empirical analyses of resource scarcity is by Barnett and Morse (1963), relating US data on extractive, agricultural and mineral resources in the period 1870–1957. They consider two alternative hypotheses (strong and weak) of resource scarcity. By observing trends of real costs of extractive products per unit (in terms of labour–capital input), they conclude that the strong hypothesis of increasing economic scarcity (in which economic scarcity of resources increases despite technological progress) has to be rejected in all cases except forestry (Table 4.4). Population pressure has not increased the absolute costs of extractive products; on the contrary, labour and capital increased their prices relative to natural resources.

Table 4.4   Indices of labour–capital input per unit of extractive output

	Total extractive	Agriculture	Minerals	Forestry
1929 = 100				
1870–1900	134	132	210	59
1919	122	114	164	106
1957	60	61	47	90

Source: Barnett and Morse (1963).

However, the most revealing trend is the relative movement in factor prices rather than trends in absolute prices. A weak hypothesis is thus assessed by Barnett and Morse with relative costs of extractive goods per unit of labour and capital, evaluated with respect to costs of non-extractive goods. The scarcity hypothesis measured in this weaker version also fails in the agricultural and minerals sectors and is supported only in the forestry sector (Table 4.5). Scarcity also declines, by this measure, in the aggregate of all three extractive sectors.

While these findings are unambiguous up to the 1950s, trends of declining extraction costs are less marked in the following two decades, as measured by Barnett (1979). However, evidence of resource scarcity in this shorter interval is dismissed by the author as simply 'a transient phenomenon in market economies because its appearance induces economic forces, that is, technical change, substitution and so on, which tend to mitigate the long term effect' (Barnett, 1979, p. 182).

Table 4.5   *Labour–capital input per unit of extractive output relative to unit costs of non-extractive goods*

	Total extractive	Agriculture	Minerals	Forestry
1929 = 100				
1870–1900	99	97	154	37
1919	103	97	139	84
1957	87	89	68	130

Source: Barnett and Morse (1963).

Insights into indicators of resource scarcity in more recent years are provided by Nordhaus (1992), who again deals mainly with US data. He is primarily interested in assessing whether the substantial slow-down in output per capita and labour productivity of the last two decades in all major industrialized countries can be attributed to two specific sources: the exhaustion of high-grade or low-cost natural resources which force the use of high-cost substitutes, and the need to divert part of productive capacity to reduce pollution and eliminate wastes. Estimates of productivity in extractive industries, which are taken to indicate depletion of high-grade and low-cost resources, show upward trends except for crude oil and natural gases (Table 4.6). On the whole this data seems to confirm the optimistic view that growth in resource harvesting has not required increasing capital and labour per unit of output. It is then suggested by Nordhaus that the two potential sources of growth slow down stated above are responsible for only about one-quarter of a percentage point of the 1.5 per cent slow down in productivity from 1948–73 to 1973–80.

Table 4.6   *Productivity trends in extractive industries*

Sector	Annual percentage increase			
	1938–47	1947–65	1965–73	1973–89
Iron mining	1.5	3.6	3.7	4.3
Copper mining	1.8	3.4	–0.3	6.0
Coal mining	1.2	6.1	–1.0	3.4
Non-metallic minerals	—	—	4.0	1.2
Petroleum and natural gas	—	3.5	4.3	3.5
Non-farm business	1.9	2.6	2.0	0.7

Source: Nordhaus (1992).

Resource prices relative to labour prices in the US since the 1970s sometimes show an irregular pattern, with occasional increases for petroleum, coal, copper and sulphur. Land prices, which have been declining for over a century, show no clear trend after the 1940s. However, the conclusion of Nordhaus is that a generalized increase in the relative scarcity of resources does not seem to have occurred to date.

Furthermore, neoclassical economists are confident that the inevitable reduction of some natural resources does not pose serious intertemporal equity problems, since future generations are compensated by higher levels of knowledge, capital and technology which leave them no worse off. The issue is dealt with by referring not to the division of natural resources between present and future generations, but to a comprehensive concept of welfare which, in their view, need not shrink because of a decrease in natural resources. In essence, a society's assets are the aggregate of all its resources: natural, human and man-made. To the extent that 'mined' natural resources are invested in other forms of capital, a society's income may be sustained (the Hartwick–Solow rule).

The economists' view of the growth debate is one implying a struggle between the drag to economic growth arising from population growth and resource exhaustion on the one side, and compensating advances in technology and new discoveries on the other. Data from the last two centuries inform us that not only have many resources not declined in an economic sense, but that technological change has managed to increase both the quality and the quantity of resources at human disposal. It may be that past successes justify the confidence that the same mechanisms of markets and technological progress will be able to expand the 'total stock of capital' available for society's use in the future. However, there are very real reasons for concern that the economists' analysis to date has been too narrowly focused upon specific natural resource commodities (such as minerals) and that it does not apply well to more complex natural services and systems.

The concept of scale of the economy: meta-resources and sustainable development

A more complex version of the limits to growth points less to the limitations of specific natural resources and more to the general relationship between human society and the ecosystem supporting it. To place this relationship between humanity and its environment at the centre of the analysis, some economists have introduced the concept of 'scale' (Georgescu-Roegen, 1971; Boulding, 1966; Daly, 1972 re-edited in 1992). These economists argue that neoclassical economics has failed to distinguish the problem of efficiency from that of the optimal scale of the economy (Daly, 1987; Foy and Daly, 1992). Neoclassical economics is concerned with the optimal allocation of given resources within a certain distribution. In this approach it is the market mechanism (governed by price movements which function as signals of relative value) which allocates resources efficiently, provided there are no externalities (see Chapter Two).

The scale approach instead analyses the dimension of the whole economy, which is considered as an open subsystem, within the larger ecosystem. Seen from this perspective it becomes quite clear that the growth of the economy is limited by the finite size of the total ecosystem, specifically by its dependence on the earth as a source of inputs and as a sink for waste outputs. The approach focuses attention on the intricate ecological connections, which suffer from disruption as the subsystem becomes larger relative to the total system.

In traditional economic modelling, flows in the economy are represented in a circular fashion. For example, the value of the production of goods and services from firms is equal to the purchases of holders of factors of production: money simply flows around the economy in a continuous circle. An alternative approach sees the energy flow of matter as ultimately undirectional, because recycling, although possible, is never 100 per cent complete and energy is inevitably dispersed in all processes as stated by the fundamental second law of thermodynamics. It is these leakages which affect the environment in the form of depletion and pollution. Depletion and pollution in turn interfere with life-supporting services rendered to the economy by other species and by the natural biogeochemical cycle. The feedback from the total system represents a form of external costs which cannot be solved simply by resort to the price mechanism.

The scarcity at issue in this context is global scarcity referring to all resources, to be distinguished from relative scarcity to which the solution may be the substitution of abundant resources for relatively scarce ones. Absolute scarcity increases as growth in population and per capita consumption pushes the economy closer to the limit where all the possible substitutions are already made. The fact that prices cannot deal with absolute scarcity is easily seen by the impossibility of raising the relative price of all resources. At the global level, the incorporation of environmental costs into market prices is not a sufficient environmental policy, as the market is not able to set its own boundaries automatically within the larger ecosystem. In other words, the market mechanism can seek to achieve an efficient allocation of resources within the economic subsystem, but it cannot determine the size of this subsystem relative to the whole ecosystem.

Although the most severe problems lie with global living resources, there are specific aspects concerning relative scarcity which raise serious concerns, for instance regarding fossil fuels. If cheap and non-polluting substitutes are not found, a shortage of energy sources rather than food shortages will soon create enormous problems for economic growth. Goeller (1979) calculated that substantial increase in world demand may shorten to only 100 years the ratio of reserves to demand for fossil fuels. Moreover, he questions the validity of recycling as a fundamental conservation measure since, unless the process attains at least 90 per cent recovery, it is relatively ineffective over many recycles.

Despite the optimism of many studies, there are also identifiable limits to substitution opportunities and serious drawbacks associated with them:

> As a single example, plastic can now substitute for metals or other materials in many applications, but disposal of plastics (and the toxic wastes generated in their manufacture) creates extremely serious environmental problems. In the long run, the plastics industry will suffer from the depletion of (and competition for) petro-leum and other fossil fuels from which plastics are made, or of wood from which they can be made. Plastics are a prime example of a substitution that has pushed the T factor in the I=PAT equation in precisely the wrong direction.
> (Ehrlich and Ehrlich, 1990, pp. 166–7. For the impact equation see section VI.)

According to the global perspective, which carefully considers the interactions between economic and ecological systems, the real concerns relate to the degradation of living resources, both sea and land based, whose supply is more limited and less elastic with respect to productivity and prices, and less prone to augmentation through technology. These are termed 'meta-resources' – forms of natural capital providing unique and irreplaceable services. Their continued depletion (extermination of populations and species, depletion of aquifers, destruction of forests and erosion of soil) may seriously impair the survival capacities of human societies (Ehrlich, 1989).

An idea of the magnitude of human impact on the biosphere is given by the disproportionate share of net primary production (NPP) appropriated by humans *vis-à-vis* other species. 'NPP is the amount of energy left after subtracting the respiration of primary producers (mostly plants) from the total amount of energy (mostly solar) that is fixed biologically' (Vitousek et al., 1986). It provides the source of life for all animal and micro-organism species on earth (specifically of all heterotrophs: consumers and decomposers), accounting, in a way, for the total food resource on the planet. Humans consume, destroy and co-opt for their activities nearly 40 per cent of all terrestrial NPP each year (see Box 4.3), causing the extinction of a large number of species and biotic resources which constitute the genetic basis for essential applications, such as new crops, new medicines and vaccines. Although calculation of NPP exploitation does not permit us to draw inferences about the earth's carrying capacity, these results clearly indicate the dangers of continually increasing human population and the scale of its activities.

Another serious concern about the effects of population and economic growth on meta-resources focuses on 'global warming': the increase of earth's

Box 4.3   Human appropriation of NPP

NPP is measured in petagram (Pg) of organic matter, equivalent to 10^{15} grams. Total biomass is calculated at 1,244 Pg and the annual terrestrial NPP at 132.1 Pg (Ajtay et al., 1979). By considering also the potential NPP of terrestrial ecosystems (17.5), the annual NPP figure of 132.1 increases to 149.6. The total impact of humans on this global resource can be derived by summing both the direct and indirect uses. The direct uses are the destruction of organic material and land as a result of conversion to crop land and pasture land, forest clearing and burning in shifting cultivation. The indirect uses arise from the loss of potential NPP due to man's conversion of natural ecosystems into other systems whose NPP is deemed lower, such as agricultural systems, the permanent conversion of forest to pastures, desertification, and conversion of natural systems to areas for human settlements. Estimating human appropriations indicates that humans consume, destroy and co-opt 38.8% of potential terrestrial productivity. In these calculations consumption of aquatic ecosystems NPP, which is relatively small, is not included in order to focus on the major impact on terrestrial resources.

Process	NPP used (Pg)
Cultivated land	15.0
Grazing land	11.6
Forest land	13.6
Human occupied areas	0.4
Lost NPP in agriculture	9.0
Conversion of forests into pastures	1.4
Desertification	4.5
Loss to human areas	2.6
Total human appropriation	58.1
Annual terrestrial NPP	149.6
Percentage of terrestrial NPP co-opted or lost to human use	38.8%

Source: Vitousek et al. (1986).

average temperature caused by the growing accumulation in the atmosphere of carbon dioxide and other trace gases being produced by human activities, for example, burning fossil fuels, deforestation, rice cultivation, fertilizer use and production of chlorofluorocarbons. It is estimated that emissions of carbon dioxide, responsible for over half of the temperature increase, have risen by 25 per cent since the start of the industrial revolution and will continue to increase as a result of population growth and expanding consumption. There is no scientific consensus as to the expected rise in global temperature or the economic and ecological consequences of global warming and therefore as to the urgency with which to respond to the threat posed by the concentration of greenhouse gases. The role of population growth among the other interacting factors as a cause of global warming appears to be important. One estimate suggests population growth accounts for 35 per cent of the increase in global emissions and for 48 per cent in developing countries alone (Bongaarts, 1992). More generally, even if the elasticity of energy demand relative to the increase in GDP per capita is kept low, current technologies do not allow for an immediate drastic reduction of trace gases emissions (Gilland, 1988).

In the face of uncertainties about the nature and timing of long term effects, there is agreement on the costs and benefits of further increases in societal scale. Applying a high discount rate to uncertain future costs leads to the conclusion that massive reductions in the scale of human activities (through the halting of population growth and industrialization) are not cost effective (Nordhaus, 1991). However according to other experts, ignorance about the exact magnitude of future threats should induce a conservationist approach, which puts high priority on avoiding the most disastrous consequences for humankind. A sensible and far-sighted approach would imply aversion to risk, the use of very long time horizons (in the order of 250 years), the use of low discount rates and prompt policy implementation (Cline, 1992).

The concept of sustainable development which attempts to incorporate all relevant factors that interact with the socio-economic system, including those less certain and in the distant future, is promulgated as the more appropriate concept of development. It tries to ensure a real future for humankind, overcoming the limitations of the economic concept of sustainability, which sets the conditions for the maintenance of a given per capita consumption without considering the effects on, and from, the larger ecosystem. While a nation is an open system which may draw resources from other regions, the earth as a whole can only follow a path of sustainable development: the only way to borrow is by depleting its own capital, which implies jeopardizing its future life. The World Commission on Environment and Development (Brundtland, 1987) detailed the issues and urgency of moving towards sustainable development, defined as the 'development which meets the need of the present without compromising the ability of future generations to meet their own needs'. From this perspective, the 'scale' of an economy must be a significant contributor to environmental degradation. There are 'meta-resources' for which it is impossible to substitute, and human individuals and activities depend upon them. Their scarcity implies a constraint on human scale.

Some failures of technological and behavioural responses
Humans, more than any other species, are able to respond to environmental changes by using technological advances, trade (between lands with different endowments of resources), and institutional and behavioural adaptations. A vast literature has investigated the extent to which an economy is able to adapt to the negative effects of its growth within the ecosystem and whether this response is able to diminish or even reverse these effects. Theories of induced technological innovation and of demographic transition both stress a population's ability to overcome the limits of natural scarcity and enhance per capita welfare. The problem with these theories, however, is that they do not take into account the occurrence of externalities which may cause a failure in bringing about the correct responses. Environmental degradation illustrates this externality problem.

The theory of induced technical change interprets technical change as endogenous to the economic system, induced by differences or changes in the conditions of factor supply and product demand (Hayami and Ruttan, 1970, 1985 and 1991; Binswanger and Ruttan, 1978). These changes are in turn often caused by demographic changes. This theory is based on the work of Boserup (1965, 1981), who developed the idea that population growth acted as a major determinant of agricultural development in the economic history of Europe, Asia, Africa and Latin America, inducing responses which overcame the negative effects from diminishing marginal returns to a fixed amount of land.

Boserup's analysis of agricultural development is based on the concept of the frequency of cropping. The shortening of fallow periods, in order to increase the product per acre, requires a change in inputs and techniques applied to the land. The theory explains that under conditions of population pressure land use practices change gradually from extensive to intensive cultivation. In the earliest stages of civilization, the forest fallow system was used because of the extensive forest cover and the low population density. Subsequent stages saw the progressive reduction of fallow periods with the consequent decrease of forest cover and the appearance of bush, shrub and then grassland cover. In order to substitute for the lack of fallow as a soil-regenerating method, other inputs – such as labour, the plough, organic manuring and artificial fertilizers – were increasingly utilized to raise land productivity and fertility, thus enabling annual and even multiple cropping.

Historical data, reported in abundance by Boserup and the previously mentioned authors, connect changes in techniques with the rate of population growth. Population growth acted both as a demand factor, pushing for increased production, and a supply factor, by providing the labour necessary to introduce those changes.

The claim that population growth automatically generates feedback effects which are able to increase food production (hence the 'problem' generates its own solution) nevertheless cannot explain the persistence of high population growth rates, degraded land, poverty of resources and very low technology in many developing regions, especially in sub-Saharan Africa. Here, the recent declines in per capita food production and land productivity have coexisted with the highest population growth rates in the world. One of the reasons may be the adverse agro-climatic conditions. By analysing different agro-ecosystems, one can recognize that some of them may not support intensive farming technologies. Rapid population growth in these areas may thus augment pressure on resources and result in excessive exploitation without the relief offered by technological improvement. Population growth may not always be accompanied by increased productivity (Ho, 1985).

The impact of population growth on agricultural productivity can therefore be considered as the sum of two opposite effects (Pearce, 1990). There is the positive impulse given to technology and the negative impact on soil productivity due to more intense farming. Soil erosion, salinization and the counter-productive effects of pesticides can be the direct results of productivity efforts. Boserup herself warns against the 'temptation to regard soil fertility exclusively as a gift of nature, bestowed upon certain lands once and for all'. Instead soil fertility should be treated as a variable, closely associated with changes in population and agricultural methods. Given this approach, it is the relative strength of the increased technology effects versus the 'degradation of soil' conditions which ultimately determines the pace of productivity increases (or decreases).

While it is true that changing demography will alter relative opportunity costs and factor endowments, the requirement that these changes be reflected in agricultural prices, land tenure and crop research policy may not be met, with the result that factor substitution and technological change as envisaged in Boserup's theory cannot take place. Instead, population pressure may lead to 'regressive intensification'. This occurs where practices designed for fertile lands are applied to marginal lands, with the result that soil productivity falls as erosion and nutrient exhaustion occur.

The failure of the market mechanisms to convey the correct signals together with the inability to implement a land policy which ensures equal access to and participation in growth in production, may lead to regressive intensification. To illustrate, the urgency of satisfying immediate wants leads to heavy discounting of future social needs and the subsequent exploitation of current resources. The market reflects neither the future social value of these resources, nor the claims of the poor and landless. The conditions of poverty, population growth and ineffective land reform, combined with reliance on the market mechanism, may mean the only option available is to clear marginal land and deplete irreplaceable resources (soil, forest or pasture).

An example of the failure of the market mechanism is its inability to account for a divergence between private and social gains from high fertility. Poor rural countries are mainly biomass-based subsistence economies, which derive their material basis from water, plants, animals and fuelwood, with the application of high labour inputs. When these natural resources deteriorate (due to population pressure and other causes), households need to compensate for the loss with higher inputs of labour. For example, when fuelwood decreases in the neighbourhood, mothers require more child labour to search for and collect fuelwood. The interaction of rapid population growth and environmental degradation, where each element is seen as the rational response to the other, represents the trap which blocks the mechanism towards technological progress and perpetuates poverty (Dasgupta, 1993). To summarize, child labour represents an essential resource for poor households with no access to capital or land, therefore each family perceives a powerful incentive to have many children. High fertility rates, although rational at a family level, result in excessive population size, the costs of which are borne by all households with the poor usually bearing a disproportionate share (World Bank, 1984).

The potential vicious cycle of population growth and degradation is confirmed in the few empirical studies so far attempted in the area. According to an analysis applied to six African countries (Lele and Stone, 1989), extremely rapid population growth and rising densities have negative effects even for land-abundant countries, since there is a 'tendency to "mine" the land for immediate survival versus the social need to protect the soil as a productive resource'. In such conditions there are no gains in agricultural productivity. Furthermore, a World Bank (1991) study finds a positive and significant statistical correlation between fertility rates and deforestation from a cross-sectional analysis of 38 African countries. This adds to the evidence that high fertility rates and environmental degradation reinforce each other, at the expense of sustainable growth in food production and general living standards.

The role of institutional factors
Concluding that the main responsibility for environmental degradation lies with population growth is misleading if it neglects other fundamental ele-

ments which interact with population growth to endanger the earth's resources. Many of those who previously pointed only to the negative aspects
of population growth are now revising their views (National Research Council, 1986; United Nations, 1991). They are taking a broader look at the effects
of population growth, uncovering negative and positive aspects, and shedding
light on a series of factors which are themselves causes of problems and
which alter the population impact on the environment. With this perspective,
the population element may act not as a direct cause but as a 'compound'
element of environmental degradation and resource depletion.

In many regions the problem of environmental degradation is much worse
than it would be under population pressure alone. High levels of consumption
and polluting technology have already been identified as seriously undermining environmental quality and natural capital. A simple algebraic identity, put
forward by Ehrlich and Ehrlich (1981), singles out three factors which impact
on the environment: population size (P), average person's consumption of
resources (affluence, A) and technology (T), resulting in the 'impact equation':

$$I = PAT$$

This equation sheds light on the relative importance of these factors across
countries, with a predominance of the population element in poor countries
and high levels of the consumption and industrial production elements in rich
countries. The industrialized countries are those most responsible for the
injection of carbon dioxide and methane (the major greenhouse gases) into
the atmosphere, causing ozone depletion, acid raid and oceanic pollution.
Most of this waste is due to the consumption of energy (A) and to the
mobilization of it through environmentally disruptive processes (T). Focusing narrowly on numbers prevents a sound evaluation of the serious consequences of rich countries' patterns of consumption and production. Certainly
the work of Commoner (1971 and 1991) has focused attention on the role of
technology, more than affluence and population, in aggravating the negative
consequences of human impact.

Institutional variables and their effects on resource quality have much to do
with problems of efficiency and distribution. So far we have mainly addressed the question of scale (Foy and Daly, 1992). According to some
studies the main problem behind resource degradation is the existence of
'open access' resources. Many natural resources in poor countries, normally
under state management, are open access resources (Bromley and Cernea,
1989). Governments have proved financially and organizationally incapable
of regulating rights of access and use and, in addition, unable to implement
programmes of maintenance and improvement. The effect of their policies

has been mainly to disrupt pre-existing common property arrangements, which in the past defined precise rules relating to access and use for all members of the community. Local collective arrangements (common property resources), in diverse agro-climatic conditions, have usually succeeded in preserving resources and regulating the impact of population upon them. Exploitation of resources under population pressure can therefore be considered more a consequence of the shift from common property to open access management, than of the population pressure itself. Numerous systems of common property resources were successful in preserving resources from overuse, dealing both with ecologically fragile environments and population growth. Usually those lands inappropriate to intensive cultivation did not justify individual property rights and were thus put under common property management.

A statistical analysis of the causes of tropical deforestation in Ecuador (Southgate et al., 1991) shows how land clearing is positively correlated with tenure insecurity as well as population pressure. Increasing tropical deforestation in the eastern regions of the country results from the inability of the government to control access and establish definite property rights. Instead, informal agricultural use rights are assumed by whoever clears the land. The practice of fallow cultivation is discouraged by the fact that idle land may be claimed by anybody. Since there are no rewards for a practice which preserves the soil for the future, the insecurity in tenure arrangements encourages present users to exploit resources immediately and indiscriminately.

Unequal distribution of resources, besides being undesirable in itself, may also contribute to environmental problems (Repetto and Holmes, 1983). Data from poor countries point to a high degree of inequality in the distribution of the main factor, land. Often large areas of land are cultivated with low intensive techniques which further increases pressure on remaining land where most households are constrained. In frontier areas, the phenomena of marginalization of the poor and deterioration of resources are strongly interrelated. The growing numbers of landless people in poor countries live mainly on common property resources which are often subject to a privatization process or, alternatively, on newly colonized land which was idle because it was unsuitable to cultivate. The attempt to overcome the deficiencies of environmentally fragile land leads to further soil degradation and rapid reduction of forest cover. The crowding of people onto marginal resources, far from being proof of the negative impact of population pressure, derives from the policy of many governments of providing incentives for the colonization of new land in order to avoid the issue of distribution of the already cultivated areas (as in the case of Haiti described by Foy and Daly, 1992).

Conclusions

Population growth is constrained by the finite scale of the ecosystem, which sets limits to processing energy, exploiting resources and recycling wastes. A world population growing beyond these limits is unsustainable and bound to collapse.

Although there is evidence that technological advancements together with institutional and social changes may in general overcome resource scarcity, there are fundamental worries that the human population is undermining, through its growth, the very basis of its life on earth. Humans are continuously undercutting animal and plant populations by converting a larger share of land and resources for their own use. Humans are also drastically modifying environmental conditions and land quality as a result of expanded agriculture and creation of more wastes. Lastly, humans are affecting the planet's climate with large emissions of greenhouse gases into the atmosphere. According to some estimates, by the year 2000 there may be an overall rise of 4° in the average temperature since the industrial revolution.

Even if sheer numbers are not the only cause of this disruption, a global perspective on world consumption and technological impact on environmental quality requires the evaluation of the potential effects of population size, acting as a multiplier factor.

However population size is not the only problem, since even a very rapid population growth in a low density area may prevent the onset of adjustment mechanisms necessary to adapt production and social conditions to a changed demographic situation. This is very much the case for sub-Saharan Africa, which has a relatively low density but a high rate of population growth.

The failures of market mechanisms to account for the social value of conservation measures encourages the exploitation of scarce resources in order to satisfy immediate needs. Similarly, the failure to include the social costs of high fertility leads to poor rural households maintaining high fertility rates as a response to lack of capital, land, insurance and credit markets, and to a deteriorated resource base. The link between population growth and environmental degradation is therefore particularly delicate in poor countries. High growth rates represent the unresolved residue of their economic backwardness, while the inability to apply proper production methods, able to relieve the pressure on resources and on high fertility, contributes to a further deterioration of the environment.

Bibliography

Abrahamson, D.E. (1989), *The Challenge of Global Warming*, Island Press: Washington D.C.

Ajtay, G.L., Ketner, P. and Duvigneaud, P. (1979), 'Terrestrial Primary Production and Phytomass', in Bolin, B. et al. (eds), *The Global Carbon Cycle*, John Wiley and Sons: New York.

Allen, R. and Barnes, J. (1985), 'The Causes of Deforestation in Developing Countries', *Annals of the Association of American Geographers*, **75**, no.2.

Barnett, H.J. (1979), 'Scarcity and Growth Revisited', in Smith, K. (1979).

Barnett, H.J. and Morse, C. (1963), *Scarcity and Growth: The Economics of Natural Resource Availability*, Johns Hopkins University Press: Baltimore.

Binswanger, H.P. and Ruttan, V.W. (eds) (1978), *Induced Innovation: Technology, Institutions and Development*, Johns Hopkins University Press: Baltimore.

Bongaarts, J. (1992), 'Population Growth and Global Warming', *Population and Development Review*, **18**, no.2.

Boserup, E. (1965), *The Conditions of Agricultural Growth: The Economics of Agrarian Change under Population Pressure*, Aldine Publishing: New York.

Boserup, E. (1981), *Population and Technological Change: A Study of Long-term Trends*, University of Chicago Press: Chicago.

Boulding, K. (1966), 'The Economics of the Coming Spaceship Earth', in Jarret, H. (ed.), *Environmental Quality in a Growing Economy*, Johns Hopkins University Press: Baltimore.

Bromley, D.W. and Cernea, M.M. (1989), 'The Management of Common Property Natural Resources', *World Bank Discussion Paper*, no. 57.

Brown, L. (1991), *State of the World 1991*, Norton: New York.

Brown, L. et al. (1989), *State of the World 1989*, Norton: New York.

Brundtland, G.H. (1987), *Our Common Future*, World Commission on Environment and Development, Oxford University Press: Oxford.

Capistrano, A. and Kiker, C. (1990), *Global Economic Influences on Tropical Broadleaved Forest Depletion*, The World Bank: Washington D.C.

Cline, W.R. (1991), 'Scientific Basis for the Greenhouse Effect', *Economic Journal*, **101**, no.407.

Cline, W.R. (1992), *The Economics of Global Warming*, Institute for International Economics: Washington D.C.

Commoner, B. (1971), *The Closing Circle*, Knopf: New York.

Commoner, B. (1991), 'Rapid Population Growth and Environmental Stress', in United Nations (1991).

Constantino, L. and Ingram, D. (1990), *Supply-Demand Projections from the Indonesian Forestry Sector*, FAO: Jakarta.

Daly, H.E. (1987), 'The Economic Growth Debate: What Some Economists Have Learned But Many Have Not', *Journal of Environmental Economics and Management*, **14**.

Daly, H.E. (1992), *Steady-state Economics* (2nd edn with New Essays), Earthscan: London.

Dasgupta, P. (1993), *An Inquiry into Well-Being and Destitution*, Clarendon Press: Oxford.

Davis, K. (1991), 'Population and Resources: Fact and Interpretation', in Davis, K. and Bernstam, M.S. (1991).

Davis, K. and Bernstam, M.S. (eds) (1991), *Resources, Environment and Population: Present Knowledge, Future Options*, Suppl. to Population and Development Review, vol. 16, The Population Council and Oxford University Press: New York.

Ehrlich, P.R. (1968), *The Population Bomb*, Ballantine Press: New York.

Ehrlich, P.R. (1989), 'The Limits to Substitution: Meta-resource Depletion and a New Economic-Ecological Paradigm', *Ecological Economics*, **1**.

Ehrlich, P.R. and Ehrlich, A.H. (1981), *Extinction: the Causes and Consequences of the Disappearance of Species*, Random House: New York.

Ehrlich, P.R. and Ehrlich, A.H. (1990), *The Population Explosion*, Hutchinson: London.

Food and Agriculture Oganisation (1981), *Production Yearbook*, FAO: Rome.

Foy, G. and Daly, H. (1992), 'Allocation, Distribution and Scale as Determinants of Environmental Degradation: Case Studies of Haiti, El Salvador and Costa Rica', in Markandya, A. and Richardson, J. (1992).

Georgescu-Roegen, N. (1971), *The Entropy Law and the Economic Process*, Harvard University Press: Cambridge, Mass.

Gilland, B. (1983), 'Considerations on World Population and Food Supply', *Population and Development Review*, **9**, no.2.

Gilland, B. (1988), 'Population Growth and Demography 1985–2020', *Population and Development Review*, **14**, no.2.

Global Outlook 2000 (1990) (3rd edn), United Nations: New York.

Goeller, H.E. (1979), 'The Age of Substitutability: A Scientific Appraisal of Natural Resource Adequacy', in Smith, K. (1979).

Harte, J. (1988), 'Acid Rain', in Ehrlich, P. and Holdren, J. (eds), *The Cassandra Conference*, Texas A&M Press: College Station.

Hayami, Y. and Ruttan, V.W. (1970), 'Factor Prices and Technical Change in Agricultural Development: The United States and Japan, 1880–1960', *Journal of Political Economy*, **78**.

Hayami, Y. and Ruttan, V.W. (1985), *Agriculture Development: An International Perspective*, Johns Hopkins University Press: Baltimore.

Hayami, Y. and Ruttan, V.W. (1991), 'Rapid Population Growth and Technical and Institutional Change', in United Nations (1991).

Higgins, G.M. et al. (1983), 'Potential Population Supporting Capacities of Lands in the Developing World', Technical Report of FAO/UNFPA/IIASA: Rome.

Ho, T.J. (1985), 'Population Growth and Agricultural Productivity in Sub-Saharan Africa', in Davis, T.D. (ed.), *Proceedings of the Fifth Agricultural Sector Symposium. Population and Food*, The World Bank: Washington D.C.

Lee, R. et al. (eds.) (1988), *Population, Food and Rural Development*, Clarendon Press: Oxford.

Lele, U. and Stone, S. (1989), 'Population Pressure: The Environment and Agricultural Intensification', *MADIA Discussion Paper*, no. 4, The World Bank: Washington D.C.

Lovins, A.B. (1991), 'Energy, People and Industrialisation', in Davis, K. and Bernstam, M.S. (1991).

Markandya, A. and Richardson, J. (eds.) (1992), *Environmental Economics*, Earthscan: London.

Meadows, D.H. et al. (1972), *The Limits to Growth*, Universe Books: New York.

Meadows, D.H. et al. (1992), *Beyond the Limits*, Earthscan: London.

McEvedy, C. and Jones, R. (1978), *Atlas of World Population History*, Penguin Books: New York.

National Research Council (1986), *Population and Economic Development: Policy Questions*, National Academy of Science Press: Washington D.C.

Nordhaus, D.W. (1991), 'To Slow or not to Slow: The Economics of the Greenhouse Effect', *Economic Journal*, **101**, no. 407.

Nordhaus, D.W. (1992), 'Lethal Model 2: The Limits to Growth Revisited', *Brookings Papers on Economic Activity*, no.2.

Palo, M.G., Mery, G. and Salmi, J. (1987), *Deforestation in the Tropics: Pilot Scenarios based on Quantitative Analyses*, Metsatutkimuslaitoksen Tiedonantaja no. 272, Helsinki.

Pearce, D.J. (1990), 'Population, Poverty and Environment', prepared for *Pensamiento Ibero Americano Revista de Economia Politica*.

Pearce, D.J., Brown, K., Swanson, T. and Perrings, C. (1993), *Economics and the Conservation of Global Biological Diversity*, A Report to the Global Environment Facility, CSERGE: London.

Pearce, D.J. and Warford, J.J. (1993), *World without End: Economics, Environment and Sustainable Development*, Oxford University Press: New York.

Pingali, P., Bigot, Y. and Binswanger, H.P. (1987), *Agricultural Mechanisation and the Evolution of Farming Systems in Sub-Saharan Africa*, Johns Hopkins University Press: Baltimore.

Repetto, R. (1987), 'Population, Resources, Environment: An Uncertain Future', *Population Bulletin*, **42**, no.2.

Repetto, R. and Holmes, T. (1983), 'The Role of Population in Resource Depletion in Developing Countries', *Population and Development Review*, **9**, no.4.

Revell, R. (1976), 'The Resources Available for Agriculture', *Scientific American*, **235**, no.3.

Schneider, S.H. (1989), *Global Warming*, Sierra Club Books: San Francisco.

Smith, K. (ed.) (1979), *Scarcity and Growth Reconsidered*, Johns Hopkins University Press: Baltimore.

Solow, R.M. (1974), 'The Economics of Resources or the Resources of Economics', *American Economic Review*, **64**, no.2.

Southgate, D., Sierra, R. and Brown, L. (1991), 'The Causes of Tropical Deforestation in Ecuador: A Statistical Analysis', *World Development*, **19**, no.9.

Tucker, C.J., Dregne, H.E. and Newcomb, W.W. (1990), 'Expansion and Contraction of the Sahara Desert from 1980 to 1990', *Science*, **253**.

Unesco and FAO (1985), *Carrying Capacity Assessment with a Pilot Study of Kenya: A Resource Accounting Methodology for Exploring National Options for Sustainable Development*, Unesco and FAO: Paris and Rome.

United Nations, *World Population Prospects as Assessed in 1988, in 1990*, United Nations: New York.

United Nations (1991), *Consequences of Rapid Population Growth in Developing Countries*, Taylor and Francis: New York.

Vitousek, P.M., Ehrlich, P.R., Ehrlich, A.H. and Matson, P.A. (1986), 'Human Appropriation of the Products of Photosynthesis', *Bioscience*, **36**, no.6.

Wilson, E.O. (1988), *Biodiversity*, National Academy Press: Washington D.C.

World Bank (1984), *World Development Report*, Washington D.C.

World Bank (1991), *The Population, Agriculture and Environment Nexus in Sub-Saharan Africa*, World Bank Africa Region: Washington D.C.

World Bank (1992), *World Development Report*, Washington D.C.

World Bank (1993), *World Development Report*, Washington D.C.

World Resources Institute (1990), *World Resources 1990–91*, Oxford University Press: New York.

5　Poverty and degradation

Mark Rogers

Introduction

Recent estimates indicate that over 1,000 million people live in poverty (World Bank, 1992). These poor people tend to live in some of the least resilient and most threatened environments. Tropical forests, upland areas, semi-arid zones and the peripheries of large cities are the home for many of the poor. The rural areas are often at risk from soil erosion, soil infertility, flooding and drought, while urban overcrowding leads to poor water and sanitation services. The fragility of the environment can generate a vicious cycle where degradation causes falling productivity which leads to more poverty that causes yet more degradation. However the links between poverty and degradation are complex and depend on a range of other factors such as land tenurial rights, population growth and social customs.

This chapter analyses the impact of poverty on environmental degradation at the level of the individual. It develops a framework demonstrating how poverty – in the absence of income and assets – contributes to individual decision-making concerning investment in environmental resources. Chapter Six then goes on to examine the impact of low income at a societal level; specifically, the impact of indebtedness on environmental degradation. Although the evidence is inconclusive we believe that the analytical links between poverty and degradation are clear ones – people with shallow asset bases often find it necessary to mine their natural resources in times of societal stress.

World poverty and world resources

The World Bank defines 43 low income countries where per capita income is less than $610 per year. These countries account for 61 per cent of the world's population but receive only 5 per cent of the world's total income. These low income countries also cover 28 per cent of the world's land area. The low income countries combined with the 50 middle income countries (those with per capita income between $611 and $7619) share around 18 per cent of the world's income, have 83 per cent of the world's population and cover about 60 per cent of the world's land area.

The figures for per capita income growth in Table 5.1 imply an improving situation for the low and middle income countries. However individual countries have suffered negative average growth rates for the period 1965–90.

Table 5.1   Income, population and land distribution

	Population (billion)	Area (billion km^2)	per capita GNP 1990 (US$)	per capita annual growth 1965–90 (%)
Low income economies	3.06	37.8	350	2.9
China and India	1.98	12.8	360	3.7
Other countries (41)	1.08	25.0	320	1.7
Middle income economies	1.09	41.1	2 220	2.2
Lower-middle income (41 countries)	0.63	22.4	1 530	1.5
Higher-middle income (17 countries)	0.46	18.7	3 410	2.8
High income economies	0.82	31.8	19 590	2.4

Source: World Bank (1992).

There are 14 low income countries and nine middle income countries that have averaged negative growth for this period. The sub-Saharan Africa region has grown the slowest over the last 25 years with an average annual per capita growth rate of 0.2 per cent (1965–90) compared to 2.9 per cent for the low income countries as a whole. As a result an estimated one-quarter of the population of sub-Saharan Africa lives perpetually at the edge of starvation (Leonard, 1989).

The existence of poverty is not only dependent on the shares of income between countries but also on the income distribution within countries. For example, Bangladesh has a very low GNP per head ($210) but a relatively equal income distribution, while Brazil with a much higher GNP per head ($2,680) has a relatively unequal distribution of income. Both countries have large numbers of people living in poverty. The distribution of the world's poor between major regions is shown in Table 5.2.

It is estimated that half of the world's poor live in 'ecologically fragile' rural areas (World Bank, 1992). These include tropical forests, upland areas and arid and semi-arid regions. (Table 5.3 shows rates of deforestation in selected regions and countries.) These fragile areas are not resilient to stress or shocks from either natural or man-made causes. Soils may be irreversibly damaged by water and wind erosion, salinisation and inappropriate farming methods. Furthermore, these areas are often incompatible with modern farming techniques due to climatic and soil conditions.[1] Poverty and degradation are highly interlinked in these areas. Poor people are constrained in these areas since they, by definition, have no resources to obtain better land. The

Table 5.2 *Distribution of the world's poor*

Region	Population below poverty line		Number of poor	
	1985 (%)	1990 (%)	1985 (millions)	1990 (million)
All developing countries	30.5	29.7	1 051	1 133
South Asia	51.8	49.0	532	562
East Asia	13.2	11.3	182	169
Sub-Saharan Africa	47.6	47.8	184	216
Middle East and North Africa	30.6	33.1	60	73
Eastern Europe	7.1	7.1	5	5
Latin America and the Caribbean	22.4	25.5	87	108

Note: Poverty line is $370 in 1985 prices.

Source: World Bank (1992).

Table 5.3 *Estimates of annual tropical deforestation*

Region	Total forests (thousand hectares)	Annual deforestation (1981–90) (%)
Africa	4 800	1.7
Tropical Asia	4 700	0.9
Latin America	7 300	1.4
Total (62 countries)	16 800	1.2
of which:		
Brazil	1 700	0.5
Nigeria	200	6.7
India	48	0.1
Indonesia	1 200	1.1
Philippines	270	2.8
Thailand	600	7.2

Source: Barbier (1990).

fragile nature of the poor's land means that investment in soil and water preservation are vital but the poverty of the occupants may prevent this required investment. This may leave those inhabiting these areas in an extremely vulnerable position.

Table 5.4 *Countries with the greatest 'species richness'*

Mammals			Birds			Reptiles		
Country	GNP per capita ($)	Species	Country	GNP per capita ($)	Species	Country	GNP per capita ($)	Species
Indonesia	570	515	Colombia	1 260	1 721	Mexico	2 490	717
Mexico	2 490	449	Peru	1 160	1 701	Australia	17 000	686
Brazil	2 680	428	Brazil	2 680	1 622	Indonesia	570	600
Zaire	220	409	Indonesia	220	1 519	India	350	383
China	370	394	Ecuador	980	1 447	Colombia	1 260	383
Peru	1 160	361	Venezuela	2 560	1 275	Ecuador	980	345
Colombia	1 260	359	Bolivia	630	1 250	Peru	1 160	297
India	350	350	India	350	1 200	Malaysia	2 320	294
Uganda	220	311	Malaysia	2 320	1 200	Thailand	1 420	282
Tanzania	110	310	China	370	1 195	Papua N.G.	860	282

Source: McNeely et al. (1990).

In addition the poor countries of the world contain much of the world's remaining stock of natural resources, including much of its biodiversity (the collective term for all genetic information, species and ecosystems). Destruction and degradation of the environment in the poor countries will therefore involve significant losses to the world's stock of natural resources. Table 5.4 shows the ten countries with the greatest numbers of species of mammals, birds and reptiles along with their GNP/head. As can be seen all, apart from Australia, are low or middle income countries.

Links between poverty and degradation

Poverty has been described as both the cause and effect of environmental degradation. There are circumstances in which poor people over-exploit the environment in their struggle to survive and act as agents of degradation. Equally, there are situations where environmental degradation leads to falling crop productivity or increasing levels of disease that in turn create more poverty. This vicious cycle of poverty leading to degradation and worsening poverty has been stressed by various authors (for recent comments see Pearce and Warford, 1993; Bhalla, 1992; and World Bank, 1992). While the extent of poverty and the state of the environment may be closely linked this does not mean there are simple, clear lines of causation. Separating the environmental effects of poverty, population growth, inappropriate property rights and other factors is difficult. Some authors think it may be more appropriate to view poverty as the mechanism through which other factors lead to degradation (for example Pearce and Warford, 1993).

Moreover it is clear that poor people often rely directly on natural resources for their survival.[2] Soil provides food either from crops or by its vegetation which provides grazing for livestock. Forest or woodland areas provide sources of fuel and building materials. Rivers and watersheds provide water for both people and crops. These natural resources can be regarded as the 'natural capital' on which poor people rely for their living. For example, soil can provide a flow of food or income in the same way that a machine can produce a flow of manufactured goods. Both are forms of 'capital', one provided by the earth and the other man-made. Poor people usually have very small amounts of man-made capital and this means they have virtually no opportunities to generate income by producing manufactured goods. Poor people also have their own labour as a resource but employment possibilities are usually limited. Poor people generally rely upon a very limited stock of natural capital, for example, a small plot of land or access to a small communal common. Even those people who neither own nor rent land and who rely on employment for income, often supplement their income in an important way by access to some natural capital. Natural capital that can be accessed without a rental or ownership contract is called common property resources (CPRs). Examples of CPRs are woodlands, grazing areas and rivers that can be used by members of the community. A study of rural villages in India found CPRs accounted for 14 to 23 per cent of average household income (Jodha, 1992). It is this characteristic of heavy reliance upon natural, capital-based sources of income that typifies many poverty-stricken peoples. This chapter investigates its meaningfulness.

Poverty, natural capital and investment
Natural capital can be degraded by the actions of its users. For example, soil fertility can be destroyed by growing inappropriate crops and erosion can result from over-grazing. Forests and woodlands can also be destroyed if wood is extracted faster than it grows. The maintenance of the stock of natural capital requires sustainable management. In particular current resources must be invested to ensure that the capital is productive in the future. As an example, the fertilizing of soil (which ensures that the soil retains its productivity) involves not using resources today (for example the animal dung used as fertilizer could have been used as fuel) and investing them for returns to be received in the future. Irrigation schemes, tree planting and decisions on how much livestock to keep are all examples of 'investment decisions', that is, having to plan today in order to ensure future production levels.

In making any investment decision, people need some way of comparing the future benefits (for example improved soil fertility and crop yields) to the current costs (for example the cost of fertilizer). As an example, a farmer may be comparing an expected increase in crop yields of $10 in a year's time with an investment today of $5. Each person will have a 'time preference' that will determine whether such an investment is worth undertaking. Economists use 'discount rates' to indicate time preferences. A discount rate of 100 per cent per year means that $5 today is considered equivalent to $10 in a year's time; a discount rate of 50 per cent means $5 today equals $7.5 in a year's time. As the discount rate increases, the level of total investment will fall since fewer investment projects will be able to provide a sufficient return. In addition, higher discount rates mean that short-term investments are favoured over long-term investments. For example, consider a farmer's investment that costs $5 today and can yield either $100 in ten year's time or $10 in one year's time depending on the farmer's actions. With a rate of discount of 10 per cent the farmer will choose the ten year option but when the discount rate is 30 per cent the one year option is chosen.

Poor people often have relatively high discount rates. Studies in India have shown that the rate of return required by poor farmers is 30 to 40 per cent per annum (World Bank, 1992). High discount rates arise from the uncertainty that poor people face about their future. Poor health, diet and living conditions mean that people are uncertain about their future survival and work capacity. In addition, the uncertainty caused by possible drought or flooding may mean investments, especially long-term investments, are not undertaken. For example, efforts to introduce soil conservation techniques in Burkina Faso showed that adoption of new techniques was highest when returns occurred within two or three years (World Bank, 1992). Lastly, poor people may view their property entitlements as uncertain and increase their discount rate accordingly. Future tenancy agreement changes and policy changes may move poor farmers from their land and previous investment in the land would have no benefit to them.

Poverty means, therefore, that discount rates of individuals are high and the planning horizon is relatively short. Investments in natural capital often have relatively low rates of return that continue far into the future.[3] For example, planting trees yields benefits in terms of fuelwood and prevention of erosion but these only occur five and more years into the future. A poor community may, therefore, invest only a small amount in its natural capital. This lack of investment in natural capital may lead to degradation, which in turn implies that future productivity will fall.[4]

It is important to note that poverty does not always lead to degradation. There may be strong social and cultural rules for controlling the use of natural capital that override individual preferences. Such social and cultural rules may have been built up over long periods of time to ensure the survival of the community. Only when such long-standing rules break down, for example by migration to a new area or by changes in tenurial rights, may degradation become a problem. This is especially the case with the management of CPRs. Traditionally CPRs are governed by social rules established over time but the joint effects of population growth, poverty and policy changes may break down these rules (Jodha, 1992). The CPRs then become 'open access regimes' (OARs), areas where people can extract as many resources as they are able. These high extraction rates occur since there is insufficient incentive to an individual to preserve a resource that is open to all. In essence, the distinction between a CPR and an OAR is that individuals producing under an OAR act as though the discount rates were infinitely high, due to the low probability of appropriating the benefits of forgone harvests. Under an OAR the incentive to invest in the natural resources is eliminated.

Poor people's responses to shocks: mining the future
Poor people may be able to live in harmony with the environment through the combination of traditional methods and normal conditions. However such commodities are still subject to 'shocks', whether natural ones such as floods or droughts or man-made ones such as land tenure changes. These shocks

will cause poor people to either migrate from the affected area or to stay and try to survive.

If poor people stay in the affected area they are faced with the necessity of extracting sufficient resources to survive. Their poverty means they have a very limited range of resources – only their natural capital stock and their labour. The usefulness of 'human capital' under these circumstances may be limited. A shock may also lead to a fall in employment opportunities which means the poor will only have their natural resources for survival. People may be forced to over-exploit these resources. For example land may be overgrazed, crops may be planted on marginal soil, or additional fuelwood may be collected from woodlands for sale.

This type of resource exploitation is known as 'mining'. Mining means that the stock of natural capital is being reduced for current consumption at the expense of future production. Mining provides a short-term method of survival but leads to environmental degradation and adverse impacts in the future. As an example Java in Indonesia suffers from high population density and large numbers of poor people. The pressures of population and poverty led to a doubling of the upland areas planted with rice from 1981 to 1985. While this increased the output of rice in the short run such gains are not sustainable (Bilsborrow, 1992). The current gains in rice production are being 'purchased' through the losses of soil and soil fertility and, implicitly, future yields of other products.

Whether degradation will occur depends on the particular characteristics of the local environment. Environments can accommodate a certain level of exploitation and still be able to regenerate themselves to their original state. However, when environments are pushed beyond certain 'threshold levels', this leads to a decline in productivity in the future. For example land may be able to sustain some periods of overgrazing, but if the grazing is too intense land cover may be pushed below a certain threshold level and the mix of species may be altered, after which water and wind erosion may remove soil and prevent plant regeneration (Perrings and Walker, 1992).

It should be stressed that a shock affecting a community will not always lead to degradation, depending on the resources available and the social rules governing the community. For example a study in Nigeria found that the pressure of famine did not affect the smallholders' tree conservation practices (Mortimer, 1989). Also Jagannathan (1989) stresses that if additional employment can be obtained in the event of a shock then poor people may restore their income level through work rather than mining the environment. 'Mining' is one possible response to an environmental shock but by no means a necessary consequence.

Poverty, migration and degradation

Another possible response of poor people faced with increasing pressure on resources is to migrate to another region. The pressure on resources could arise from a 'shock' or from steadily worsening conditions. Historically the process of development has led to a movement of people from rural to urban areas. Such migration is one factor behind the rapidly growing cities in many developing countries. These cities often have large numbers of people living in slums and squatter settlements which have inadequate water, sanitation, power and transport services. These slums are generally located on the city's poorest land, such as steep slopes, river banks and close to rubbish dumps. The combination of overcrowding, poor services and location creates unhealthy conditions where people not only suffer from high levels of disease but are also subject to fire, flooding and landslides. Table 5.5 shows details of migration trends in selected countries, broken down by origin and destination of move.

Table 5.5 illustrates that there has also been substantial rural to rural area migration in developing countries over the recent past. Such migration has

Table 5.5 Distribution of total migrants by origin and destination

	Distribution			
Country(year)	Rural-rural	Urban-urban	Rural-urban	Urban-rural
Botswana ('85)*	60.0	8.0	29.0	3.0
Brazil ('70)*	18.0	50.4	25.7	6.0
Ivory Coast ('86)	14.8	44.2	20.3	20.7
Ecuador ('82)	16.0	46.0	18.0	21.0
Egypt ('76)	26.0	55.2	12.0	6.8
Ghana ('88)	4.6	48.5	9.5	37.3
Honduras ('83)	25.9	31.7	28.6	14.1
India ('81)*	16.7	11.9	65.4	6.1
Korea, Rep. of ('75)	43.5	28.7	14.0	13.8
Malaysia ('70)	8.8	20.0	38.8	32.4
Pakistan ('73)	17.2	38.7	33.0	11.1
Peru ('86)	11.6	51.6	13.6	23.2
Philippines ('73)	39.0	25.3	19.9	15.8
Thailand ('80)	15.4	18.5	55.9	10.1

Note: Data refers to previous place of residence except countries with * where data refers to place of birth.

Source: Bilsborrow (1992).

environmental effects in both the origin region and the destination region. A lower population in the originating area may lead to reduced pressure on natural resources and hence less degradation. The study of the environmental impacts of migration has, however, usually focused on the destination regions. In particular, the movement of people to forest areas and the subsequent deforestation caused by land clearing for agriculture has been a major factor in the loss of forests. Leonard (1989) states that about two-thirds of tropical deforestation in developing countries occurs for agricultural reasons with about 80 per cent of this attributable to slash-and-burn agriculture being practised by poor in-migrants.[5]

The new migrants often rapidly clear the land in order to make a legal claim. For example in Ecuador formal property rights are only given when the land has been cleared, as is also the case in the Sudan and other developing countries (Southgate, 1990, 1991).[6] Deforested land is usually subject to soil erosion (through water run-off or wind erosion) and loss of fertility (through leaching) and some estimates suggest that 50 per cent of the soil's fertility can be lost within three years (Leonard, 1989). Such losses of fertility may cause the migrants to clear more land locally or to move on to other areas.

Migration is not simply a response to 'push' factors in the origin region (for example poverty, natural disasters, changes in land tenure) but is also dependent on 'pull' factors from the destination region. These 'pull' factors can be the offer of free land (and the resources on or in the land) or subsidies paid by governments.[7] Moreover the rate of migration is also dependent on the ease of access in terms of transport. Mahar (1989) analyses deforestation in Brazil's Amazon region with respect to migration and states, 'Pushed by poverty and skewed land distribution in their regions of origin, the settlers have merely responded to government-created incentives in the form of access roads, titles to public lands, various public services and, in the case of the Trans Amazon scheme, subsistence allowances' (p. 109). Therefore much of the impact of migration is actually the consequence of a wide range of governmental policies (subsidies, land tenure and infrastructure). The role of government policy in generating environmental degradation is discussed in Chapter Three.

Poverty as a disabling factor
The conditions of poverty also act to disable people from taking actions that benefit their environment. Efficient and sustainable resource management often requires a range of resources: human, natural, legal and informational. Poverty implies a lack of breadth as well as depth in assets. The absence of any one of these assets may in itself lead to environmental degradation.

One disabling factor is the lack of credit available to poor people. Even if such people want to invest in their natural capital, for example by irrigating or fertilizing land, borrowing facilities may be limited and interest rates high. Limited credit and high interest rates reflect the isolation of poor areas, the high levels of uncertainty and the lack of collateral available from the poor.

Poor people may also be dissuaded from investing in the environment by reason of their lack of legal entitlements. For example, women in sub-Saharan Africa often have no right of tenure to land despite the fact that they provide 50 to 80 per cent of the labour (World Bank, 1992). Consequently the women have limited access to credit and may also have low incentives to invest due to uncertainty over future tenure.

Poor education and illiteracy among the poor means that it may be difficult to obtain information about the environmental implications of certain actions. For example a new pesticide may cause degradation if used improperly but illiteracy may prevent this knowledge being known. Pesticide use in Indonesia, Pakistan, the Philippines and Sri Lanka rose by more than 10 per cent per year from 1980 to 1985. Insufficient knowledge on how and when to apply pesticides can lead to soil and water pollution and to the destruction of wildlife. The benefits of fertilizers, tree planting and irrigation may also be unknown to poor people resulting in limited or inappropriate use. For example continued irrigation in the absence of adequate drainage for the land leads to increasing levels of salts left in the soil by evaporating water. This salinization destroys the fertility of the land and is costly to correct.[8] Environmental problems of this sort are most likely to occur when traditional methods have been replaced by new methods, or people have migrated to new agricultural areas where soils are different and hence there is no historical experience to rely upon. When this is the case and information is costly, environmental degradation may be the result.

A case study concerning fuelwood

Around 35 per cent of fuel requirements in developing countries is derived from biomass (the collective term for wood products, animal dung, crop residues and grass). Much of this biomass is used by poor people for cooking and heating. An FAO study in 1983 estimated that around 250 million people suffered from acute shortages of fuelwood resulting from deforestation (Leonard, 1989). Furthermore 1,300 million people were estimated to be cutting down trees and using wood faster than it could be regenerated.

Table 5.6 shows the reliance of households in some sub-Saharan countries on biomass fuels. As can be seen from the table all households, except in Ethiopia, rely almost exclusively on fuelwood and charcoal. Throughout developing countries poor households, whether in urban or rural areas, rely on woodfuel. For example in India an estimated 50 per cent of energy for cooking in cities is provided by fuelwood (Sethuraman, 1992). Growing consumption of fuelwood places forest and woodland areas under severe

Table 5.6   Dependence on biomass fuels in selected sub-Saharan countries

Country (year)	Percentage of household fuel met by biomass			
	Fuelwood	Charcoal	Other biomass	Total biomass
Benin ('84)	88	2	7	97
Botswana ('82)	96			96
Congo ('85)	84	3		87
Ivory Coast ('83)	86	6		92
Ethiopia ('82)	40	1	58	99
Ghana ('85)	73	14	6	93
Kenya ('85)	83	12		95
Liberia ('83)	87	11		98
Malawi ('80)	99			99
Mauritania ('83)	82	10	5	97
Niger ('81)	99			99
Nigeria ('80)	92	1		93
Senegal ('81)	86	11		97
Sierra Leone ('84)	91	4		95
Somalia ('84)	89	6	4	99
Sudan ('81)	54	35	9	98
Tanzania ('81)	96	3		99
Uganda ('80)	96	3		99
Zaire ('83)	93	6		99
Zimbabwe ('80)	85			85

Source: Pearce and Warford (1993).

pressure, especially in areas close to urban centres.[9] Deforestation leaves the soil vulnerable to erosion by water or wind. Soil erosion then has detrimental effects both locally and in other areas as the soil washed away is deposited in dams, irrigation systems and river transit systems.

The overuse of forest and woodland areas for fuelwood is caused by a number of factors. Population growth means there is a growing demand for fuelwood. Additionally many forested areas are common property resources and therefore prone to over-exploitation. Poverty is also part of the explanation of why fuelwood demand can lead to deforestation and degradation. As discussed above, poverty leads to a short planning horizon. Planting trees for fuelwood is a long-term investment with the costs incurred principally in the first year and the benefits occurring only in the future. Conditions of poverty suggest, therefore, that the planting of new trees may be insufficient for future needs.

The conditions of poverty also explain why fuelwood usage may be both inefficient and also resistant to the introduction of other fuel sources such as kerosene stoves or liquid propane gas (LPG). Poor people often use inefficient biomass stoves that require unnecessarily high levels of inputs (wood) and produce high levels of indoor air pollution. Both China and India have programmes to encourage the adoption of new, modern biomass stoves that are more efficient. Some estimates show that the benefit of using these new stoves, in terms of fuel savings, health and environmental improvements, can be $25–100 per stove per year, enough to repay the initial investment within a few months (World Bank, 1992). Given that the new stoves are apparently such a good short term investment why do poor people not invest in them? There are a number of reasons. First, some of the potential benefits may not be fully known to poor people. For example the improved health that arises from reduced indoor air pollution may be unknown given poor education and illiteracy. Secondly, some of the benefits may be shared by the whole community, for example in the case where the fuelwood comes from a CPR, and hence the individual's incentive to invest in a new stove is reduced. Thirdly, the limited investment resources and access to credit of poor households may prevent them purchasing new stoves even if they recognize their benefits. Finally, due to distance and poor infrastructure the supply of such fuels to remote areas may be uncertain, causing people to continue with fuel wood.

Table 5.7 gives data from a study in Malawi which showed that traditional stoves were much less efficient than an improved stove (which could be produced locally).

Table 5.6 also shows the importance of charcoal as a household fuel. Studies have shown that most of the charcoal in Africa is produced using

Table 5.7   Efficiency of traditional and improved stoves in Malawi

Type of charcoal	Average consumption of fuel (kg)	
	Traditional stove	Improved stove
Pine	2.10	1.18
Indigenous	3.15	2.23

Source: Armitage and Schramm (1989).

earth kilns which convert wood into charcoal at an efficiency of 10 to 12 per cent (by weight). In contrast brick or steel kilns, which are used widely in Latin America, have a 28 to 35 per cent efficiency rate (Armitage and Schramm, 1989). Armitage and Schramm report the reasons for the lack of adoption of more efficient kilns as being that kiln owners are small scale and part-time with limited resources and access to credit, combined with the fact that the owners are often illiterate and unaware of new methods. The use of inefficient kilns means that more wood is required to provide the same amount of charcoal, further increasing pressure on forest resources.

There are two other aspects to fuelwood use in poor communities that should be stressed. First, the use of fuelwood in inefficient stoves causes high levels of indoor air pollution which in turn leads to increased health risks. The smoke from biomass burning contributes to the acute respiratory infections that cause an estimated four million deaths a year among infants and children (World Bank, 1992). Therefore replacing inefficient stoves would not only reduce pressure on resources but improve health, a major stop to reducing poverty.

Secondly, the requirement to collect and search for fuelwood often takes substantial amounts of time, reducing time available for tending crops and other activities. Sousan at al. (1991) stress this as a problem in the Dhanusha region of southern central Nepal.[10] Children and women in poor communities often undertake the collection of fuelwood. By the age of six children in India collect fuelwood, tend animals, fetch water and look after younger siblings (Dasgupta 1982). The fact that children can help with the work load of a poor family is important in understanding the decision to have large families. Reducing fuelwood consumption would reduce, to some extent, the desire to have as many children. Therefore using more efficient stoves would not only reduce pressure on resources but may also reduce population pressure. These issues were addressed further in Chapter Three.

Poverty, policies and aid

Government policies often seek to alleviate poverty through a range of measures. These may include subsidies to agricultural inputs, irrigation projects, rural credit schemes, changing tenurial rights and migration programmes. The effect of such policies on the environment can be complex and diverse, and requires analysis of the specific policies as well as the characteristics of the region.

Government migration policies have had major environmental impacts in a number of developing countries. Indonesia's transmigration programme has been one of the largest in the world and had as its principal goal 'the alleviation of rural poverty and unemployment/underemployment problems' (Bilsborrow, 1992, p. 26). In the period 1980–87 it sponsored over one million families to move from densely populated rural areas in Java, Bali, Madura and Lombok to other relatively under-populated, rural regions (Bilsborrow, 1992). Reducing the population in origin areas may reduce pressure on natural resources and reduce degradation. However, the destination plots for the sponsored Indonesian families were in forested lands which were subsequently cleared. Estimates suggest that around 110,000 hectares of forest were cleared per annum in the 1980s by migrants, although perhaps only one-third of this was due to government sponsored migrants with the remainder due to 'spontaneous' migrants (Bilsborrow, 1992). Moreover, the new lands often proved to have low soil fertility that was soon exhausted, causing the migrants to clear more land for crops or to increase firewood collection for sale (Bilsborrow, 1992).

In the last forty years Thailand has also sought to reduce rural poverty by means of government policies to settle people in public forest reserves. From 1959 to 1988 about 108 million rai of forest land was cleared and 90 per cent of this converted to agriculture. In the 1980s around 1.2 million families were settled on forest land (Reed, 1992). The fact that land tenure on the new land is often only five to twenty five years (and is not transferable) means the farmers may have an incentive to over-exploit the soil. The deforestation also leads to greater downstream flooding, landslides and wider climatic and biodiversity impacts. The Brazilian government has also promoted the deforestation of large areas of the Amazon tropical forest. The building of such roads as the Cuiaba-Porto highway in Brazil is judged to have allowed substantial migration. Brazil also used subsidies to promote land clearance and encourage cattle ranching, although many of these subsidies were not directed at poor farmers. These policies are reviewed in Chapter Three.

Government changes to land tenure systems may lead some poor people to lose their access to land. Their response may be to move to marginal lands or urban areas which in turn may result in degradation. Similarly, changes in incentives for poor farmers may also lead to degradation. For example, Haiti's government policy in the 1970s encouraged the growth of bean and grain crops in preference to coffee. As a result the soil fertility may have suffered as coffee is better at stabilising soil quality. However Haiti also suffered from severe uncertainty over property rights at this time, which reduced the incentive to invest in soil conservation.

External (aid) policies designed to alleviate poverty in poor countries may also cause environmental degradation in certain cases. To illustrate, the European Union (EU) has arrangements with various developing countries to import certain quotas of goods. As an example, the EU guarantees the import of a certain quantity of beef from Botswana at higher than world prices. Botswana exports 85 per cent of the beef it produces and around one half of this goes to the EU. The guarantee of exports to the EU at high prices has contributed towards the expansion of ranches in Botswana and between 1964 and 1984 the national herd probably doubled in size (Pearce and Warford, 1993). This has led to overgrazing and range depletion in many areas (Arntzen and Veenendaal, 1986; Ringrose and Matheson, 1986). In addition to the EU policies there are also domestic policies (for example, subsidies for slaughterhouses and tax write-offs for agricultural investments) which contribute to the increased herd sizes (Pearce and Warford, 1993).

Policies that are designed to alleviate poverty may therefore cause degradation. In particular, policies that have been hastily implemented or poorly analysed may be especially likely to cause degradation. Bilsborrow (1992) considers that site appraisals of new land for the in-migrants in Indonesia were often inadequate with the result that soils could only support crops for a few years, after which the migrants had to move or clear more land.

Conclusion

Poverty and degradation have particularly close links, most obviously because the poor people of the world tend to live in ecologically fragile areas. When we view the environment as a form of natural capital which is used by poor people we can identify a number of reasons why degradation might occur. The first is the fact that the 'discount rate' used by poor people may be high with the result that investment in natural capital may be low in poor societies and biased towards short-term projects. Secondly, poverty means people have no surplus resources and this implies that any 'shocks' may result in the 'mining' of the environment. Lastly, poverty acts as a disabling factor; poor health, poor education, illiteracy and lack of legal rights may all act to reduce the ability and incentive to prevent degradation. The fact that degradation may lead to more poverty, for example falling crop yields as soils are eroded, means that a vicious circle can develop with disastrous consequences.

Despite the close links between poverty and degradation it is wrong to always connect the two. Population pressure, land tenure arrangements and government policies act in conjunction with poverty to cause degradation. Even in conditions of poverty the existence of traditional methods and forms of co-operation may prevent degradation if there is an absence of other malign factors.

Notes

1. In an analysis by Leonard (1989), out of 780 million people in the world defined as poor only 280 million are on land that could be responsive to modern, productivity-increasing farming methods.
2. Dasgupta (1993) states, 'Poor countries are for the most part biomass-based subsistence economies, in that their rural folk eke out a living from products obtained directly from plants and animals' (p. 273).

3. A quote from the Venator et al. (1992) article on land management practices in Latin America illustrates, 'Unfortunately, but not unexpectedly, concepts of resource conservation are hard to promote among farmers living under subsistence conditions. Terraces are excellent for the recuperation of eroded agricultural lands, but these are expensive to build and may take centuries to recuperate the investment' (p. 289).
4. Underinvestment, degradation and productivity decline may be linked through a number of distinct resources. For example, see Newcombe's (1989) study of deforestation in Ethiopia. As fuelwood became scarce the poor switched to dung and straw for energy supplies. This in turn reduced soil fertility and land productivity.
5. Furthermore, Southgate (1990) states, 'Although destructive logging also takes place in Latin America, deforestation in the region is primarily an agricultural phenomenon' (p. 1). Reed (1992), in case studies of both Thailand's and the Ivory Coast's deforestation history, considers land clearing for agriculture to be a principal factor in both countries.
6. Svanqvist (1992) states in the period 1971–75 over 400,000 hectares of Ecuador's forests were occupied by farmers who used newly built petroleum industry roads for access, yet only 2 per cent of the timber cut in the clearance process was used by timber mills.
7. Hecht (1992) states that a powerful 'pull' factor into the Amazonian forests in recent years is the returns on growing cocoa.
8. An estimated 10 per cent of all the world's irrigated land is affected by salinization caused by poor irrigation management (World Bank, 1992). Moreover the area of land removed from cultivation by salinization throughout the world is thought by some to equal the additional land added through irrigation (see Dasgupta, 1993).
9. The word 'close' can be misleading. Sethuraman (1992) states that 223,600 tons of fuelwood in 1981–2 was transported to New Delhi from the forests of Madhya Pradesh (700 km away). Cline-Cole et al. (1990) in a study of fuelwood consumption in Kano, Nigeria also find that tree stocks in regions closest to Kano were in fact increasing and that while deforestation was occurring further out from Kano this was not simply a result of fuelwood demand from Kano as land clearing and local fuelwood demands were also important factors.
10. This study in Nepal also found that fuel wood shortages caused a switch to other biomass fuels such as dung and crop residues, which in turn reduced manure available for the soil.

Bibliography

Anderson, D. (1987), *The Economics of Afforestation*, Johns Hopkins University Press: Baltimore.

Anderson, D. and Fishwish, R. (1984), 'Fuelwood Consumption and Deforestation in African Countries', World Bank Staff Working Paper 704, World Bank: Washington D.C.

Armitage, J. and Schramm, G. (1989), 'Managing the Supply of and the Demand for Fuelwood in Africa', in Schramm, Gunter and Warford, J. (eds) *Environmental Management and Economic Development*, Johns Hopkins University Press: Baltimore.

Arntzen, J. and Veenendaal, M. (1986), *A Profile of Environment and Development in Botswana*, Institute for Environmental Studies, Free University of Amsterdam.

Barbier et al. (1992), 'Timber Trade, Trade Policies and Environmental Degradation', London Environmental Economics Centre, DP 92–01.

Bhalla, A.S. (1992), 'Environmental Degradation in Rural Areas', in Bhalla, A.S. (ed.), *Environment, Employment and Development*, International Labour Office: Geneva.

Bilsborrow, R.E. (1992), 'Rural Poverty, Migration, and the Environment in Developing Countries', World Bank Policy Research Working Paper 1017, Washington D.C.

Cline-Cole, R.A., Main, H.A.C. and Nichol, J.E. (1990), 'On Fuelwood Consumption, Population Dynamics and Deforestation in Africa', *World Development*, 18 (4), 513–27.

Dasgupta, P. (1982), *The Control of Resources*, Basil Blackwell: Oxford.

Dasgupta, P. (1993a), *An Inquiry into Well-Being and Destitution*, Clarendon Press: Oxford.

Dasgupta, P. (1993b), 'Public Neglect and Private Deprivation', in Cahill, K. (ed.), *A Framework for Survival: Health and Human Rights in Conflicts and Disasters*, Basic Books: New York.

Dasgupta, P. (1993c), 'The Economics of Destitution', in Aart de Zeeuw (ed.), *Advanced Lectures in Quantitative Economics, Volume II*, Academic Press: New York.

Downing, C. (1992), 'Two Peasants Discuss Deforestation', in Downing, T.E. et al. (ed.), *Development or Destruction*, Westview: Colorado.

Ehui, S.K., Hertel, T.W. and Preckel, P.V. (1990), 'Forest Resource Depletion, Soil Dynamics, and Agricultural Productivity in the Tropics', *Journal of Environmental Economics and Management*, **18**, 136–54.

Hecht, S.B. (1992), 'Logics of Livestock and Deforestation: the Case of Amazonia', in Downing, T.E. et al. (ed.), *Development or Destruction*, Westview: Colorado.

Foy, G. and Daly, H. (1989), 'Allocation, Distribution and Scale as Determinants of Environmental Degradation: Case Studies of Haiti, El Salvador and Costa Rica', World Bank Environment Working Paper No. 19, World Bank: Washington D.C.

Jagannathan, N.V. (1989), 'Poverty, Public Policies, and the Environment', World Bank Environment Department Working Paper 1990–8, World Bank: Washington D.C.

Jodha, N.S. (1992), 'Common Property Resources', World Bank Discussion Paper, August 1992, Washington D.C.

Laceres, R. et al. (ed.) (1989), *Stoves for People: Proceedings of the Second International Workshop on Stoves Dissemination*, Intermediate Technology Publications: London.

Leonard, H.J. (1989), *Environment and the Poor: Development Strategies for a Common Agenda*, Overseas Development Council: Washington D.C.

Mahar, D.J. (1989), 'Deforestation in Brazil's Amazon Region: Magnitude, Rate and Causes', in Schramm, Gunter and Warford (ed.), *Environmental Management and Economic Development*, Johns Hopkins University Press: Baltimore.

Malton, P.J. (1991), 'Farmer Risk Management Strategies: The Case of the West African Semi-Arid Tropics', in Holden, D. et al. (ed.), *Risk in Agriculture. Proceedings of the 10th Agricultural Sector Symposium*, World Bank: Washington D.C.

Markandya, A. and Pearce, D. (1988), 'Environmental Considerations and the Choice of Discount Rate in Developing Countries', World Bank Environment Department Working Paper No. 3, World Bank: Washington D.C.

McNeely, J. et al. (1990), *Conserving the World's Biological Diversity*, International Union of the Conservation of Nature: Gland, Switzerland.

Mortimer, M. (1989), 'The Causes, Nature, and Rate of Soil Degradation in the Northernmost States of Nigeria', World Bank Environment Department Working Paper No. 17, World Bank: Washington D.C.

Newcombe, K. (1989), 'An Economic Justification for Rural Afforestation: The Case of Ethiopia', in Schramm, Gunter and Warford (ed.), *Environmental Management and Economic Development*, Johns Hopkins University Press: Baltimore.

Norgaard, R.B. (1990), 'Sustainability as Intergenerational Equity', Asian Development Bank Discussion Paper, ADB: Manila.

Pearce, D. (1990), 'Population, Poverty and Environment', *Pensamiento Ibero Americano, Revista de Economia Politica*, Osvaldo Sunkel: Madrid.

Pearce, D. and Warford, J.J. (1993), *World Without End*, Oxford University Press: New York.

Pearce, D., Brown, K., Swanson, T. and Perrings, C. (1993), 'Economics and the Conservation of Global Biological Diversity', A Report on the Global Environment Facility, Centre for Social and Economic Research on the Global Environment: London.

Perrings, C. and Walker, B. (1992), 'Biodiversity Loss and the Economics of Discontinuous Change in Semi-Arid Rangelands', Discussion Paper at the Second Conference on the Ecology and Economics of Biodiversity Loss, Beijer International Institute of Ecological Economics: Stockholm, Sweden.

Reed, D. (1992), *Structural Adjustment and the Environment*, Earthscan: London.

Rhodes, S.L. (1991), 'Rethinking Desertification: What Do We Know and What Have We Learned?', *World Development*, **19** (9), 1137–43.

Ringrose, S. and Matheson, W. (1986), 'Desertification in Botswana: Progress Towards a Viable Monitoring System', *Desertification Control Bulletin*, **13**, 6–11.

Sarris, A. and Shams, H. (1991), *Ghana Under Structural Adjustment*, New York University Press: New York.

Sethuraman, S.V. (1992), 'Urbanisation, Employment and the Environment', in Bhalla, A.S. (ed.), *Environment, Employment and Development*, International Labour Office: Geneva.

Soussan, J., Gevers, E., Ghimire, K. and O'Keefe, P. (1991), 'Planning for Sustainability: Access to Fuelwood in Dhanusha District, Nepal', *World Development*, **19** (10), 1299–1314.

Southgate, D. (1990), 'The Causes of Land Degradation along "Spontaneously" Expanding Agricultural Frontiers in the Third World', *Land Economics*, **66** (1), 93–101.

Southgate, D. (1991), 'Tropical Deforestation and Agricultural Development in Latin America', Discussion Paper, Department of Agricultural Economics, Ohio State University.

Southgate, D., Sierra, R., Brown, L. (1991), 'The Causes of Tropical Deforestation in Ecuador: A Statistical Analysis', *World Development*, **19** (9), 1145–51.

Sundrum, R.M. (1990), *Income Distribution in Less Developed Countries*, Routledge: London.

Svanqvist, N.H. (1992), 'The Timber Industry Perspective', in Downing, T.E. et al. (eds), *Development or Destruction*, Westview: Colorado.

United Nations (1993), *The Global Partnership for Environment and Development. A Guide to Agenda 21 Post Rio Edition*, United Nations: New York.

Venator, C., Glaeser, J. and Soto, R. (1992), 'A Silvopastoral Strategy', in Downing, T.E. et al. (eds), *Development or Destruction*, Westview: Colorado.

Wilken, G.C. (1989), 'Transferring Traditional Technology: A Bottom-Up Approach for Fragile Lands', in Browder, J.O. (ed.), *Fragile Lands of Latin America*, Westview Press: San Francisco and London.

World Bank (1991), *World Development Report: The Challenge of Development*, Oxford University Press: New York.

World Bank (1992), *World Development Report: Development and Environment*, Oxford University Press: New York.

6 Societal poverty: indebtedness and degradation

Mark Rogers

Introduction

The last decade has seen the issues of developing country indebtedness and the global environment become increasingly important in the debate on the world's future. The rise in importance of these issues leads naturally to a discussion of the connection between the two. Some authors claim that the indebted developing countries are locked into a cycle of high debt repayments that necessitates environmental degradation which, in turn, prevents economic growth. Their argument is that the huge burden that debt repayments place on a country force it to rapidly exploit its natural resources. While this reasoning contains elements of truth, care must be taken when attributing degradation to the debt burden. The relation between debt and degradation is far more complex than this simple argument would indicate. There is little doubt that the struggle to repay debts has caused great changes and hardship in indebted countries; however, there is still much to understand concerning the effects of these changes on the environment.

Background to the debt crisis

In 1982 Mexico brought the debt situation to the attention of the world by renegotiating its debt repayment obligations. Before this, in the 1970s and early 1980s, there had been huge increases in lending to developing countries, mainly from commercial banks in the developed countries.[1] Many of these loans were used in ambitious public sector investments that would later have difficulty in generating sufficient returns to pay back the loans. In addition some of the loans in the 1970s were used to finance current consumption rather than investment.[2] The decisions of the developing countries to borrow so extensively were supported by the commercial banks. In fact even in the years 1979 to 1981 when world economic conditions were beginning to deteriorate (suggesting that countries might have difficulty in making repayments), the banks nearly doubled lending to the major debtors (see Table 6.1).[3] In the early 1980s changing world economic conditions caused further problems for the debtor countries in making their debt repayments. The principal changes in the world economy were rising interest rates, a world recession originating in the major industrial countries, and the falling prices of commodities.

Table 6.1   Net liabilities of countries to international banks

	Dec 1979 ($ billion)	Dec 1981 ($ billion)
Argentina	5.3	16.3
Brazil	28.8	44.8
Mexico	22.5	43.5

Source: Sachs (1989).

The repayments on foreign loans must come from foreign exchange earned by the country in its foreign trade. The foreign exchange that is available depends to a large extent on the difference between exports (receipts of foreign exchange) and imports (payments of foreign exchange). The rise in world interest rates meant that a greater difference between exports and imports was required in order to pay the higher interest repayments.[4] Similarly, the fall in commodity prices meant that debtor countries were receiving less for their exports (see Table 6.2).[5] Lastly, the world recession meant demand for their exports was falling. Debtor countries were, therefore, put under severe repayment pressure both from the combination of changes in the world economy and the poor performance of the original investments made

Table 6.2   Changes in export prices and terms of trade

	Average annual percentage change		
	1965–73	1973–80	1980–87
Export prices			
Low and middle income economies	6.1	14.7	−4.6
Primary Goods	5.8	18.5	−6.9
Foods	5.9	8.3	−2.7
Fuels	9.0	29.5	−9.7
Nonfood Primary	3.1	9.8	−3.9
Manufacturers	5.8	6.8	−0.9
Terms of Trade			
Low and middle income economies	0.1	2.1	−3.7
Severely indebted middle income economies	2.8	0.5	−2.8

Note: 'Terms of trade' measures the relative movement of export prices against that of import prices.

Source: World Development Report (1991).

Table 6.3   Debt burden in 1990 and 1980

	Total debt	External debt/ GNP ratio		Debt service/ exports ratio	
	1990 ($ billion)	1990 (%)	1980 (%)	1990 (%)	1980 (%)
Argentina	61.1	61.7	48.4	34.1	37.3
Bolivia	4.3	100.9	93.3	39.8	35.0
Brazil	116.2	25.1	31.2	20.8	63.1
Egypt	39.8	126.5	97.8	25.7	14.8
Indonesia	67.9	66.4	28.0	30.9	13.9
Mexico	96.8	42.1	30.5	27.8	49.5
Nigeria	36.1	110.9	10.0	20.3	4.2
Peru	21.1	58.7	51.0	11.0	46.5
Philippines	30.5	69.3	53.8	21.2	26.6
Poland	49.4	82.0	16.3	4.9	17.9
Venezuela	33.3	71.0	42.1	20.7	27.2

Source: World Bank (1992).

with the loans. This combination of factors was behind the debt crisis of the early 1980s. Once Mexico in August 1982 had announced its inability to meet repayments, other countries rapidly followed. By the end of 1983, forty-three countries were behind with their debt repayments (Moran, 1992). Table 6.3 illustrates the debt burden for selected countries in 1990 and 1980.

The severe pressure on debtors to meet their repayments led to a number of changes in their economies. These we can classify as trade related changes, domestic economy adjustments and the effect of 'Structural Adjustment Reforms' (implemented by the World Bank and IMF). Under these categorizations we can investigate the links to degradation.

Trade-related changes
A central part of the argument that the debt crisis has increased the level of degradation is that the pressure to rapidly increase exports has led to the over-exploitation of natural resources such as hardwoods, fisheries and minerals. In addition countries may be forced to increase the exports of food products such as coffee, groundnuts and beef. These food exports may lead to degradation by exhausting soil or by causing deforestation (to make way for cattle ranches or new crop land). The Brundtland Commission's view is as follows:

The promotion of increased volumes of commodity exports has led to cases of unsustainable overuse of the natural resource base. While individual cases may not fit this generalisation, it has been argued that such processes have been at work in ranching for beef, fishing in both coastal and deep-sea waters, forestry, and the growing of some cash crops.
(World Commission on Environment and Development, 1987, pp. 80–81.)

In many debtor countries natural resources are a significant part of export earnings, as can be seen from Table 6.4. However there is considerable variation, for example, 99 per cent of Nigeria's exports are derived from natural resources compared with only 38 per cent of the Philippines.

More importantly for our purposes we would like to know the changes in growth rates of exports of natural resources in the 1980s to see what effect the debt crisis may have had. Table 6.5 shows figures that compare primary goods export volume growth with manufactures export volume growth. These figures show that the growth rate of primary exports for the severely indebted countries was higher in the 1980–87 period than the two previous periods. This indicates some support for the argument that exploitation of natural resources was increased in this period. However, we also note that the growth rate of manufacturers has been greater than primary goods in all periods. For low and middle income countries as a whole, the primary export growth rate

Table 6.4   Structure of merchandise exports in 1990

| | Percentage share of merchandise exports | | | | |
| | Natural resource sector | | Other | | |
	FMM	OPC	MTE	OM	TC
Bolivia	69	27	0	5	1
Peru	55	29	2	10	2
Argentina	6	59	7	29	3
Mexico	43	13	3	19	2
Brazil	16	31	18	35	3
Nigeria	97	2	0	0	0
Philippines	12	26	10	52	7

FMM – Fuels, minerals and metals   OM – Other manufacturers
OPC – Other primary commodities   TC – Textiles and clothing
MTE – Machinery and transport equipment

Source: World Bank (1992).

Table 6.5   Growth of export volume

	Average annual percentage changes		
	1965–73	1973–80	1980–87
Low and middle income economies			
Primary goods	4.0	1.2	2.8
Manufactures	10.9	13.0	7.0
Total	5.1	3.5	4.6
Severely indebted middle income economies			
Primary goods	−1.4	0.9	2.5
Manufactures	15.6	10.9	7.4
Total	0.6	2.8	3.6
World			
Primary goods	6.9	2.8	1.9
Manufactures	10.7	6.2	4.2
Total	9.2	4.9	3.6

Note: Severely indebted middle income countries are Argentina, Bolivia, Brazil, Chile, PR of Congo, Costa Rica, Ivory Coast, Ecuador, Egypt, Honduras, Hungary, Mexico, Morocco, Nicaragua, Peru, Philippines, Poland, Senegal, Uruguay and Venezuela.

Source: World Bank (1991).

was lower in 1980–87 (when the debt burden was high) than in 1965–73. Given the level of aggregation we cannot read too much into these broad figures, but we can see that the hypothesis that debt burden causes a rise in natural resource exports oversimplifies the situation. Countries may in fact respond to indebtedness by increasing manufactures exports rather than primary goods exports. Moreover, increased levels of primary goods exports do not necessarily imply degradation which depends more on the techniques used to produce increased exports.

The difficulty of linking degradation to increased primary exports can be seen clearly if we consider cash crop exports. Developing countries are the world's leading exporters of many cash crop products, for example, cocoa (92 per cent of world total exports), coffee (92 per cent), cotton (45 per cent), groundnuts (60 per cent), sugar (69 per cent) and tea (85 per cent). If countries are to increase exports of these goods they must either increase productivity or expand the land area devoted to their cultivation (or reduce domestic consumption). Expanding the land area under cultivation may lead to degradation of soils (through nutrient exhaustion or increased erosion) if the crops are not suited to that land. Crops such as groundnuts, maize and cotton are potentially hazardous to soils, especially if the soils are on marginal, less fertile land (Pearce and Warford, 1993; Hansen, 1990). However, other cash crops such as coffee, palm oil and tea can help protect soils if planted on hilly terrain and managed properly (Hansen, 1990). Therefore it is difficult to make any generalizations about the effect of increasing exports of cash crops on degradation without having full knowledge of local conditions.

The possibility that exports of beef from Latin American countries have caused increased rates of deforestation has been investigated by various authors (for example Hecht, 1992; Gullison and Losos, 1993). There is little disagreement that much of the land deforested in Latin America's lowland tropics is utilised as pasture for cattle (Hecht, 1992). However the beef produced by these areas is often a small part of the countries' total production (usually less than 5 per cent) and, moreover, frequently unsuitable for export to the major US market (Hecht, 1992). Gullison and Losos (1993) have analysed whether rising debt burdens have caused increased beef exports and find that they have not. Instead they find that the increased beef production has gone to domestic markets.

Many studies have used statistical techniques to analyse the factors that cause deforestation. The studies use data on, for example, the rate of population growth, population density, income, agricultural productivity and international indebtedness, and investigate whether these are correlated with the rate of deforestation. The results from some of these studies are summarized in Table 6.6. These studies show that population density and growth rates are important in explaining rates of deforestation. The evidence for the role of international indebtedness is less clear. Many studies can find no significant correlation and those that do find significant effects reach conflicting conclusions.

Some countries, in their attempts to increase exports, have also set up 'export processing zones' to attract foreign investment. It has been claimed that these zones have low pollution standards and therefore attract foreign companies who wish to avoid the tighter controls in their home country. If this is the case the net result would be that industrial water, air and noise pollution would be increased both in the debtor country and in the world overall. The Maquiladora export processing zone in Northern Mexico has been criticized in this way.[6] Grossman and Krueger (1992) study the possibility that foreign firms locate in Maquiladora because of the low pollution standards and find that this is not a significant factor. Similarly, Pearce and Warford (1993), in a review of evidence on the existence of 'pollution havens' in countries with low pollution standards, find little to support the view that a firm's location is dependent on environmental regulations. These studies are analysed in Chapter Seven.

Table 6.6   Econometric studies of deforestation

Author		Rate of population growth	Population density	Income	Agricultural productivity	International indebtedness
		Deforestation significantly related to				
Burgess, 1991	(a)	–		+		+
	(b)	–				+
Capistrano &	(a)			+		
Kiker, 1990	(b)			+		–
	(c)	+		+		–
Kahn and McDonald, 1990		–				+
Perrings, 1992	(a)	+	+	+		+
	(b)	–	+			

Note: In the table above a minus sign (–) means that an increase in the variable (given by column) leads to a decrease in deforestation. A plus sign (+) means an increase in the variable leads to an increase in deforestation.

Source: Pearce et al. (1993).

Indebted countries also adjusted to the debt burden by reducing imports. For the severely indebted countries imports fell an average of 2.2 per cent per year in the 1980s (World Bank, 1992). Around two-thirds of these imports are manufactures. The adjustment of an economy to reduced imports may involve the cancellation or scaling back of investments and projects that rely on foreign goods. The effect of these changes on the environment is difficult to determine. Projects that were likely to cause degradation – such as building roads into virgin regions – may be cancelled but, alternatively, environmentally beneficial projects may be stopped. Therefore assessing the environmental impacts of import reductions at an aggregate level is impossible.

To conclude, the effect on the environment of the trade-related changes induced by higher debt burdens is uncertain. Whether more degradation has been caused by the pressure to increase exports and reduce imports depends critically on the exact nature of the particular country's trade. In most cases the trade-related changes will cause both positive and negative effects on the environment. The overall net effect is therefore difficult to assess, as is indicated by the various empirical studies.

Domestic economy adjustments
The pressure of debt repayments combined with the difficult world economic conditions meant the severely indebted countries experienced falls in per capita income in the mid-1980s. The fall in income increased hardship and poverty for millions of people. As discussed in the previous section the effects of poverty on degradation are not clear since a range of other factors are involved. In some countries the poor may have been forced onto marginal lands or caused to over-exploit soil, fisheries and forests resulting in degradation. Table 6.7 reports some figures for growth, inflation and capital formation in the heavily indebted countries during this period.

Table 6.7   Changes in domestic economic indicators for severely indebted countries (1982–86).

	1982 (%)	1983 (%)	1984 (%)	1985 (%)	1986 (%)
Per capita GDP (annual change)	–2.7	–5.5	–0.1	0.9	1.4
Inflation (annual rate)	57.7	90.8	116.4	126.9	76.2
Gross capital formation/GDP	22.3	18.2	17.4	16.5	16.8

Note: Figures for the fifteen most heavily indebted countries.

Source: Krugman (1989).

The Table shows that gross capital investment fell in the indebted countries. At the aggregate level, assessing the effects on the environment of a decline in investment is difficult, as indicated previously. Government expenditure also had to be cut in many countries due to the lack of foreign exchange and declining tax revenues. From an environmental point of view the expenditures lost may have had both positive and negative effects. Some government projects – in particular large dam and road building projects – may cause damage to the environment and their cancellation would lead to less degradation. For example, Hansen (1989) states that the massive road building programmes in the 1960s and 1970s in Brazil, which opened up some of the Amazonia, were largely financed by foreign loans. On the other hand some government expenditure, such as that on sanitation services, may directly improve the environment.

The fact that per capita income in the severely indebted countries was falling in the early years of the debt crisis leads some authors to raise the possibility of a link between income levels and environmental degradation (Pearce and Warford, 1993; Reed, 1992). Such a relationship is often called the 'environmental Kuznets curve'. The Kuznets curve suggests there is a relationship between the level of per capita income and the quality of the environment. Specifically, the relationship suggests that as income rises from a low level the environment will suffer, as the process of growth causes degradation. However as income per capita rises higher, people begin to demand environmental protection (in the form of pollution controls, conservation areas and so on). The result is that when income per head reaches a certain level, any further income growth leads to an improvement in the environment. Falling incomes associated with debt burden may therefore have led countries to reduce expenditure on pollution controls and other environmental safeguards. In Mexico the budget of the Bureau of Urban Development and Environment fell faster than overall government expenditure (Reed, 1992), suggesting that a Kuznets curve effect may indeed exist.

Structural adjustment reforms

As severely indebted countries have attempted to adjust to the debt crisis, they have been forced to negotiate new repayment terms with the banks. The International Monetary Fund (IMF), as the focal point of negotiations, typically insists that the debtor country introduces a range of reforms as a condition for new repayment terms and new loans from the IMF and multilateral banks. These conditional reforms are known as 'structural adjustment reforms' and are designed to improve efficiency and growth prospects for the debtor's economy. Loans that are conditional on such reforms – Structural Adjustment Loans (SALs) – are not made only to the severely indebted countries. From 1981 to 1991 an estimated $28.5 billion in SALs flowed into 64 developing countries (Pearce and Warford, 1993). Attention has been focused on the environmental impact of the loans and their associated reforms.

The range of reforms that can be included in SALs includes trade liberalization, financial liberalization, tax reforms, privatization, land reforms and price reforms. The possible environmental consequences of these reforms can be diverse. Moreover it is not until very recently that lending institutions have specifically included environmental concerns in their planning, so we might well expect their environmental effects to be variable.

Adjustment reforms frequently seek to change agricultural output prices, which are often affected by government subsidies or taxes. Pearce and Warford (1993) review the impact of such changes in 43 cases. They found a mixture of environmental effects, both good and bad, as the result of reforms. For example, in Haiti, SALs attempted to remove export taxes on coffee, encouraging its planting on hillsides in the place of more erosive grain crops. In Malawi export taxes on tea were increased, reducing the incentives to grow tea. Despite tea being better for the soil it is cured by using fuelwood. Therefore a reduction in the need of fuelwood is likely to reduce deforestation and hence the overall environmental effect of the tax increase may be beneficial.

Developing countries often subsidize the use of agricultural inputs such as fertilizers, pesticides, irrigation and mechanization. These subsidies may encourage overuse of inputs and subsequent environmental damage. For example overuse of pesticides may lead to water pollution and the destruction of wildlife. Panayotou (1990) reports that overuse of a pesticide to protect rice in Indonesia wiped out natural predators and led to an overall fall in rice output. Similarly, the widespread subsidy of irrigation can lead to water logging, salinization, increased health risks and flooding (Hansen, 1990). In the 43 SAL cases studied by Pearce and Warford (1993) they find that 65 per cent reduced agricultural input subsidies. This may imply that degradation was lessened. Energy subsidies are also often made in developing countries and again SALs tend to reduce these. Since energy subsidies may encourage the wasteful use of fuels and high levels of pollution, their reduction may lessen degradation.

Institutional reforms are also important features of most SALs. Such reforms include privatization, reforming land tenure, improving crop marketing and encouraging foreign investment. Land tenure rights can be a critical factor in degradation. In Jamaica farmers were given land tenure that encouraged them to invest in soil conservation. Conversely in Brazil the granting of land rights in return for the clearance of forest areas has led to extensive deforestation. Land tenure is essential for the avoidance of degradation but it must not be conferred on a basis that systematically discriminates against environmental benefits.

In conclusion, the environmental effects of SALs are diverse. However the fact that SALs generally remove subsidies and price distortions implies an environmentally beneficial effect. Hansen (1990) reviews 83 World Bank adjustment lending operations (up to 1988) and ten Asian Development Bank operations (since 1987), finding that the reforms, overall, have a bias in favour of the environment. Pearce and Warford (1993) also conclude that the environment has probably gained in aggregate from the introduction of SALs. There is, however, still much debate over the full effects of SALs on the environment.

Table 6.8 *Debt-for-nature agreements*

Debtor country	Date	Face value (US$ million)	Market price (%)	Cost US$ million)	RDM (%)	Cons funds (US$ million)	Cons inv	Local fund admin
Philippines[a]	01/89 (Part1)	0.39	51.3	0.20	100	0.39	WWF-US	Haribon Foundation
	08/90 (PartII)	0.9	48.9	0.44	100	0.90	WWF-US	Haribon Foundation
Poland[b]	01/90	0.05	23.0	0.01	100	0.05	WWF	n.a.
Costa Rica[c]	01/91	0.60	60.0	0.36	90	0.54	RFA MCL TNC	n.a.
Mexico[d]	02/91 (Part I)	0.25	72.0	0.18	100	0.25	CL	n.a.
	08/91 (Part II)	0.25	Bank donation			0.25	CL	n.a.

	Date	Face value	Market price	RDM	Cons funds		Cons inv	
Ecuador[e]	12/87 (Part 1)	1.00	35.4	0.35	100	1.00	FN/ WWF	Fundación Natura
	04/89 (Part II)	9.00	11.9	1.07	100	9.00	FN/ WWF TNC/MBG	Fundación Natura
Madagascar[f]	01/91	0.12	50.0	0.06	100	0.12	CL	n.a.

Abbreviations:

Date – date debt exchange executed

Face value – face value of debt acquired

Market price – secondary market price

RDM – redemption price as % of face value

Cons funds – conservation funds generated

Cons inv – conservation investor: WWF – World Wildlife Fund, RFA – Rain Forest Alliance, MCL – Monteverde Conservation League, TNC – The Nature Conservancy, CL – Conservation International; FN – Fundación Natura, MBG – Missouri Botanical Garden.

Notes:

(a) The Philippines' agreements were used to contribute to the implementation, management and training of conservation groups.

(b) This agreement was set up as part of a larger Swedish scheme that aimed to clean up the River Vistula.

(c) Costa Rica has had six previous agreements dating back to 1987. This agreement led to the purchase of 2,023 ha of land for the Monteverde Cloud Forest Reserve and to improve local protection.

(d) These two agreements were part of a US$4 million programme to fund ecosystem conservation data centres to assess the distribution, status and conservation priority of Mexico's key species and habitats.

(e) These agreements supported management plans for six protected areas in the Andes and Amazon.

(f) Madagascar had a previous two-stage debt agreement in 1989/90. This particular agreement was the start of an agreement with Conservation International that it would exchange US$5 million of the nation's debt over the next five years. The proceeds of the swaps are to support various conservation activities.

Debt-for-nature swaps

As part of the solution to the debt problem there have been a number of so-called 'debt-for-nature swaps'. These involve the exchange or 'swap' of an amount of outstanding debt for an obligation to conserve a natural resource in the debtor country. For example the first debt-for-nature swap was in Bolivia where a US-based foundation swapped $650,000 of face value Bolivian debt for an agreement to establish and preserve 3.7 million acres of forest (Hansen, 1989). The mechanism by which swaps occur is that the interested foreign party will initially purchase debt in the secondary market. (Banks sell debt in a secondary market at prices, in most cases, well below face value. Bolivian debt in 1987 was selling at about 6 cents per $1 of face value in the secondary market and the low price reflects the fact that people think it very unlikely that Bolivia will ever pay back all its debt at face value.) The foreign party will then swap their purchased debt with the debtor's government for some form of environmental project. From 1987 until 1992, 17 countries partici-pated in debt-for-nature swaps which removed $100 million of face value debt at a cost of $16 million dollars. Table 6.8 details some recent debt-for-nature agreements.

However, while the end result of the debt-for-nature swaps is beneficial for the environment, there is criticism about the method used. Some authors criticize any purchase of debt by the debtor countries (in the above case Bolivia effectively purchased its debt by 'giving up' its rights to exploit the forest area) as reducing the face value of its debt by a small amount may not reduce the actual amount a debtor country will finally have to repay. For example in 1988 Bolivia repurchased $308 million of face value debt on the secondary market at a cost of $34 million. The total *market* value of Bolivia's debt only dropped from $40.2 to $39.8 million but basically, the creditors thought that Bolivia would only ever repay about $40 million and the total face value of the debt outstanding was irrelevant (see Bulow and Rogoff (1988) for the argument against debt buybacks). Given this argument it is claimed that a debtor may be better off negotiating directly with the foreign party interested in protecting the environment and not involve debt reduction and the creditor banks.

To date debt-for-nature swaps have had only a small direct effect on both the environment and the debt burden since the monetary amounts involved and areas covered are small. Whether larger debt-for-nature swaps are possi-ble in the future is uncertain. Even if the scale of swaps remains small Hansen (1989) sees an important role for them in promoting awareness of the issues of degradation.

Conclusion

The debt crisis which began in the early 1980s caused falling incomes and hardship in many countries. Debt repayments necessitated changes in the trade patterns of countries and, importantly, many countries had to plan adjustments in conjunction with international lending organizations. The environmental effects of these changes and adjustments are varied. Any simple statement that debt causes degradation is misleading in that it ignores the complex nature of the linkages involved. In evaluating the debt impact on any particular country there are perhaps three primary areas for investigation: firstly, whether the pressure to increase exports in a short space of time has led to increased degradation; secondly, whether falling incomes have caused degradation through increased poverty and migration; and lastly, what effects the adjustments in government policies, forced by falling revenues and international organizations, have had on the environment.

Notes

1. To illustrate the importance of commercial bank lending, in 1970–72 69.3 per cent of Brazil's long term debt was owed to private sources while in 1980–82 the figure was 88.1 per cent. The equivalent figures for Argentina were 87.4 per cent (1970–72) and 91 per cent (1980–82), for Mexico 80.5 per cent and 89.1 per cent and for Venezuela 69.2 per cent and 96.4 per cent.
2. For example, the rise in consumption spending from an additional $1 of foreign loans in the 1960s and 1970s was estimated to be 99 cents for Columbia and 88 cents for Bolivia (World Bank, 1991, p. 123).
3. Total bank gross lending to the non-oil-producing developing countries rose by 24 per cent in 1980 (over the previous year), 19 per cent in 1981 and 7 per cent in 1982 (Sachs, 1989).
4. Rising world interest rates were an important factor because much of the debts outstanding had 'floating rate' interest repayments. For example, in 1989 Brazil had 66.3 per cent of its long term debt under floating rates; likewise Mexico 75.3 per cent, Argentina 80.4 per cent, Costa Rica 43.7 per cent and Ivory Coast 35.4 per cent (World Bank, 1991).
5. Table 6.2 also shows that export prices were rapidly increasing in the 1973–80 period. This combined with the fact that real interest rates were low in the 1970s explains, to some extent, why banks lent so freely.
6. The Maquiladora programme in 1991 had 1,963 plants and employed 500,000 workers, earning an estimated $5 billion a year in foreign exchange (Reed, 1992).

Bibliography

Bulow, J. and Rogoff, K. (1988), 'The Buyback Boondoogle', *Brookings Papers on Economic Activity*, **2**.

Burgess, J. (1991), 'Economic Analysis of Frontier Agricultural Expansion and Tropical Deforestation', MSc Dissertation, University College London.

Capistrano, A. and Kiker, C. (1990), *Global Economic Influences on Tropical Broadleaved Forest Depletion*, World Bank: Washington D.C.

Carmichael, J. (1989), 'The Debt Crisis: Where Do We Stand After Seven Years?' *Research Observer* **4**, 2, World Bank: Washington D.C.

Coote, B. (1992), *The Trade Trap: Poverty and the Global Commodity Markets*, OXFAM: Oxford.

Fri, R.W. (1993), 'Environment and Development: The Next Step', *Resources Winter*, 1993, 16–18.

Grossman, G. and Krueger, A. (1992), 'Environmental Impacts of a North American Free Trade Agreement', Centre for Economic Policy and Research, Working Paper 644.

Gullison, R.E. and Losos, E.C. (1993), 'The Role of Foreign Debt in Deforestation in Latin America', *Conservation Biology*, **7**, 1, 140–47.

Hansen, S. (1989), 'Debt For Nature Swaps – Overview and Discussion of Key Issues', *Ecological Economics*, **1**, 77–93.

Hansen, S. (1990), 'Macroeconomic Policies and Sustainable Development in the Third World', *Journal of International Development*, **2**, 4, 533–57.

Hecht, S. (1992), 'Economic Causes of Degradation' in Downing, T. et al. (eds), *Development or Destruction: The Case of Amazonia*, Westview: Boulder, Colorado.

Kahn, J. and McDonald, J. (1990), *Third World Debt and Tropical Deforestation*, Department of Economics, SUNY: Binghamton, New York.

Krugman, P. (1989), 'Financing vs. Forgiving a Debt Overhang', *Journal of Development Economics*, **29**, 253–68.

Krugman, P. (1992), *Currencies and Crises*, MIT Press: Cambridge, Mass.

Lagos, R.A. (1992), 'Debt Relief through Debt Conversion: Chile', *Journal of Development Studies*, **28**, 3, 473–99.

Miller, M. (1991), *Debt and the Environment*, UN Publications: New York.

Moran, K. (1992), 'Debt-For-Nature Swaps: A Response to Debt and Deforestation in Developing Countries?' in Downing, T.E. et al. (eds.), *Development or Destruction*, Westview: Boulder, Colorado.

Occhiolini, M. (1990), 'Debt-for-Nature Swaps', World Bank Working Paper 393, World Bank: Washington D.C.

Panayotou, T. (1990), 'Economic Incentives in Environmental Management and their Relevance to Developing Countries', in Erocal, D. (ed.), *Environmental Management in Developing Countries*, OECD: Paris.

Pearce, D. and Warford, J. (1993), *World Without End*, Oxford University Press: New York.

Reed, D. (1992), *Structural Adjustment and the Environment*, Earthscan Publications: London.

Rogoff, K. (1992), 'Dealing with Developing Country Debt in the 1990's', *World Economy*, **15**, 4, 475–86.

Sachs, J.D. (1989), *Developing Country Debt and the World Economy*, University of Chicago Press: Chicago.

Shilling, J. (1992), 'Reflections on Debt and the Environment', *Finance and Development*, **29**, 2, 28–30.

Varangis, P.N., Primo Braga, C.A. and Takeuchi, K. (1993), 'Tropical Timber Trade Policies', World Bank Working Paper No. 1156, World Bank: Washington D.C.

World Bank (1991), *World Development Report: The Challenge of Development*, Oxford University Press: New York.

World Bank (1992), *World Development Report: Development and the Environment*, Oxford University Press: New York.

World Commission on Environment and Development (1987), *Our Common Future*, Oxford University Press: Oxford.

7 International trade and environmental quality

Nick Johnstone

Introduction

The relationship between international trade and environmental quality is exceedingly complex, requiring careful analysis. In effect, there are two primary means by which economic and environmental systems interact on the international stage. First, relative cost effects arising from domestic natural endowments and social regulation of the use of the environment affect international trade patterns. Secondly, international trade in natural resources and pollution-intensive products affects the global incidence of environmental effects. In effect, environmental factors (endowments, preferences and regulations) are both outcomes and causes of international trade and investment patterns. Given this complexity it is not surprising that the question of whether or not international trade is benign or malign with respect to environmental degradation has been a subject of much debate between economists and environmentalists. Loosely speaking, whereas many economists assert that international trade tends to encourage the conservation of environmental resources and the preservation of environmental quality, many environmentalists see international trade as a proximate cause of natural resource over-exploitation and environmental degradation. The tone of the debate has been marked as much by acrimony as it has been by mutual misunderstanding. In this light, the controversial and polemical words of Lawrence Summers, former chief economist of the World Bank, serve as a useful introduction to both the issues involved and the tone of the debate:

> Just between you and me, shouldn't the World Bank be encouraging more migration of the dirty industries to the LDC's? I can think of three reasons:
>
> 1. A given amount of health-impairing pollution should be done in the country with the lowest cost, which will be the country with the lowest wages...I think the economic logic behind dumping a load of toxic waste in the lowest-wage country is impeccable and we should face up to that.
> 2. The costs of pollution are likely to be non-linear as the initial increments of pollution probably have very low cost. I've always thought that under-populated countries in Africa are vastly under-polluted.
> 3. The demand for a clean environment for aesthetic and health reasons is likely to have very high income-elasticity.... Clearly trade in goods that embody aesthetic pollution concerns could be welfare-enhancing. While production is mobile the consumption of pretty air is a non-tradeable.[1]

Although intended as an internal document for World Bank staff, the memo received wide circulation. Not surprisingly, reaction to the tone of the piece was a mixture of incredulity and opprobrium. It is, however, the logic of the arguments involved which must be addressed and in this respect Summers points out a number of inter-related factors which determine the relationship between international trade and the environment, namely the importance of international differences in the marginal social cost of environmental degradation, in the stocks of natural capital, and in the demand for environmental goods. The discussion of these factors which affect that relationship will begin by characterizing, at the risk of over-simplification, the respective arguments of economists and environmentalists. It should be emphasized, however, that this serves more as an introduction to the issues involved than as an accurate portrayal of the respective positions.

International trade and the environment: the economists' argument
The belief of some economists in the benign role played by international trade in the exploitation of the global environment can be attributed to two theoretical notions, one demand-determined and 'static' and the other supply-determined and 'dynamic'. The static argument rests upon a belief in the role played by international trade in the allocation of resources. According to orthodox economic theory, international trade encourages the efficient exploitation of resources across trading nations. Since the production of goods involves the use of different 'factors of production' (labour, physical capital, natural capital and human capital), trade enables countries to export those goods which incorporate proportionately more of those factors of production which it possesses in relative abundance, since greater abundance will lead to lower prices and a competitive advantage in such goods relative to other trading nations. Thus a free international trading regime will enable each country to produce and export those goods which are best suited to its relative resource endowments. Trade in goods can, therefore, be considered in terms of trade in embodied factors of production. With respect to the environment, this implies that a given level of global material welfare can be attained at less factor input (including environmental input) than would be the case if each country attempted to satisfy its own consumption patterns purely through domestic production. Consequently it is argued that the inhibition of trade flows arising from trade restrictions, whether explicit (tariffs and import restrictions) or implicit (subsidies and non-tariff barriers), will result in greater levels of resource requirements than would be the case in a free international trading regime.

This analysis may be extended to include all natural resource inputs and pollution emission outputs directly within the production process and indirectly through input-output linkages. The environmental significance of such processes is, perhaps, best illustrated by the European Union's Common Agricultural Policy (CAP). CAP producer subsidies, estimated at 39 per cent of output value (Anderson and Blackhurst, 1992) encourage European specialization in the cultivation of agricultural products which are significantly more chemical and energy-intensive than agricultural output in those countries whose production has been displaced (see Table 7.1).

Table 7.1 Agricultural subsidies and the chemical and energy intensity of agricultural production in selected countries

	Agricultural subsidy equivalent 1979–89 (%)	Chemical fertilizer use 1987–89 (kg/ha of arable land)	Tractors and harvesters 1987–89 (per ha of arable land)
Denmark	39	243	0.078
France	39	312	0.087
Germany	39	405	0.212
Netherlands	39	662	0.214
Italy	39	172	0.117
Spain	39	101	0.037
Ireland	39	717	0.177
UK	39	359	0.085
Argentina	–38	5	0.007
Brazil	22	46	0.009
India	–2	62	0.005
Indonesia	11	113	0.002
Thailand	–4	33	0.006
Australia	11	26	0.008
Canada	35	47	0.020
US	30	95	0.028

Source: Anderson and Blackhurst (1992); WRI (1992).

The dynamic argument in support of the environmental consequences of free trade is related to the effect of international trade on income levels and the consequent effect of increased income levels on the demand for environmental preservation. The argument is predicated upon two propositions. First, it is argued that international trade tends to increase income levels. Recent studies conducted by the World Bank and the Organization for Economic Cooperation and Development indicate that annual global income levels will rise by as much as $213 billion (1992 prices) in the event of a successful completion of the Uruguay Round of negotiations for trade liberalization

(Goldin et al., 1993). It is then argued that increased income levels tend to result in greater environmental quality due to the increased notional demand for environmental goods and to the role that increased national income plays in bringing about increased capacity to meet such demand.

Although the latter point is controversial and will be discussed in greater detail below, empirical evidence tends to support this view. More precisely it appears that 'environmental wear' – the precise meaning of which will be discussed in greater detail below – rises with income levels until it reaches a certain point beyond which it begins to fall, generating an inverse U relationship (see Figure 7.1). This is borne out by more comprehensive studies. In a cross-section study involving 80 countries, Lucas, Wheeler and Hettige (1992) found that there was an inverse U relationship between GDP per capita and total toxic emissions relative to GDP, such that the pollution-intensity of economies increased until a certain point beyond which emissions fell. This relationship is also borne out by time-series studies which indicate that the relative toxic intensity of economies in individual countries tends to rise over a portion of the development path before falling. Grossman and Krueger (1992) reach similar results in their analysis of concentrations of sulphur dioxide, dark matter and particulates relative to income levels in different countries. It was concluded that sulphur dioxide and dark matter concentrations tend to rise until countries reach a GDP of approximately $5,000 (1985 US dollars), at which point they begin decreasing. The study also indicated that concentrations rise again once income levels reach approximately $14,000.

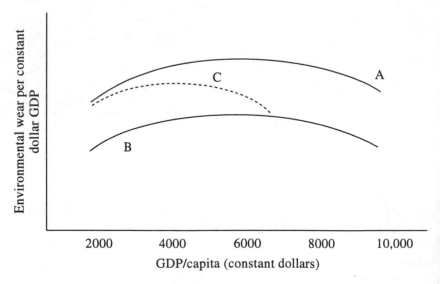

Figure 7.1   The intensity of environmental wear hypothesis

Conversely, concentrations of suspended particles tend to fall until GDP per capita reaches $9,000 at which point they stabilize. On the basis of results such as these, it is argued that a free international trading regime will result in increased environmental preservation and arrest the process of degradation by encouraging countries to engage in relatively less pollution-intensive production.

International trade and the environment: the environmentalists' argument
Environmentalists, differing from economists, usually assert that international trade increases environmental degradation. In some instances these arguments are based upon a more general antipathy toward the processes of industrialization and development as usually defined. However in this discussion it will be implicitly assumed that such objectives are desirable in their own right. The discussion is, therefore, only concerned with differences in beliefs about the environmental effects of achieving given objectives through international trade and not with differences in the objectives themselves. The latter point is clearly beyond the scope of such a discussion.

To a great extent environmentalists' belief in the fundamentally malign effects of international trade on the environment is predicated upon a belief that the expansion of international trade will encourage developing countries to mirror the development path of industrialized countries (Arden-Clarke, 1991). Thus on the one hand it is argued that international trade, by enabling the separation of the act of consumption from the environmental consequences of that consumption, reduces demand-derived incentives for environmentally sustainable production processes. In effect it is argued that international trade allows certain countries to import the sustainability of domestic environmental systems at the expense of other countries which are exporting their environmental sustainability. For example, it is asserted that the level of exports of hazardous waste is related to the relative stringency of domestic regulations which protect surface waters and groundwater in the exporting countries (see Table 7.2). Countries which are concerned about toxic wastes are able to continue to produce goods which are intensive in the generation of such wastes since they can rely upon other countries with less stringent regulations to dispose of it (see Moyers, 1991; French, 1990; Gupta, 1990 and Spalding, 1990). It has been estimated that the total annual trade of toxic waste is 2.2 million tons (Moyers, 1991).

Given the paucity of data it is difficult to develop a full picture of the trade in hazardous waste. However it is clear that trade between European countries with stringent regulations (principally West Germany but also Switzerland and Denmark) and neighbouring countries with less stringent regulations (principally East Germany, Belgium and France) is particularly significant.

Table 7.2   Major hazardous waste importing and exporting countries

	Imports (thousand tons)	Exports (thousand tons)
Belgium	914.1	13.2
Brazil	40.0	n.a.
Canada	130.0	65.0
Denmark	n.a.	20.0
France	95.9	25.0
W. Germany	75.0	1 695.0
E. Germany	814.3	n.a.
Netherlands	320.0	250.0
Switzerland	7.1	68.0
United Kingdom	82.5	n.a.
United States	45.3	203.4

Source: WRI (1990).

Another, more direct, example of international trade in environmental re-sources involves trade in endangered species and related products. Thus countries with relatively little species diversity are able to import large num-bers of animals from regions which are more species-rich: the total interna-tional trade in live species and animal products in 1987 was estimated to be $5 billion (World Resources Institute, 1990). For instance Japan, with its stringent domestic conservation laws, is the second largest importer of live primates in 1988 (7,133), the largest importer of cat skins (34,696) and the second largest importer of reptile skins (950,047) (World Resources Institute, 1992). Indeed, the CITES convention lists thousands of species as being potentially endangered as a consequence of commercial trade. This would therefore constitute another example of international trade enabling countries with demand for 'environmental' goods to obtain their supply from overseas, with little consideration of the impact upon the resource.

It is also argued that international trade, by encouraging national speciali-zation in the production of a limited number of goods, results in a depend-ence on a rather narrow resource base. Thus the trade-induced specialization which economists see as being environmentally benign, has the potential to be malign. For instance international trade tends to encourage agriculture-based economies to specialize in the cultivation of a limited number of crops (that is, coffee, maize, cassava, bananas) in order to maximize foreign ex-change earnings. This brings about the 'homogenization' of natural systems, whereby regions which had once been rich in species-diversity are increasingly

Table 7.3 Homogenization of the resource base in the agricultural sector

	Area devoted to modern rice varieties (thousand ha)	Percentage of rice area using modern varieties (%)	Change in degree of specialization
Sri Lanka	612	71	2000 varieties in 1959 to five in 1991. 75% of varieties from one maternal parent.
India	18 495	47	From 30000 varieties to 75% of total production from less than ten varieties.
Bangladesh	2 325	22	62% of varieties from one maternal parent.
Indonesia	5 416	60	74% of varieties from one maternal parent.

Sources: Hazel (1985); WCMC (1992).

characterized by a limited number of species (see Table 7.3). Not only does this specialization threaten the genetic pool of the region itself, and indeed the world, but it also increases the instability of the ecological system, eventually undermining the productivity of the crop itself. Thus average yield variability (measured as the coefficient of variation) has increased from 0.028 to 0.034 between 1960 and 1983 (Hazell, 1989). Although it may be possible to mask this decline in productivity for a certain number of years through increased inputs of chemical fertilizers and 'mining' of the soil's nutrients, the limits of such specialization are eventually breached (see World Resources Institute, 1990; Pearce and Warford, 1993; World Bank, 1992).

Clearly then the relationship between international trade and environmental degradation is complex and requires careful analysis. Although international trade may improve the allocation of economic processes which use environmental resources and increase effective demand for environmental preservation, it may also undermine the sustainability of ecosystems and insulate societies, at least temporarily, from the effects of environmental degradation. Given the complexity of the issues involved therefore, a more thorough theoretical discussion is required.

Environmental factors, comparative advantage and international trade
The potential effect of environmental factors with respect to international trade patterns has been discussed extensively in the literature on international environmental economics.[2] Thus, as noted above, according to classical trade theory a country will tend to specialize in the export of goods involving production processes which are relatively more intensive in the use of those factors of production which it possesses in relative abundance. The theory of environmentally determined comparative advantage is merely an extension of this theory in the sense that the environment is introduced as a factor of production, analogous to the classical factors of production, labour and capital. Thus a country with a relative abundance of natural capital will specialize in the production of goods which are intensive in the use of natural capital.

In what sense might the environment be considered a factor of production? On the one hand natural resources could be used directly, either in processed form or as inputs in the production of other goods. For instance the exploitation of non-renewable natural resources (such as minerals and fossil fuels) has a direct effect on the available stock of such resources for future use. In addition, a harvest rate of renewable natural resources (such as forests and marine species) which exceeds the resource's natural growth rate will also reduce the stock of natural capital available for future use. Less obviously, but analogously, the environment can also be considered a factor of production through the use of its capacity to absorb the waste arising from production processes. For example to the extent that a body of water is able to render a limited concentration of industrial pollutants benign, the production process which generates the waste water flow uses the river's assimilative capacity. A similar point can be made with respect to climatic patterns which disperse air pollutants sufficiently to obviate adverse environmental effects. However, as is the case with the use of renewable resources as inputs in production, this capacity can be exceeded such that there is a permanent loss in the capacity of the environmental medium to process future streams of waste.

Thus the production of goods which use the environment 'intensively' (whether as natural resource inputs or as pollution emission outputs) will reduce the stock of natural capital which is available for future use in economic processes. Indeed, the distinction between goods which are intensive in the use of natural resources inputs and those which are intensive in pollution outputs is, in some sense, artificial. Irrespective of whether a country specializes in the exploitation of natural resources or the production of pollution-intensive goods, the country is exporting goods which embody significant amounts of natural capital. In this sense a factory which pollutes a body of water, destroying fish stocks, is no different from a fishery which over-exploits the species, rendering it extinct. The manufactures produced by the factory embody the river's natural capital no less than the fishery's output.

The real distinction lies between the use of natural resources which are priced and those which are not. It is for this reason that the amount of natural capital which is available for productive processes must be recognized as a social, and not strictly natural, phenomenon. Stated somewhat differently, the use of natural capital is a function not only of supply conditions in terms of natural capital endowments, but also of demand conditions. This arises from the fact that environmental quality is a final good in its own right and not solely a factor of production. The value which a society places on environmental quality – as a final good – might be the result of the value attached to it for recreational purposes, aesthetic reasons, or even merely due to awareness of its existence. Thus the maximum capacity of a river to absorb waste is defined not only by its natural properties but also by the uses to which it is put. A river which is used for recreational purposes (fishing, boating, swimming) will, effectively, have much less assimilative capacity than an identical river which is used for other purposes (industrial process water, irrigation for agriculture, hydroelectric plants). The cost associated with the use of its assimilative capacity will be correspondingly higher.

To a great extent however, the price associated with the use of the environment as a source of environmental quality is not expressed directly in the market but usually manifests itself indirectly through state intervention in economy-environment interactions. Through such intervention the state affects the extent and means by which agents in the economy are able to employ the environment for productive purposes. This may manifest itself in a rather direct sense (effluent taxes, pollution permits, technology-based standards) or by more indirect means (land use constraints, user charges for sewer systems, liability regimes for environmental damages). Indeed, some forms of state intervention of economy-environment interactions may not even be recognized as explicitly environmental (public investment in different forms of transportation infrastructure and sales taxes on domestic fuels and petrol). Nonetheless, to the extent that they restrict the employment of the environment in productive processes, there is an implicit price assessed to its use. The 'price' assessed will correspond to the cost of compliance with direct environmental regulations and other less direct restrictions.

The price assessed will, however, differ between regions (and thus between countries) depending on 'natural' factors such as the availability of natural resources, the composition of the soil and the speed and direction of prevailing winds and currents, as well as 'anthropogenic' factors such as the political, social and economic factors which determine the means by which the state mediates interactions between the economy and the environment. In an ideal system the assessed price would be equal to the marginal cost of value forgone to society as a consequence of the decline in environmental quality. However in reality the price may bear little relation to the actual value forgone (and the consequences will be discussed in greater detail below). In any event, countries place very different 'prices' on the use of their natural and environmental resources and, to some extent, this determines the direction of resulting trade flows.

International trade and South-North transfers of environmental resources

The theoretical discussion above highlights the potential for environmental factors to be determinants of international trade patterns. This theory implies that some countries will tend to specialize in the production of pollution-intensive goods and the exploitation of natural resources. Moreover it is often argued that relatively poorer countries will tend to be those countries which undertake such specialization, for two related reasons. First, since developing countries generally possess relatively limited stocks of physical capital (such as machinery and equipment), it is argued that natural capital is frequently substituted as a means to secure improved development prospects. Secondly, since environmental quality appears to increase with income levels, it is felt that developing countries are less likely to place stringent restrictions on the exploitation of natural capital. Thus it is argued that poorer countries tend to export their environmental resources, whether directly as natural resources or indirectly as pollution-intensive products. In the event that the nature of the exploitation and production results in a permanent depletion of the natural stock, developing countries are, effectively, exporting the sustainability of their environmental systems. The implications, indeed validity, of such an argument must be discussed more fully.

The first question which must be addressed is whether or not relatively poorer countries have a tendency to substitute significant reliance upon natural capital for a lack of physical capital. In order to determine whether or not this is so it is necessary to compare not only rates of natural resource exploitation but also potential rates of physical capital accumulation, since the central issue is whether or not poorer countries are required to exploit their natural resource base relatively more intensively than richer countries. Thus, assuming that *potential* physical capital accumulation rates are related to *actual* financial savings rates, a high rate of natural capital stock depreciation relative to financial savings rates would indicate that a country is substituting natural capital for physical capital. In effect, a relatively high rate would indicate that the country concerned was *mining* its natural capital for consumption rather than *converting* it into physical capital stocks. In the event that this tendency is related to income levels one would therefore expect the ratio of natural capital depreciation to savings rates to increase as income levels fell. To a great extent this is borne out by the empirical evidence (see Figure 7.2). In the figure, the vertical axis compares the ratio of natural capital stock depreciation relative to financial savings rates in twenty countries (five high income countries, nine middle income countries and six low

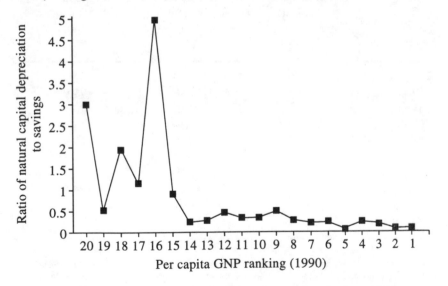

Figure 7.2   *Income and the substitutability of natural capital for physical capital*

income countries), while on the horizontal axis the countries are ranked from poorest to richest.[3] The figure indicates that poorer countries are 'mining' their natural resources at a much faster rate than richer countries. Thus, there does seem to be a clear relationship between income levels and tendencies to substitute natural capital for physical capital.

Moreover the studies cited earlier appear to support the claim that beyond a certain income level countries tend to engage in economic processes which are relatively less intensive in their use of the environment, whether through natural resource exploitation or pollution-intensive production. The next question which must be addressed therefore is whether or not this is reflected in international trade flows. Are poorer countries exporting goods which are relatively more environment-intensive? With respect to the export of natural resources, it does indeed appear to be the case that much of the basis for natural resource base exploitation can be attributed to exports. For instance, those countries with exceptionally high deforestation rates tend to be both open to international trade and reliant upon primary products (see Table 7.4).

Table 7.4   Deforestation, per capita income and trading regimes in selected developing countries

	Deforestation (% lost)	Per capita income 1992 ($)	Trade openness 1992
Ivory Coast	36.0	770	57.9
Costa Rica	22.6	1 690	71.9
Thailand	19.8	1 000	70.7
Philippines	19.6	630	48.5
Nicaragua	18.9	NA	40.9
Togo	18.4	370	74.8
Ecuador	18.3	1 120	55.1
Malaysia	14.6	1 940	124.6
Honduras	14.5	860	51.5
Paraguay	14.2	1 180	54.6

Notes:
(a)   Deforestation is defined as the percentage of forest area lost from 1966–68 to 1986–88.
(b)   Trade openness is the sum of exports and imports over gross domestic product. In the case of the United Kingdom the equivalent figure is 46.1.

Source: Pearce, Fankhauser, Adger and Swanson (1992).

A similar pattern is also characteristic of many developing countries with high rates of soil degradation and significant agricultural commodity exports. Thus 24 per cent of soil degradation in Africa is attributable to agricultural practices with much of the erosion occurring in countries with significant agricultural exports such as Morocco, the Ivory Coast, Malawi and Senegal (WRI, 1992).

It is important to stress however that such correlations do not imply causality. Although high deforestation and soil erosion rates certainly coexist with open trading regimes, international trade should not necessarily be considered a causal factor in such processes of natural resource depletion. The relevance of this point to the deforestation rates cited above will be discussed in greater detail in the final section. However attempts have been made to determine causality in the pollution-intensity of trade in manufactures. Thus Tobey (1990) conducted a study to test directly for the importance of natural capital factor endowments as determinants of trade patterns for pollution-intensive sectors such as basic and processed metals, chemicals and pulp and paper. In one test an index of the relative stringency of environmental regulations was introduced into the model (along with a number of other factors such as capital and labour costs) as a proxy for the environmental endowment in 23 countries with widely divergent income levels. However the environmental variable was not found to be significant, indicating that environmental abundance was not a determinant of international trade patterns. In a second test 58 countries were divided into three broad groups depending on the relative stringency of their environmental regimes, and similar regressions were run, in this case omitting the environmental variable. In effect the author was attempting to determine whether or not there was an explanatory factor missing (that is, natural capital) in such tests. However once again the hypothesis that pollution control measures have no effect on trade patterns could not be rejected. Similarly in a study of Mexican-American trade flows Grossman and Krueger (1992) were also unable to uncover significant evidence of environment-induced changes in trade flows in pollution-intensive sectors. A number of other recent studies broadly support the conclusion that environmental factors are not significant determinants of trade and investment patterns. For instance McConnell and Schwab (1990) and Bartik (1988) found little evidence of environmental regulations playing a significant role in business location decisions.

The empirical evidence of environmentally determined trade effects is, therefore, quite limited. Part of the reason for this can certainly be attributed to the fact that the cross-sectional methodology used assumes implicitly that sectors with the heaviest pollution abatement and control expenditures will be those sectors which are most affected by environmental regulations in terms of competitive displacement. However since most such sectors (chemicals, basic metals, processed metals, pulp and paper) possess structural characteristics such as demand and supply elasticities and input-output linkages which discourage territorial restructuring of production, cross-sectional studies and studies which concentrate on the most pollution-intensive sectors may not be an appropriate means of testing such hypotheses. Moreover such studies tend to emphasise regulatory costs of production associated with the use of the environment at the expense of non-regulatory environment-related production costs. This latter point is particularly important since *ex post* liability regimes, public infrastructure finance mechanisms, and land use control institutions and objectives may vary between countries even more than the stringency and enforcement of direct regulations.

Although it is difficult to attribute causality to environmental factors as determinants of the pattern of trade flows from South to North, there is little question that many countries are, in some sense, exporting their environmental sustainability. In a study conducted by Pearce and Atkinson (1992), more than half of the developing countries included did not possess net physical capital accumulation rates sufficient to offset natural capital depreciation. This implies that economic processes in such countries are not only environmentally unsustainable but economically unsustainable as well. Conversely, all of the developed countries in the study had rates of physical capital accumulation sufficient to offset the relatively lower rates of natural capital depreciation. To some extent then the export of environment-intensive goods is a short-term response to economic necessity rather than a long-term manifestation of comparative advantage (see Chapter Six). This does not, however, imply that developing countries should never specialize in the production and exploitation of environment-intensive goods, merely that the means by which many countries are doing so is not sustainable

Economic development and state intervention in economy-environment interactions

From the above, although it is clear that international trade encourages the exploitation of natural resources in many developing countries, the unsustainability of many forms of such exploitation should not necessarily be attributed to trade *per se*, but is instead attributable to the practices themselves. Trade may facilitate and accelerate environmental degradation but it does not, in and by itself, cause such degradation. However the importance of the role played by international trade in many processes of environmental degradation is such that it is not sufficient merely to attribute blame for such degradation on a simple inability or unwillingness of many states 'to get the prices right'. Indeed, there are fundamental criticisms of arguments that international trade is, by its very nature, environmentally benign.

Uncertainty, irreversibility and the pricing of environmental resources

The first point to be addressed is related to the difficulties of pricing environmental resources in the context of economic processes which frequently have both far-reaching and unknown environmental consequences. In such a context international trade based on existing constraints on the use of environmental resources may play an important role in restricting the options of future generations to enjoy the benefits of environmental goods. This will be briefly discussed in the context of hazardous waste exports from North to South, the extent of which can be alarming. It has been estimated that annually there are over 600,000 tons of net exports of hazardous waste from OECD countries, with at least eleven developing countries being significant recipients of such waste (Richardson, 1991). As a particularly alarming case, Guinea-Bissau imported $600 million of hazardous waste from American and European sources over the course of a five-year period in the late 1980s, a figure which was approximately equal to its gross domestic product (Richardson, 1991). Environmentalists might cite such exports as evidence of the pernicious nature of international trade, with relatively wealthier countries importing their environmental sustainability at the expense of the environmental sustainability of other countries. Conversely many economists would assert that restrictions on such trade, such as the Lomé IV Convention and the Bamoko Convention, distort trade flows and reduce efficiency since they constrain the capacity for those countries with comparative advantage in hazardous waste treatment and disposal to exploit such advantages.

The truth certainly lies somewhere in between these two views. The price associated with the use of the environment is a reflection of three factors: endowments of natural capital, social preferences for environmental quality and the extent to which state interventions reflect the first two factors. Some trade in such waste may be a reflection of relative natural endowments (for example differences in the permeability of the soil and local climatic conditions) as well as relative domestic preferences (for example the relative importance attached to small risks of cancer in countries with very different income levels) in the exporting and importing countries. However, much of the waste is certainly more of a reflection of the extent to which state interventions actually reflect the true cost associated with the use of the environment in economic processes. Given that the environmental consequences of the treatment and disposal of many forms of hazardous waste are frequently uncertain, it is exceedingly difficult (if not impossible) to determine an appropriate 'price', particularly for countries with limited experience in the treatment, management and disposal of such waste. Moreover given the capital intensity of such facilities, it is distinctly unlikely that labour-rich developing countries will have an authentic comparative advantage in the sector.

Moreover, many of the adverse effects arising from hazardous waste are long-lived or even irreversible, resulting in permanent damage to the environment. Given the presumed income elasticity of demand for environmental quality, this latter point is particularly important for developing countries. Thus any trade in hazardous waste from richer countries to poorer countries arising from existing constraints placed on the use of domestic environmental resources must, to some extent, discount either the environmental preferences of future generations in the recipient country and/or the development prospects of the country itself. It is, at best, disingenuous to assert that the recipient countries should specialize in environment-intensive production in order to secure development, but that the very process by which such development is secured denies future generations the option of expressing demand for the environmental goods which have been degraded in the process. Thus much of the trade is based not so much on actual endowments and underlying preferences but on more fundamental issues such as relations of economic dependency and the complexities involved in mediating economy-environment interactions.

Environmental quality, economic development and income distribution
The second point is concerned with the relationship between environmental quality and income levels. Although it is widely assumed that the generally positive nature of this relationship reflects increased demand for environmental quality, this point requires careful qualification. On the one hand, such a relationship is primarily a reflection of transformations in the structure of the economy as development proceeds. Although demand for environmental quality may play a small role in affecting the path of development, relative emission levels certainly reflect more fundamental underlying economic processes which are, in all likelihood, unrelated to environmental factors. Thus concentrations of particulate matter tend to fall as income levels rise, reflecting increased paving of roads and reduced reliance on wood and dung as fuel sources. Conversely, high income countries appear more than willing to emit higher levels of carbon dioxide and generate larger quantities of solid waste. Thus it is likely that any improvements in environmental quality as income levels increase arise not so much from increased demand for environmental quality but from transformations in economic structure as development progresses.

Similarly relatively lower access to safe water and adequate sanitation in developing countries, the most important cause of surface water pollution in many countries, should certainly not be construed as a reflection of free choice with respect to environmental quality (see Figure 7.2). For instance, studies conducted in Ghana, Burkina Faso, Pakistan, Thailand and Brazil indicate that residents are, in principle, willing to pay significant amounts for improved wastewater collection and treatment but are often stuck in a low-level equilibrium whereby poor quality service is met with little demand for improvement due to low aspirations (World Bank, 1992). Indeed a more significant relationship than that between income levels and environmental quality may be that between income distribution (as opposed to levels) and environmental degradation. Thus residents of shanty towns frequently pay significantly more for clean water than residents of wealthier neighbourhoods as they do not have access to public services and are forced to buy bottled water from street vendors. In Lima lower income families pay 18 times as much for water as a middle-class family and in some shanty towns in Nigeria and Haiti, 18 to 20 per cent of household income is devoted to water costs (World Bank, 1992). Thus the proximity of low income households to the adverse effects of the degradation of surface waters would indicate that demand for environmental quality is, if anything, greater than that of high income households. Unfortunately such households are not in a position to make such demand effective and as such are required to purchase bottled water. More equal access to environment-related public services (potable water and waste water treatment) would result in less environmental degradation and, paradoxically, lower expenditures on environmental goods.

A case study of international trade in wood-based products
The fundamental cause of environmental degradation is, therefore, related to the inability of different societies to provide an institutional context wherein the true cost associated with the use of environmental resources is accurately reflected in prices. International trade, although not strictly a causal factor can, however, play an important role in contributing to processes of environmental degradation. First, international trade may accelerate such processes by providing increased opportunities for more extensive exploitation of environmental resources. Secondly, in the context of a global economy wherein endowments (environmental and economic) are unequally distributed, such opportunities are likely to be significant given large international differences in the cost associated with the use of the environment. These questions will be analysed in the context of international trade in wood-based products.

The sustainability of timber exploitation and environmental externalities
While temperate countries have reported a net increase of 2 per cent in the extent of forest cover since the Second World War, in tropical countries there has been an average annual decrease in the extent of forest cover of 0.6 per cent in the years between 1976 and 1985 and this rate appears to be increasing. It has been estimated that the overall annual rate of deforestation for the 1980s was 1.2 per cent, with 1.4 per cent in Asia, 1.6 per cent in Latin America and somewhat less for Africa (Barbier et al., 1992). Although there

is a great deal of uncertainty about the accuracy of these figures, there is little question that the rates of deforestation in developing countries are both high and increasing. However the contribution of timber exploitation to such degradation appears to be limited. Indeed, only a rather limited proportion of such deforestation (less than 10 per cent) can be attributed to forestry practices themselves, with the overwhelming majority attributable to the agricultural sector (more than 80 per cent) (Amelung, 1991). In addition there are some notable examples of sustainable timber management (India, Malaysia and the Philippines) and even reafforestation (China) (Barbier, 1992).

Unsustainable timber exploitation is significant not only in terms of increased scarcity of timber supplies but also in terms of environmental externalities associated with timber exploitation. Perhaps the most important externality is associated with species loss. It has been estimated that 50 to 90 per cent of the total number of species are to be found in tropical forests. Additionally, deforestation exacerbates the problem of global warming in two ways: the burning of timber stands results in significant carbon emissions and reduced forest cover inhibits the role played by the forest as a carbon store. Deforestation may also weaken the important role played by timber stands in the protection of watersheds and result in significant soil erosion. Finally, deforestation may result in microclimatic changes with unforeseen consequences on neighbouring ecosystems (Burgess 1992). Thus the effects of environmental externalities associated with deforestation have local, regional and global components.

International trade in timber products
The Food and Agriculture Organization (FAO) divides forest products into five broad categories: roundwood, sawnwood, wood-based panels, wood pulp and paper products. In 1990 total trade in forest products was $123.36 billion (Barbier et al., 1992). However exports from North America and Western Europe represented 31 per cent and 49 per cent of the world total respectively in 1990 (see Table 7.5). In addition developed country exports were much more heavily weighted toward products involving relatively more processing (wood-based panels, wood pulp and paper products) than exports from developing countries (Barbier et al., 1992). Only a relatively small number of LDCs have a positive trade balance in wood-based products: ten out of 18 tropical African countries, five of 19 Central American and South American tropical countries, and eight of 17 tropical countries from Asia and Oceania (Burgess, 1992). Those LDCs which have net exports greater than $100 million in 1990 were Congo, Ivory Coast, Gabon, Liberia, Zaire, Brazil, Indonesia, Malaysia and Papua-New Guinea (Barbier et al., 1992).

International trade represents a rather small proportion of global production: 7.5 per cent of industrial roundwood, 19.5 per cent of sawnwood, 23.4

Table 7.5   Exports of wood-based products

	Industrial roundwood	Sawnwood & sleepers	Wood-based panels	Wood pulp	Paper products	Total
			All figures in 1990 $			
North America	3 161	6 938	1 280	8 380	10 707	30 467
Europe	1 833	6 378	4 050	5 338	29 687	47 286
Oceania	502	130	101	256	274	1 264
Other DCs	36	27	77	267	1 675	2 082
Africa	493	231	104	120	5	953
Latin America	209	426	317	962	830	2 743
Near East	14	20	10	0	30	74
Far East	1 727	1 711	3 921	126	1 516	9 001
Other LDCs	142	12	4	0	0	159

Source: Barbier et al. (1992).

per cent of wood-based panels, 16.3 per cent of pulp and 22.9 per cent of paper by volume in million cubic metres (see Table 7.6). As a proportion of production in LDCs, trade represented 11 per cent for industrial roundwood, 12 per cent of sawnwood and 69 per cent of wood-based panels, with the rest consumed locally (Burgess, 1992).

Given the previous analysis and the above information one would not expect international trade to be a particularly significant cause of deforestation. Indeed, in a cross-sectional study of 45 countries from 1967 to 1985 conducted by Capistrano (1990), the export price of tropical timber was a significant determinant of deforestation rates only in the period from 1967 to 1971. In a cross-sectional study of 72 countries in 1980, Palo, Mery and Salmi (1987) did not find that forest product exports were a significant determinant of forest cover. The evidence is therefore mixed, but the weight of the evidence does not support the contention that the timber trade is the primary cause of tropical deforestation (Brown and Pearce, 1994).

Table 7.6   Exports of wood-based products as a proportion of production in tropical regions

	1961 (%)	1970 (%)	1980 (%)	1990 (%)
Tropical Africa				
Roundwood	23.8	23.3	16.3	9.5
Sawnwood	32.1	28.5	12.7	12.3
Wood-based panels	34.0	33.0	28.6	21.9
Tropical C. and S. America				
Roundwood	1.6	1.0	0.2	0.2
Sawnwood	14.7	13.6	6.9	3.9
Wood-based panels	34.0	33.0	15.3	19.4
Tropical Asia and Oceania				
Roundwood	22.2	44.2	8.25	20.4
Sawnwood	11.9	18.5	24.5	17.5
Wood-Based Panels	40.5	39.9	49.4	89.7

Source: Barbier et al. (1992).

Trade regulation and environmental externalities
Although international trade is, at most, a contributory factor in processes of deforestation, the regulation of trade as a means of ensuring the sustainability

of timber exploitation is likely to be a subject of significant and increasing concern for two related reasons: the importance of international economic effects (trade competitiveness) arising from domestic environmental policies and the importance of international environmental effects (global externalities) arising from domestic economic processes. Given the dominant role played by the General Agreement on Tariff and Trade (GATT) on trade regulation, GATT policies on the relationship between trade regulation and the environment are of particular significance. It is however only relatively recently that the GATT has begun to address some of these issues. The basic tenets of the GATT can be summarized under two fundamental principles:

1. The Most Favoured nation (MFN) principle (Article I), which asserts that any trade advantage conferred by one country on another country must automatically be extended to all other GATT signatories.
2. The National Treatment (NT) principle (Article III), which asserts that each country must treat imported goods in the same way as 'like or competing' domestic goods.

In addition Article II specifies maximum tariffs for particular goods and obliges states to negotiate their decline in successive rounds, Article XI forbids the use of quantitative restrictions on imports, and Article XVI specifies the conditions under which subsidies can be applied.

Exceptions to the basic free trade principles of the GATT can be applied in specific circumstances. Although the environment was not a pressing issue at the time of the GATT's inception in 1947, two clauses in Article XX have proved relevant to environmental concerns: Clause XX(b) allows exceptions for measures which are 'necessary to protect human, animal or plant life or health' and Clause XX(g) allows exceptions for measures 'relating to the conservation of exhaustible natural resources if such measures are made effective in conjunction with restrictions on domestic production or consumption'.

Three cases which have been brought before the GATT serve to clarify the precise meaning of these clauses. In 1982 the US placed restrictions on the import of Canadian tuna, claiming that the exhaustible resource was being exploited in an unsustainable manner. Canada took the US to the GATT, arguing that the restriction was in fact merely retaliation for the seizure of American fishing vessels. The GATT Panel ruled that the measure was legitimate in so far as it was not discriminatory and that it related to the conservation of resources. However the restriction was not valid in that equivalent domestic regulations on exploitation of the resource had not been applied in accordance with Clause XX(g). In 1987 the European Community, Mexico and Canada took the US to the GATT when tariffs were placed on imports of petroleum and chemical feedstocks in order to finance the clean-up of hazardous waste sites under the 1982 Superfund Act. The plaintiffs argued that the tax was illegitimate in that while the motivation for the tax was environmental, the damages were extra-territorial and the tax represented a departure from the 'Polluter Pays Principle' since foreign manufacturers were already paying for pollution controls under domestic regulations. The Panel found in favour of the US, ruling that the motivation for the tax was irrelevant in the case and that border tax adjustments were legitimate since the measure was a simple product tax. Finally, in 1988 Mexico took the US to the GATT over American restrictions on the import of tuna caught with the use of purse-seine nets which result in mammal (principally dolphin) catch rates greater than those of the American fleet. The Panel found in favour of Mexico, ruling that the US could not restrict imports in order to conserve extra-territorial resources. Moreover it was reaffirmed that trade restrictions could only be applied on the basis of products and not production or process methods.

In general the decisions of the GATT Panel indicate that trade restrictions based on pollution arising from consumption are legitimate, whereas those based on pollution arising from production processes are not. The distinction is based upon interpretations of sovereignty. Thus it is felt that import restrictions are illegitimate in the event that they rest upon concerns about the technological processes employed within foreign countries or upon concerns about the use to which foreign resources are put. The relevant clauses do however require clarification, particularly since recent discussions concerning the 1979 Agreement on Technical Barriers to Trade (the Standards Code) indicate that there is some confusion amongst member countries about the relevance of Article XX to production and process methods (Low and Safadi, 1991). In addition, the extra-territoriality principles expressed in GATT Panel decisions have never been fully tested since most decisions were rejected on the basis that they were first and foremost protectionist, and only incidentally conservationist. The Panel has consistently stated that conservationist principles are adequate grounds for departure from free trade but that such principles must be developed and agreed on a multilateral basis.

Although none of the GATT Panel decisions which have included environmental components have been related to the timber trade explicitly, they do give insight into the potential for trade policies to be used as a means of attaining environmental objectives. This is important since there have been attempts (both unilateral and multilateral) to regulate trade in timber for environment-related reasons. For instance, the Netherlands has advocated the use of unilateral bans of imports from countries whose exploitation is not managed sustainably. Although the International Tropical Timber Organization (ITTO) has not advocated the use of bans, there have been discussions about the use of surcharges for imports from countries whose exploitation is not sustainable (Poore, 1989).

The effectiveness of trade policies as a means of attaining environmental objectives

Given these developments, an analysis of the relative effectiveness and desirability of trade policies (import bans and tariffs) as a means of attaining environmental objectives is in order. A number of points merit discussion. First, since trade is not a cause of environmental degradation but only a contributory factor, restrictions on trade do not address the fundamental cause of deforestation. Indeed the experience of Indonesia is instructive in this regard. In an attempt to encourage resource-based industrialization, the Indonesian government taxed and later banned the export of raw timber, thus granting an effective subsidy to those domestic sectors which use timber as an input in production. The ban has been successful in so far as wood-processing sectors in Indonesia have been dynamic in recent years (Primo Braga, 1992). However the environmental consequences have been less positive. On the one hand the processing sectors in Indonesia require more logs per unit of output than sectors elsewhere (Primo Braga, 1992). Similarly, many of these same processing sectors are particularly pollution-intensive. For instance it has been found that less pollution-intensive thermomechanical technology has been adopted by the pulp and paper sector in countries with relatively more open trading regimes (Wheeler and Martin, 1992). Thus protection, by distorting trade flows, has encouraged the development of production processes requiring relatively greater environmental throughput. Since the trade effects would be equivalent, there is little reason to suspect that the imposition of trade restrictions by importing countries would not have equivalent environmental effects. It would appear therefore that it is exceedingly complex to use international trade policies to attain environmental objectives in a predictable manner since such policies are not directed toward the externality itself. Indeed, depending on input-output linkages the effects may even be perverse.

Even within the primary timber sector itself it may be exceedingly difficult to develop objective criteria by which to determine whether or not timber is being sustainably managed in a manner which is acceptable to both producer and consumer countries. Environmental externalities are complex phenomena arising out of both natural and social contexts. Thus in the case of timber, the relative sustainability of exploitation depends upon the extent and nature of felling, the regenerative capacity of the resource, the alternative uses to which the ecosystem can be put and a host of other factors. Efforts on the part of importing countries to determine whether, and the extent to which, exploitation in exporting countries is sustainable will require subjective evaluations relating to production process methods. The ability of foreign governments to make such evaluations is questionable. Moreover such evaluations will raise concerns about the sovereign rights of states to use resources as they see fit, an issue which the GATT has been reluctant to address.

As an alternative to import bans and surcharges, the formation of a cartel amongst timber exporting nations has also been discussed (Guppy, 1984). Thus it is asserted that cartels in natural resource sectors are environmentally beneficial to the extent that they lower the rate of exploitation or extraction. As Solow states, 'the monopolist is the conservationist's friend' (Solow, 1974, p. 8). There are, however, a number of points which should be made with regard to this assertion. First, there is some question as to the effect of monopolization on exploitation rates in the long run. From a theoretical perspective it would appear that the only environmental benefits of increased market power arise from the potential for lengthened planning horizons and not cartelization *per se* (Rauscher, 1990). Secondly, there is little reason to suspect that the effect of market power on exploitation rates coincides with the optimal rate from an environmental perspective. A congruence between the two would be fortuitous but unlikely, particularly given the instability of cartels. Finally, since cartelization would only reduce the rate of exploitation (if that) and not the nature of exploitation the environmental benefits are necessarily limited. Deforestation arises from unsustainable timber management and not timber exploitation in and of itself.

Therefore it is clear that an internationally implemented policy of price enhancement alone is not sufficient to address domestically based environmental problems such as deforestation. What is required is a policy that both (i) confers enhanced compensation for the flow of benefits from forest resources; and (ii) directs this compensation only to those states investing in the sustainable management of these flows (Rauscher, 1990; Swanson, 1994). That is, an international trade policy must confer increased *flows* of compensation upon those states investing in their *stocks* of natural resources. Such a policy combines the 'capital-based' solution with a discriminating mechanism for determining membership of the cartel; thus creating incentives to sustainable management in order to enter and remain within the cartel. Such a mechanism is in the nature of an 'Exchange' (Swanson and Pearce, 1989; Barbier et al., 1990).

Some economists have gone so far as to assert that product labelling and increased transparency in the market is all that is required to ensure that prices accurately reflect costs. Consumers will recognize the real costs of consumption and make choices accordingly (Primo Braga, 1992). However such a market-based system relies too heavily on the uncoordinated actions of consumer states. Although it is in the joint interest of those states to purchase timber only from sustainably managed forests, individual states will have a greater incentive to allow other states to do so while they themselves purchase the least expensive timber products. The role of an exchange is to eliminate such 'free-riders' by rendering transparent all transactions in the regulated commodity. Each consumer sees the exchange-based purchases by other consumer states as its own compensation for using the exchange, then joint use of the exchange provides the reward for the sustainable purchases of forest products. Therefore it is possible for trade-based policies to form the basis for addressing environmental problems, although it is essential that these policies be undertaken on a *multilateral* rather than a unilateral basis (as required by GATT) and that they be *stock-* rather than flow-orientated (as required for sustainability). An exchange-based policy of price enhancement is one example of a form of international system that fulfils these requirements.

Conclusion

It would appear that economists who assert that international trade is benign with respect to environmental degradation due to its beneficial allocation and income effects, while attributing blame for such processes to society's inability to 'get the prices right', are being, at best, wilfully disingenuous. At the same time environmentalists who attribute environmental degradation to international trade flows are mistaking coexistence for causality and attaching a peculiar importance to the borders of the nation state. Although international trade is not the proximate cause of environmental degradation, it can certainly play an important role in facilitating and accelerating such processes and this role must be recognized. There may indeed be instances when it is necessary to restrict or regulate trade in order to attain environmental objectives, with trade in hazardous waste and live species being notable examples. However, a more general policy of protectionism cannot be justified on environmental grounds since trade is neither a causal factor in processes of environmental degradation nor an appropriate instrument by which to attain environmental objectives.

The ideal solution rests of course with enlightened and far-sighted state intervention in economy-environment interactions, attributing appropriate costs to the exploitation of natural capital. However given global inequality in both natural resource endowments and stages of economic development, as well as the transborder nature of many environmental systems, some form of international co-operation is often necessary and desirable in order to ensure that international trade flows do not reflect flows of environmental sustainability from some countries (principally the South) to others (principally the North). Given global income inequality, some of this co-operation will necessarily require a transfer of financial resources from North to South. This chapter has outlined the basis by which these transfers might be systematically instituted to alter domestic policies regarding national resources. Specifically, what is required is the development of international institutions which would transfer resources to those states who invest in their natural resources and generate global benefits. It is possible (but not necessary) for such institutions to be trade based.

Notes

1. Excerpts taken from 'Let Them Eat Pollution' in the *Economist*, 8 February 1992.
2. See d'Arge and Kneese, 1972; Walter, 1972 and 1975; Grubel, 1976; Pethig, 1976; Siebert, 1980 and 1985; McGuire, 1982; Baumol and Oates, 1988; Merrifield, 1988; and Snape, 1992.
3. The rates of natural capital stock depreciation were obtained from Pearce and Atkinson, 1992.

Bibliography

Amelung, T. (1991), 'Tropical Deforestation as an International Economic Problem', Paper presented at the Egon-Sohmen-Foundation Conference on Economic Evolution and Environmental Concerns, Linz, Austria, 30–31 August 1991.

Anderson, K. and Blackhurst, R. (eds) (1992), *The Greening of World Trade Issues*, Harvester Wheatsheaf: London.

Anderson, K. and Tyers, R (1992), *Global Effects of Liberalizing Trade in Farm Products*, Harvester Wheatsheaf: London.

Arden-Clarke, C. (1991), *The General Agreement on Tariffs and Trade, Environmental Protection and Sustainable Development*, WWF: Gland.

Barbier, E., Burgess J., Swanson, T. and Pearce, D. (1990), *Elephants, Economics and Ivory*, Earthscan: London.

Barbier, E. et al. (1992), 'Timber Trade, Trade Policies and Environmental Degradation', London Environmental Economics Centre, Discussion Paper DP 92–01.

Bartik, T.J. (1988), 'The Effects of Environmental Regulation on Business Location in the United States', *Growth and Change*, **19**, (1), 22–44.

Baumol, W.J. (1971), *Environmental Protection: International Spillovers and Trade*, Almqvist and Wicksell: Stockholm.

Baumol, W. and Oates, W. (1988), *The Theory of Environmental Policy*, Cambridge University Press: Cambridge.

Brown, K. and Pearce, D. (eds) (1994), *The Causes of Tropical Deforestation*, UCL Press: London.

Burgess, J.C. (1992), 'The Timber Trade as a Cause of Tropical Deforestation', Paper presented at the Biodiversity Programme Workshop, The Beijer Institute for Ecological Economics of the Swedish Royal Academy of Sciences, Stockholm, 29–31 July, 1992.

Capistrano, D. (1990), 'Macroeconomic Influences on Tropical Forest Depletion: A Cross-Country Analysis', PhD, University of Florida.

Cartwright, J. (1989), 'Conserving Nature, Decreasing Debt', *Third World Quarterly*, **11**, (2), 114–27.

Castleman, B.I. (1979), 'The Export of Hazardous Factories to Developing Nations', *International Journal of Health Services*, **9**, 569–606.

Castleman, B.I. (1985), 'The Double Standard in Industrial Hazards', in Ives, J.H. (ed.), *The Export of Hazard*, Routledge and Kegan Paul: Boston.

Chapman, D. (1991), 'Environmental Standards and International Trade in Automobiles and Copper: The Case for a Social Tariff', *Natural Resources Journal*, **24**, (3), 219.

Chase Econometrics (1975), *The Macroeconomic Impacts of Federal Pollution Control Programs: 1976 Assessment*, CEQ/EPA: Washington D.C.

Controy, E.D. (1974), 'Will Dirty Industries Seek Pollution Havens Abroad?', *SAIS Review*, **18**, (3).

D;'Arge, R.C. (1971), 'International Trade, Domestic Income, and Environmental Controls: Some Empirical Estimates', in Kneese, A.V., Rolfe, S.E. and Harned, J.W. (eds), *Managing the Environment: International Economic Co-operation for Pollution Control*, Praeger: New York, 289–315.

D'Arge, R.C. and Kneese, A.V. (1972), 'Environmental Quality and International Trade', *International Organization*, **26**, (2) (Spring), 419–65.

Data Resources Incorporated (1979), *The Macroeconomic Impact of Federal Pollution Control Programs, 1978 Assessment*, EPA/CEQ: Washington D.C.

Dean, J. (1992), 'Trade and Environment: A Survey of the Literature', prepared as Background Paper for the *World Development Report 1992*, World Bank: Washington D.C.

Duerkesen, C. (1983), *Environmental Regulations and Plant Siting*, Conservation Foundation: Washington D.C.

Ferguson, W.S. (1973), 'International Trade Implications of Pollution Control', *Cornell Law Review*, **58**, 368–82.

French, H.F. (1990), 'A Most Deadly Trade', *World Watch*, **3**, (4), 11–17.

Goldin, I., Knudsen, O. and van der Mensbrugghe, D. (1993), *Trade Liberalisation: Global Economic Implications*, document prepared for the World Bank and the OECD, OECD: Paris.

Grossman, G.M. and Krueger, A.B. (1992), 'Environmental Implications of a North American Free Trade Agreement', Centre for Economic Policy Research, Discussion Paper No. 644, April.

Grubel, H.G. (1976), 'Some Effects of Environmental Controls on International Trade: The Heckscher-Ohlin Model', in Walter, I.W. (ed.), *Studies in International Environmental Economics*, John Wiley: New York, 9–27.

Guppy, N. (1984), 'Tropical Deforestation: A Global View', *Foreign Affairs*, **62**, 928–65.

Gupta, J. (1990), *Toxic Terrorism: Dumping Hazardous Wastes*, Earthscan: London.

Haverman, Robert H. and Smith, V.K. (1978), 'Investment, Inflation, Unemployment and the Environment', in Portney, P.R. (ed.), *Current Issues in United States Environmental Policy*, Johns Hopkins Press: Baltimore, 164–200.

Hazell, P.B.R. (1985), 'The Impact of the Green Revolution and the Prospects for the Future', *Food Review International*, **1**, (1).

Hazell, P.B.R. (1989), 'Changing Patterns of Variability in World Cereal Production', in Anderson, J. and Hazell, P. (eds), *Variability in Grain Yields*, World Bank: Washington.

Ives, J.H. (ed.) (1985), *The Export of Hazard*, Routledge and Kegan Paul: Boston.

Khan, R. (1980), 'Redeployment of Industries to Developing Countries – Environmental Considerations', in *Trends in Environmental Policy and Law*, Erich Schmidt Verlag: Berlin, 287–309.

Koo, A.Y.C. (1974), 'Environmental Repercussions and Trade Theory', *The Review of Economics and Statistics*, **56**, (2), 235–44.

Lee, Joon Koo and Gill Chin Lim (1983), 'Environmental Policies in Developing Countries: A Case of International Movements of Polluting Industries', *Journal of Development Economics*, **13**, (1), 159–73.

Leonard, H.J. (1984), *Are Environmental Regulations Driving US Industry Overseas?*, Conservation Foundation: Washington D.C.

Leonard, H.J. (1988), *Pollution and the Struggle for the World Product*, Cambridge University Press: Cambridge.

Leonard, H.J. and Duerkesen, C.J. (1980), 'Environmental Regulations and the Location of Industry: An International Perspective', *Columbia Journal of World Business*, **15**, (2), 52–68.

Low, P. (1991), 'Do Dirty Industries Migrate?', Paper presented at Symposium on International Trade and the Environment, World Bank, Nov. 1991.

Low, P. (1992), 'Trade Measures and Environmental Quality: The Implications for Mexico's Exports', in Low, P. (ed.), *International Trade and the Environment*, Discussion Paper No. 159, World Bank: Washington D.C., 105–20.

Low, P. and Safadi, R. (1991), 'Trade Policy and Pollution', Paper presented at Symposium on International Trade and the Environment, World Bank, Nov. 1991.

Lucas, R.E.B., Wheeler, D. and Hettige, H. (1992), 'Economic Development, Environmental

Regulation, and the International Migration of Toxic Industrial Pollution: 1960–1988', prepared as Background Paper for the *World Development Report 1992*, World Bank: Washington D.C.

Magee, S.P. and Ford, W.F. (1972), 'Environmental Pollution, the Terms of Trade and Balance of Payments of the United States', *Kyklos*, **25**, (1), 101–18.

McConnell, V.D. and Schwab, R.M. (1990), 'The Impact of Environmental Regulation on Industry Location Decisions: The Motor Vehicle Industry', *Land Economics*, **66**, (1), 67–81.

McGuire, M. (1982), 'Regulation, Factor Rewards and International Trade', *Journal of Public Economics*, **17**, 335.

Merrifield, J.D. (1988), 'The Impact of Selected Abatement Strategies on Transnational Pollution, the Terms of Trade, and Factor Rewards: A General Equilibrium Approach', *Journal of Environmental Economics and Management*, **15**, (3), 259–84.

Moyers, B. (1991), *Global Dumping Ground: The International Traffic in Hazardous Waste*, Lutterworth Press: Cambridge.

Mutti, J.H. and Richardson, J.D. (1977), 'International Competitive Displacement from Environmental Control: The Quantitative Gains from Methodological Refinement', *Journal of Environmental Economics and Management*, **4**, (1), 135–52.

Myers, N. (1991), 'The World's Forests and Human Populations', in Davis, K. and Bernstam, M.S. (eds), *Resources, Environment and Population*, Oxford University Press: Oxford.

Nunnenkamp, P. (1992), 'International Financing of Environmental Protection', Kiel Working Paper No. 512, Kiel Institute of World Economics: Kiel.

OECD (1985), *The Macro-Economic Impact of Environmental Expenditures*, OECD: Paris.

Palo, M., Mery, G. and Salmi, J. (1987), 'Deforestation in the Tropics: Pilot Scenarios Based on Quantitative Analysis', in Palo, M. and Salmi, J. (eds), *Deforestation or Development in the Third World*, Finnish Forest Research Institute: Helsinki.

Pasurka, C.A. (1984), 'The Short-Run Impact of Environmental Protection Costs on US Product Prices', *Journal of Environmental Economics and Management*, **11**, (4), 380–90.

Pearce, D. (1992), 'Should the GATT be Reformed for Environmental Reasons?', CSERGE Working Paper GEC 92–06, UCL: London.

Pearce, D. and Atkinson, G. (1992), 'Are National Economies Sustainable?: Measuring Sustainable Development', CSERGE Working Paper GEC–11, UCL: London.

Pearce, D. and Warford, J. (1993), *World Without End*, Oxford University Press: Oxford.

Pearce, D., Brown, K., Swanson, T. and Perrings, C. (1992), 'Economics and the Conservation of Global Biological Diversity: A Report to the Global Environmental Facility', UCL: London.

Pearce, D., Fankhauser, S., Adger, N. and Swanson, T. (1992), 'World Economy, World Environment', CSERGE Working Paper PA 92–07, UCL: London.

Pearson, C.S. (ed.) (1987), *Multinational Corporations, Environment, and the Third World*, Duke University Press: Durham, N.C., 3–31.

Pearson, C. and Pryor, A. (1978), *Environment: North and South, an Economic Interpretation*, John Wiley: New York.

Perrings, C. (1992), 'Biotic Diversity, Sustainable Development and Natural Capital', Paper presented to the International Society for Ecological Economists, Stockholm, 25 August.

Pethig, R. (1976), 'Pollution, Welfare and Environmental Policy in the Theory of Comparative Advantage', *Journal of Environmental Economics and Management*, **2**, (2), 160–69.

Piggott, J., Whalley, J. and Wigle, R. (1992), 'International Linkages and Carbon Reduction Initiatives', in Anderson, K. and Blackhurst, R. (eds), *The Greening of World Trade Issues*, Harvester Wheatsheaf: London, 115–29.

Poore, D. (1989), *No Timber Without Trees: Sustainability in the Tropical Forest*, Earthscan: London.

Portney, P.R. (1981), 'The Macroeconomic Impacts of Federal Environmental Regulations', *Natural Resources Journal*, **21**, (3) (July), 459–88.

Primo Braga, C.A. (1992), 'Tropical Forests and Trade Policy: The Case of Indonesia and Brazil', in Low, P. (ed.), *International Trade and the Environment*, Discussion Paper No. 159, World Bank: Washington D.C., 173–94.

Radetzki, M. (1992), 'Economic Growth and the Environment', in Low, P. (ed.), *International*

Trade and the Environment, Discussion Paper No. 159, World Bank: Washington D.C., 121–34.

Rauscher, M. (1990), 'Can Cartelization Solve the Problem of Tropical Deforestation', *Weltwirtschaftliches Archiv*, **45**, 378–87.

Rauscher, M. (1991), 'Foreign Trade and the Environment', in Siebert, H. (ed.), *Environmental Scarcity: The International Dimension*, J.C.B. Mohr: Tübingen, 17–31.

Rauscher, M. (1992), 'On Ecological Dumping', Kiel Working Paper No. 523, Kiel Institute of World Economics, August 1992.

Richardson, J.A. (1991), 'Introducing Sustainability into the International Trade in Natural Resource Services: The Case of Hazardous Waste Disposal', paper presented for the 4th joint conference between the European Association of Law and Economics and the Geneva Association, Paris, 4–5 April, 1991.

Richardson, J.D. and Mutti, J.H. (1976), 'Industrial Displacement Through Environmental Controls: The International Competitive Aspects', in *Studies in International Environmental Economics*, Wiley: New York, 57–102.

Robison, H. (1988), 'Industrial Pollution Abatement: The Impact on the Balance of Trade', *Canadian Journal of Economics*, **21**, (1), 187–99.

Royston, M.G. (1979), 'Control by Multinational Corporations: The Environmental Case for Scenario 4', *Ambio*, **8** (2/3), 84–9.

Rubin, S.J. and Graham, T.R. (eds) (1982), *Environment and Trade: The Relocation of International Trade and Environmental Policy*, Frances Pinter: London.

Shrybman, S. (1990), 'International Trade and the Environment: An Environmental Assessment of the General Agreement on Tariffs and Trade', *The Ecologist*, **20**, (1), 30–34.

Siebert, H. (1977), 'Environmental Quality and the Gains from Trade', *Kyklos*, **30**, (4), 657–73.

Siebert, H. (1985), 'Spatial Aspects of Environmental Economics', in Kneese, A.V. and Sweeney, J.L. (eds), *Handbook of Natural Resource and Energy Economics*, North-Holland: Amsterdam.

Siebert, H. (1992), *Environmental Scarcity: The International Dimension*, J.C.B. Mohr: Tübingen.

Siebert, H., Eichberger, J., Gronich, R. and Pethig, R. (1980), *Trade and Environment: A Theoretical Inquiry*, Elsevier: Amsterdam.

Solow, R.M. (1974), 'The Economics of Resources or the Resources of Economics', *American Economic Review*, **64**, 1–14.

Spalding, H. (ed.) (1990), *The International Trade in Wastes: A Greenpeace Inventory*, Greenpeace: London.

Snape, R.H. (1992), 'The Environment, International Trade and Competitiveness', in Anderson, K. and Blackhurst, R. (eds), *The Greening of World Trade Issues*, Harvester Wheatsheaf: London, 73–92.

Sutton, T.C., Whitmore, T.C. and Chadwick, A.C. (eds) (1983), *Tropical Rain Forest: Ecology and Management*, Oxford University Press: Oxford, 459–63.

Swanson, T. (1994), *The International Regulation of Extinction*, Macmillan: London.

Swanson, T. and Barbier, E. (1993), *Economics for the Wilds*, Island Press: Washington D.C.

Swanson, T. and Pearce, D. (1989), 'The Economics of an Ivory Exchange', Paper prepared for the Conference of the Parties to the Convention on International Trade in Endangered Species, IUCN: Lausanne.

Tobey, J.A. (1990), 'The Effects of Domestic Environmental Policies on Patterns of World Trade', *Kyklos*, **43**, (2), 191–209.

UNCED (1987), *Our Common Future*, Oxford University Press: Oxford.

UNCTAD (1976), *Implications for the Trade and Development of Developing Countries of US Environmental Controls*, United Nations Publication: New York, TD/B/C.2/150/add.1/Rev.1.

UNCTAD (1991), *Environment and International Trade*, UNCTAD: Geneva.

Walter, I. (ed.) (1975), *The International Economics of Pollution*, Macmillan: London.

Walter, I. (ed.) (1976), *Studies in International Environmental Economics*, Wiley: New York.

Walter, I. (1972), 'Environmental Control and Patterns of International Trade and Investment: An Emerging Policy Issue', *Banca Nazionale del Lavoro Review*, **25**, (100), 82–106.

Walter, I. (1973), 'The Pollution Content of American Trade', *Western Economic Journal*, **11**, (1) (March), 61–70.

Walter, I. and Ugelow, J. (1979), 'Environmental Policies in Developing Countries', *Ambio*, **8**, (1), 102–9.

Whalley, J. (1991), 'The Interface Between Environmental and Trade Policies', *The Economic Journal*, **101**, (2), 180–89.

Wheeler, D. and Martin, P. (1992), 'Prices, Policies and the International Diffusion of Clean Technology: The Case of Wood Pulp Production', in Low, P. (ed.), *International Trade and the Environment*, Discussion Paper No. 159, World Bank: Washington D.C., 197–224.

World Bank (1992), *World Development Report 1992: Development and Environment*, Oxford University Press: Oxford.

World Conservation Monitoring Centre (1992), 'Valuing Biodiversity', in WCMC *Global Biological Diversity*, Chapman and Hall: London.

World Resources Institute (1990), *World Resources 1990–91*, Oxford University Press: Oxford.

World Resources Institute (1992), *World Resources 1992–93*, Oxford University Press: Oxford.

Yezer, A. and Philipson, A. (1974), *Influence of Environmental Considerations on Agricultural and Industrial Decisions to Locate Outside of the Continental United States*, Council on Environmental Quality: Springfield, Virginia.

Conclusion – tragedy for the commons?

Timothy M. Swanson

The decline of nature and natural resources is seen everywhere – in the deterioration of the ambient resources (air and water) in industrialized countries, in the deforestation occurring in developing countries, and in the demise of thousands of naturally-evolved species across the globe. There is no question that human societies are responsible for most of these changes, nor that these changes are occurring on a grand scale. It is right that changes on this scale should be met with questioning and concern by all the informed peoples of the planet.

In the first instance it is important to recognize that not all of these changes to nature and natural resources necessarily constitute 'environmental degradation' – situations in which societies are worsening their own position by reason of their failure to co-operate in the commons. One facet of human development has always been (and might necessarily always need to be) the rearrangement of assets with which the earth was initially endowed. Those societies which are now developing must have an equal right to alter their environment in this process, just as did those who developed their lands and resources in the past. In addition it is not possible to refer to some parts of the earth as 'natural' and others as not. Humans have been choosing the uses to which land, waters and living things are put for many thousands of years in almost all parts of the world. To the extent that 'nature' requires the absence of any impact from human choices, there are few if any terrestrial portions of the world that remain wholly natural. So for these reasons it is not adequate to equate the existence of human-initiated change with environmental degradation; there must be something more before alterations to the environment constitute a social form of costliness.

When environmental problems are defined as institutional failures, a clear conceptual line is drawn between those changes which are of positive benefit and those which bear a social cost. However this does not ease the identification of degradation and to some extent the task becomes even more complex. It is no longer possible to identify degradation with simple natural resource decline. Instead it is necessary to look beyond the observable circumstances at the underlying conditions. Environmental degradation exists when the environment is suffering due to an underlying social problem such as poverty, unrest, inequality, or other sources of non-co-operation. It is the social problem that creates the conditions that give rise to a social cost while, in the case of environmental degradation, it is the natural environment that is the recipient of this costliness.

It is not surprising to an economist that the environment is the dumping ground for the costs of many social problems as many environmental resources are 'unowned' in the legal sense. More precisely, however, these resources are owned and used by all, rather than any one group in society, and this makes it difficult for the owners to organise and protect their interests in those resources. Once again the story from Stockholm (see Chapter Two) is apropos. In that instance an automobile manufacturer negotiated with an oil refinery in order to schedule its most corrosive emissions for those times when the wind was blowing away from the factory but toward a nearby residential neighbourhood. Of course a large group of people living in a residential neighbourhood make substantial use of the air supply around their homes, certainly as many and as valued uses as an automobile factory. However, the factory was effectively the single bargaining unit regarding the air surrounding its premises and hence it was able to negotiate effectively the maintenance of the purity of the resource it accessed, to the detriment of the local residents. The social cost arising from the placement of the oil refinery in Sweden was dumped precisely where it was most costly to combat it. This is a good illustration of why it is unsurprising that environmental resources become dumping grounds for social costs. Environmental resources (air, water, marginal lands) are precisely those resources which are too expensive to protect from such abuses.

Are these systematic reasons to believe that environmental resources will always bear such costs? One approach to this important question would focus on the potential to unilaterally appropriate society's resources and the resulting benefits therefrom. When it is costly to deny access to certain resources used by all, this renders them available for appropriation by any one. Opportunism is the systematic reason that environmental resources are often the sink for the costs of various social problems and, because it is probably a significant facet of the human character, there will always be commons problems.

Why do these opportunities exist in the context of what we call 'the environment'? The answer to this question is embedded in the complex nature of the resource and the regulatory institution involved in its management. A good example of an opportunistically generated social problem was the early toxic waste disposal industry that arose several years ago within the developed countries. The unregulated proprietors within this industry unilaterally appropriated many years' worth of groundwater through the careless disposal of wastes resulting in the leakage of highly toxic substances into water supplies. The costliness of early detection and the resultant unlikelihood of prosecution brought about an industry in which corporations collected large fees for the haphazard disposal of wastes, and then dissolved and disappeared. These social costs were essentially created by the costliness of managing the environmental resource of groundwater. Opportunists saw the availability of the resource (by reason of its relatively unguarded nature) and appropriated much of its value for themselves through its contamination. Hence in some instances the relatively unguarded state of the resource alone engenders the conditions sufficient for degradation to occur.

At other times social costs and problems arise for reasons wholly disso-ciated with the nature of the resource that winds up bearing their brunt. The inequalities that exist within and across countries create social problems whose costliness is often borne by the environment and its users. For example, poor peoples living on the margins of poor countries require investment for their development and survival, but governments' traditional response to their desperation is to grant them access to marginal lands within the country. These lands are seldom easily managed in the absence of significant investment, and the combination of poor peoples and poor lands frequently results in uncontrolled degradation. The problem of inad-equate social investment in certain segments of society is shunted onto the resource, rather than resolved.

An analogous phenomenon occurs at the international level when gross inequalities in wealth result in some countries' natural resources being con-sidered comparatively inexpensive to access, not because of their relative abundance but due to the lack of resources available for their proper manage-ment. Continuing with the example of toxic wastes, the response of devel-oped countries such as the US to the earlier predicament has been the estab-lishment of costly 'cradle to grave' waste disposal regulation, which requires careful disposal of most toxic wastes. Developing countries however do not have the resources required for managing and monitoring waste disposal in this fashion and so it is far less complicated or costly to dispose of them there. The resultant movement of noxious substances to those societies with relatively free environmental resources once again places a social problem requiring investment into a situation where such investment is virtually cer-tain *not* to occur. Thus a global social problem – vast inequalities in wealth – is translated into an environmental problem.

There are many other examples of social problems whose costliness is unrelated to the environment but nevertheless often resides there ultimately. It is frequently the case that social problems such as civil unrest and poverty manifest themselves as environmental degradation when the environmental resource is the only one available to peoples in distress. In these cases there are few assets to select from and once again the environmental resources are the least well protected within the society. Dire circumstances of any form often translate into tragedy for the commons.

Therefore, the underlying causes of environmental degradation are social problems of all types. Put simply, environmental resources are some of the least exclusively held valuables within a society and hence they become the repository of more than their share of social ills and their costliness. What can be done about this? It seems important that a society – in order to remain a society – must retain some portion of its resources in common, that is, there should be some baseline of resources that remain available to all members of that society. This much is necessary in order to recognize the rights of existence of all members and to maintain some manner of 'commonality' between all parts of society. So long as some resources remain more available for access than others, it will never be possible to eradicate environmental degradation without first addressing the root social problems. Environmental degradation must be seen as the outcome of more fundamental social problems – poverty, inequality, unrest – which must be addressed if the environmental problem is to be resolved.

Can the continuing evolution of institutions keep the deleterious effects of human opportunism at bay, or will it be necessary to address this problem in order to forestall ultimate tragedy for the human race? Hardin placed this facet of human nature at the very core of the 'tragedy of the commons' and many deep ecologists argue that it is only by changing human nature that tragedy will be avoided. Institutional economists on the other hand take this facet of human nature as a fixed parameter and then use this predictability within human nature to guide the development of institutions that will channel aggregate behaviour in a constructive direction. Is the institutionalists' framework adequate to all tasks or will the approach potentially end in tragedy if relied upon too extensively? It seems more likely that the latter is indeed the case; there are certain types of resources that exist only as very complex systems, for example the carbon cycle, that are ill-fitted to the institutionalists' framework. These systems cannot be readily broken down into institution-sized components to which relative 'prices' may be applied and so it is difficult to see how opportunistic instincts regarding the utilization of resources of this type could ever be constructively 'channelled'.

The institutionalist paradigm is based upon the idea that the complex relationship between human society and the living world may be appropriately regulated through achieving ever finer definition of the interfacing institutions. When it is inconsistent with reality to conceive of certain resources as separate components but only as part of a larger system, then the pursuit of finer definition in institutions is probably not very useful. For the regulation of this interface, very crude sorts of instruments may indeed be the only practicable approach. So, for example, complex systemic resources such as the climate and food production may be best regulated by means of crude measures controlling the scale and growth of human impacts on these systems. There is an important role for measures controlling aggregate human impacts on the earth even within the institutionalists' paradigm, as a means of redressing the predictable failures of this approach.

The regulation of the commons is an ongoing struggle in a dynamic world. The issues concern the ability of institutions to change as rapidly as do human societies, and whether they are able to evolve the complexity to match that of the resources they must regulate. Tragedy occurs whenever institutions are ill-suited to the natural environment or outpaced by social changes. We must continue to push the institutional frontier forward in hopes of keeping pace in this contest, while simultaneously recognizing the inherent limitations to this approach. The real tragedy would occur if we failed to recognize and realize our common interest in these aspects.

Index

Abrahamson, D.E. 89
acid rain 1, 13, 41–5, 52, 89, 103
ADB 53
Adger, N. 154
Africa, Sub-Saharan
  biomass fuel consumption in 119–20, 121–2
  carrying capacity of 90
  deforestation in 111, 159
  fertility rates in 86, 102
  food production per capita in 87, 101
  income per capita in 85, 110
  population of 85, 110
  poverty statistics for 111
  property rights in 119
  wood-based products exported from 160, 161, 162
  see also African elephant, decline of; Middle East/North Africa; *and under names of individual African countries*, e.g. Zambia
African elephant, decline of 1, 17, 59, 65–70, 77
Agreement on Technical Barriers to Trade (Standards Code) (1979) 164
agricultural chemicals 36–8, 52, 87, 101, 119, 137, 145, 150
agricultural land, conversion to 16, 58, 59–60, 67, 69–70, 77–8, 87–8, 118, 123, 125, 130–31, 132–3, 160
  subsidies for 15, 71, 73–6, 77, 123, 124, 125, 136–7, 145
agricultural productivity 100–102, 133, 134, 150
agricultural resources, scarcity of 93–4
agricultural specialization, trade-induced 148–50
air pollution 1–2, 3, 13–14, 31, 41–5, 52, 89, 99, 103, 105, 121, 122, 146–7, 151, 158, 160, 174
Albon, S. 69
Allen, R. 88
Amelung, T. 160
America, Latin *see* Latin America
America, North
  acid rain in 41, 52

wood-based products exported from 160, 161
  see also Canada; United States
Anderson, D. 11, 53
Anderson, K. 145
Arden-Clarke, C. 147
Argentina
  agricultural subsidies in 145
  chemical fertilizers in 145
  debt burden of 129, 130, 141
  export structure of 131, 132
  tractors and harvesters in 145
Armitage, J. 121–2
Arntzen, J. 124
Arrow, K.J. 48
Asia
  carrying capacity of 90
  deforestation in 111, 159
  fertility rates in 86
  food production per capita in 87
  income per capita in 85
  population of 85
  poverty statistics for 111
  wood-based products exported from 160, 161, 162
  see also under names of individual Asian countries, e.g. Philippines
Asian Development Bank 137
Atkinson, G. 156
Atrazine 37, 38, 52
Australia
  agricultural subsidies in 145
  chemical fertilizers in 145
  income per capita in 112
  species richness of 112
  tractors and harvesters in 145

Balick, M. 78
Bamoko Convention 157
Bangladesh
  agricultural specialization in 149
  income per capita in 110
bank loans, to developing countries 128–9, 141
Barbier, E.B. 39, 67, 111, 159, 160, 161, 162

179

cartels 166
cash crop exports 132–3
cattle ranching 15, 58, 67, 71, 73–6, 77,
    123, 130–31, 133
Caughley, G. 67
Central African Republic (CAR)
    African elephant population in 66
    park management spending in 68
Cernea, M.M. 103
charcoal, as household fuel 119, 120,
    121–2
chemicals
    agricultural 36–8, 52, 87, 101, 119,
        137, 145, 150
    disposal of 24, 30–31, 35–6, 40, 97,
        143–4, 147–8, 157–8, 174–5
    see also acid rain; pollution
Chile
    export structure of 132
China
    fuelwood consumption in 121
    income per capita in 110, 112
    land area of 110
    population of 110
    reafforestation in 160
    species richness of 112
Cirancy-Wantrup, S. 2
Clark, C. 56–7, 62
    see also over-exploitation, Clark
        model of
Cline, W.R. 99
Cline-Cole, R.A. 125
Club of Rome 10, 89, 91
coal mining 94–5
Coase Theorem 30–31, 33–4, 36, 38, 42,
    45–6, 52
Colombia
    debt burden of 141
    income per capita in 112
    species richness of 112
Common Agricultural Policy (CAP) 145
Commoner, B. 103
common property resources (CPRs) 104,
    113–14, 115, 120, 121
commons management *see* tragedy of
    the commons
comparative advantage 23–4, 150–52
concessions 71, 72–3
Congo
    biomass fuel consumption in 120

export structure of 132, 160
Constantino, L. 88
consumption levels 103, 105
Convention on International Trade in
    Endangered Species (CITES) 67,
    70, 148
conversion 15–18
    forces for 60–65
    land use conversion rates and
        locations 59–60
    policies promoting 59–60, 69–70
        non-exploitation policies 70–71
        subsidies *see* subsidies to conver-
            sions
    sources of 58–9
    unmanaged *see* unmanaged resources
Conway, G.R. 36, 52
copper mining 94–5
Costa Rica
    debt burden of 141
    debt-for-nature swaps in 138, 139
    deforestation in 59, 72, 154
    export structure of 132
    income per capita in 154
    trade openness of 154
cost/benefit streams, uncertainty
    regarding 49–50, 51
credit, availability of 118–19
cropping, frequency of 100–101
crops, cultivated, range of 23
Cummings, D. 68
Czechoslovakia
    acid rain in 43, 44

Daly, H.E. 95, 103, 104
dark matter concentrations 146
Dasgupta, P. 102, 122, 124, 125
Davis, K. 91
DDT 37
death rates 86, 122
debt-for-nature swaps 138–40
deforestation 1, 2, 5–6, 10, 15, 16, 17,
    22, 58, 125
    in Africa 111, 159
        *see also under names of individual
            African countries*, e.g. Nigeria
    agricultural productivity and 133, 134
    agricultural subsidies and 15, 71, 73–
        6, 77, 123, 125
    in Asia 111, 159